Celebrating 10 years of Engaging New Students

The 2009 Book Connection Program is supported by:
The Office of the President, Office of the Vice Provost
Department of Athletics, Department of English, Honors
Program, Learning Assistance Programs, Division of Student
Affairs, Steely Library, and NKU Presidential Ambassadors.

The Book Connection Program is sponsored and administered
by the Office of First-Year Programs.

This publication was prepared by Northern Kentucky University and printed with state funds (KRS 57.375).
Equal Education and Employment Opportunities M/F/D. 00785

D1566589

THIRTEEN WOMEN STRONG

THIRTEEN WOMEN STRONG

THE MAKING OF A TEAM

ROBERT K. WALLACE

AFTERWORD BY NANCY WINSTEL

THE UNIVERSITY PRESS OF KENTUCKY

Scholarly publisher for the Commonwealth,
serving Bellarmine University, Berea College, Centre
College of Kentucky, Eastern Kentucky University,
The Filson Historical Society, Georgetown College,
Kentucky Historical Society, Kentucky State University,
Morehead State University, Murray State University,
Northern Kentucky University, Transylvania University,
University of Kentucky, University of Louisville,
and Western Kentucky University.
All rights reserved.

Editorial and Sales Offices: The University Press of Kentucky
663 South Limestone Street, Lexington, Kentucky 40508-4008
www.kentuckypress.com

12 11 10 09 08   5 4 3 2 1

Library of Congress Cataloging-in-Publication Data

Wallace, Robert K., 1944–
  Thirteen women strong : the making of a team / Robert K. Wallace ;
afterword by Nancy Winstel.
      p. cm.
  Includes index.
  ISBN 978-0-8131-2515-2 (hardcover : alk. paper)
  1. Northern Kentucky University—Basketball. 2. Basketball for
women—Kentucky. 3. Women basketball players—Kentucky. 4. Norse
(Basketball team) I. Title.
  GV885.43.N69W35 2008
  796.323'630976947—dc22
                                        2008028020

This book is printed on acid-free recycled paper meeting
the requirements of the American National Standard
for Permanence in Paper for Printed Library Materials.

Manufactured in the United States of America.

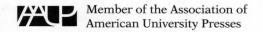 Member of the Association of
American University Presses

*To Nancy Winstel and all the women
who played or coached basketball in Regents Hall
between 1974 and 2008*

CONTENTS

Illustrations follow page 160

INTRODUCTION

The Challenge

I took my power in my hand
And went against the world.
—*Emily Dickinson*

She thinks she is playing good defense this time. But the girl gets around her. She knows why the coach is putting her on the bench. That look in the coach's eye is enough.

Next time the coach puts her on a different player. This one gets around her too. This time she gets more than the silent stare. "You're already on the worst player out there. You don't guard her because she's outhustling you. I move you to somebody else, they put in another player, she beats you to the basket, and she's not as good as the person you were guarding before. WHO DO YOU WANT ME TO PUT YOU ON?"

Today the intensity of this is too much for the player. She begins to cry.

"What are you crying about? YOU'RE CRYING BECAUSE YOU'RE NOT GUARDING ANYBODY! You're not mad at me. MY FEET aren't guarding anybody. Go ahead and cry. Fine. Go ahead and cry."

At halftime, hurt and angry, the player keeps a bit to herself in the locker room. This burns the coach even more. She thinks to herself, "It's not you, kid. We're a team. We don't act that way."

In the second half, when the coach gets ready to put the player back in, she sees she is still crying. She tells her to sit down. After

1

the player has calmed down, the coach puts her in. She now plays better; she is not being outhustled. Next time she comes to the bench, the coach puts an arm around her and says, "That's all. That's all I want you to do. We might fight, but this isn't about you. It's about *us*."

Every player who has played for Nancy Winstel has experienced some version of this moment, with or without the tears. The intensity of the coach's challenge is relentless, exceeded only by her desire for the player to succeed. When the player does meet the challenge, she and the coach have advanced together. They have taken another step in the process of building a team.

Winstel's voice still quivered with emotion as she told me about this event long after it had occurred. She apologized for revealing such a difficult moment for her player. Their encounter had also touched something deep within herself. "You have to really care about someone," she said, "to tell them something they don't want to hear."

Nancy Winstel is a tall, imposing woman in her 50s. She is a tough-love, hard-nosed competitor with a not-so-buried heart of gold. When she is not challenging a player on the sidelines she is likely to be hugging her. Often she does both at the same time, draping a long arm around the player's back as she explains a mistake or praises a play.

At the dismal low point of the 2006–07 season, when the team was working hard but performing poorly, Winstel told me, "I'd like to hug them all but I can't." As she writes in the afterword to this book, "your players have to know that you love them." Sometimes you show this "with a hug and, yes, sometimes with a kick."

This book is about 12 young women and the woman who coaches them. The young women are strong, smart, and highly competitive. They are true student-athletes, seeking full development of body and mind. On game days, basketball in hand, they strive to please their fans by defeating their opponents. Every other day they live out a competitive, supportive sisterhood among themselves. As long as they are together their individual success will be measured by the success of the whole. Whatever the result at the end of a season, each will be able to say with her teammates, but in her own way, "I took my power in my hand / And went against the world."

Thirty years earlier the woman who coaches them was exactly as young as they are, playing the same game for the same university. The 30 years that separate her from her players encompass the history of Title IX basketball in the United States. The day-by-day work that she and her players share exemplifies the continuity of the game as it is being played by thousands of players on hundreds of campuses across the country as each new season begins. Here, on Winstel's court, 13 women have one common goal: to be the best they can be. In this case, to be the best in the nation, if the ball bounces their way.

Three of the young women are the senior cocaptains of Winstel's 2006–07 team at Northern Kentucky University. As juniors the year before, Karmen Graham, Karyn Creager, and Brittany Winner led their seniorless team to a 27–5 record. After winning the Great Lakes Valley Conference (GLVC) Tournament, they advanced to the National Collegiate Athletic Association (NCAA) Great Lakes Regional and won their first game, losing in the second round to the eventual national champion. From the end of that spring semester throughout the summer months, the entire team set a voluntary schedule of weights and conditioning, open gyms, and summer league ball. During the first seven weeks of the new fall semester, they worked six days a week with weights, conditioning, and individual drills. Finally, October 15 came, the day of the first official practice. The three-hour practice began at 10 on a Sunday morning. It had special meaning for the seniors. Brittany Winner wrote in her journal:

> Practice today was one of the strangest ones I've ever had. I think we were a little bit nervous to begin with, while at the same time knowing that this day marked the real beginning of our season. The next 6 months of our lives will seem to drag on as we go through them; there will be days when each of us will dread practice and just wish we could be somewhere else. But when we get to March, we will each, without a doubt, look back and wonder where the season went.
>
> On top of the nervousness, I had this unspoken sense that this day

marked the beginning of the end. I think the other seniors did too. There's no getting around the fact that this is our last year of basketball. Ever. So with that, I am trying to approach this year with the attitude that my future high school coach started teaching me when I was in the second grade: "Don't count the days. Make the days count." If I can keep this positive mentality throughout the season, I know it will be a good year.

So great had been the previous season that Brittany and her returning teammates were expecting to be contenders for the national championship. Among the goals they set for 2006–07 were to win all their games at home, defend their GLVC championship, return to the NCAA Tournament, and this time make it at least to the Final Four. A team could hardly have higher expectations. To anticipate a season like this is what young athletes dream of from the time they begin to bounce the ball. Yet Brittany and her fellow seniors, before their dream season got under way, could not avoid the feeling that it was already ending.

All three cocaptains showed they were exceptional athletes as juniors.

Six-foot-one center Karmen Graham was first-team All-Conference, first-team All-Region, and honorable mention All-American. She averaged 15.7 points a game and led the nation in free throws made (177 of 210, for 84.3 percent).

Six-foot guard Karyn Creager was honorable mention All-Conference after scoring 9.7 points a game. She made 86.4 percent of her free throws and excelled on defense, using her long legs and arms to deny the pass, deny the drive, and intimidate opposing shooters.

Five-foot-ten guard Brittany Winner was Most Valuable Player (MVP) of the conference tournament, scoring 30 points, 20 of them in the first half, as we upset Drury in the championship game. This was the first time she had ever taken over a game so completely. It was not to be her last.

If these young women had been playing this well on a top-tier Division I team in NCAA college basketball, they might still be dreaming of a career in the pros, hoping for a spectacular senior year that would land them positions in the WNBA draft or at least professional contracts in Europe. As top-tier Division II players, however, they do not have dreams or expectations of a professional career. They are true student-athletes, playing for their education and their love of the game. Brittany is a Spanish education major who will be teaching in South America after she graduates. Karmen is a secondary education major who plans to be a high school social studies teacher. Karyn is a recreation and fitness major who plans to go on for a master's degree in health promotion and administration.

As juniors, Brittany and Karyn led the team academically with cumulative grade point averages of 3.89 and 3.90. The entire team finished the 2005–06 season with a grade point average of 3.524, fifth highest in the nation. These students are ambitious and diverse in their career goals, with nearly half planning to be teachers. Others are preparing for careers in radio-TV, marketing, banking, mathematics, sports business, or personal training. Coaches and writers like to say that college basketball prepares its players for life beyond the game. Playing for Winstel does do that.

Most of the fans in the stands are not particularly aware of the academic majors or grade point averages of these student-athletes. We admire them, enjoy them, and love them for what they do on the court. We marvel when Brittany Winner sprints the whole length of the court to catch from behind the opponent who has stolen the ball and is heading for a game-winning layup, stripping the ball clean to keep the game alive. We are flooded with admiration when we see flush-faced Karmen Graham taking it up against a much taller player with the game on the line, drawing the foul that gives her the two shots she then makes to win the game. We are enthralled by those long arms of Karyn Creager as she swishes all five three-pointers in one game or makes 34 consecutive free throws during her senior year to shatter the school record of 27 she set in her sophomore year, accompanying every made shot with a smile that mirrors the inner joy even more than the outer success.

Fans have the pleasure of watching this team from the home opener in November through the postseason in March. Yet what we see in the games they play is only the external story of what these young women do and who they are. The action on the court shows the result but not the source of the extraordinary drive they have to compete at the highest level they can reach, to defeat everyone they play, to bring out the best of their teammates in every possible way. On the court we see the result but not the process of the offseason conditioning and the preseason preparation by which these players have reached such an exceptional level of play.

This book tells the story not only of the team but also of the making of the team. It shows the process by which 12 young women came together under a powerful coach to play with exceptional skill and devotion, with and for one another. It illustrates Winstel's belief that success in coaching requires three loves: "love of your players, love of the game, and love of the process." This book shows how one woman's love of coaching is helping 12 talented teenagers become mature young women ready for life. This team is the 24th that Nancy Winstel has coached on the same court on which she herself came of age as a young woman.

This story begins in August 2003, when three of the eventual seniors arrive as first-semester freshmen, to be joined by nine new teammates in the next three years. All 12 of these young women have played basketball not only in high school and middle school but on organized teams as early as the third grade. Born in the mid-1980s, they represent a generation of American girls for whom the option of playing basketball has never been in doubt. This was not the case for their coach, born in northern Kentucky in the 1950s, for whom there was no girls' basketball team in grade school, middle school, or even high school.

Northern Kentucky State College (NKSC) opened as a four-year school in Highland Heights in 1972, the year in which Congress passed the Title IX legislation that mandated gender equality in education. Nancy Winstel enrolled as a student on the brand-new campus. She was a history major working two jobs to pay her way through school. When NKSC created its first women's basketball team in 1974–75, Nancy tried out and made the team. She did so even though she had never played on such a team before. She was asked to try out by members of the basketball team who also played in the intramural volleyball league Winstel had helped organize as one of her part-time jobs. They asked her because the basketball team had only seven players. Winstel was 5-foot-10 and Coach Marilyn Scroggin needed some height, so she took her on. Before long, Winstel was the starting center. She recalls that when Scroggin first asked her to set a pick, she said, "Okay, but what's a pick?"

Nancy Winstel and her teammates gave the new program an auspicious start. During the 1974–75 season they compiled a 19–8 record. They went all the way to the Association of Intercollegiate Athletics for Women (AIAW) National College Division Tournament in Pueblo, Colorado, beating such schools as the University of Louisville (70–59) and Xavier University (63–34) along the way. The next year was even better. Their record was 28–2; they won the Kentucky Women's Intercollegiate Conference (KWIC) championship and two of three games in the AIAW Regional Tournament. Nearly everyone was back, and hopes were high for Winstel's senior year. But several key players were injured, including Winstel herself for a while, and the team finished with a disappointing (to them) 19–11 record.

As a player Winstel showed her power as a rebounder. She still ranks third on the school's all-time list with her cumulative average of 8.3 per game for the 1974–77 seasons. She could also score, averaging 10.3 points per game in her first season (including 26 in an overtime loss to the University of Cincinnati). She was a walk-on her first year but got some money for books the next year; she thought that was "the greatest thing in the world." NKSC was one of the first colleges in the region to offer partial scholarships for women's basketball. On a campus created during the same year as Title IX, the women's athletic program had relative parity with the men's from the beginning. Winstel played all her home games in Regents Hall—one of two buildings on campus when she arrived in 1972, and still the home court for her team in 2006–07. Over the years the team has been called the Norsewomen, the Lady Norse, and now the Norse.

Northern Kentucky State College became Northern Kentucky University (NKU) in 1976. One year later Nancy Winstel graduated as a double major in history and physical education. She had originally planned to be a high school teacher. Now, however, she wanted to be a college basketball coach like Marilyn Scroggin (now Marilyn Scroggin Moore). In spite of Title IX, there were very few positions for female college basketball coaches. To be eligible for one of those positions, Winstel would need to get a master's degree. She decided to go to Indiana University in Bloomington, where Coach Scroggin Moore had gotten her degree.

Nancy Winstel had been raised in a very close family whose daughters were not expected to move away, even for a year of graduate school. This was the decisive moment in which she took her power in her hand, and went against the world. The gamble paid off. In 1978, immediately after receiving her degree from Indiana, she was hired as head basketball coach at Midway College in Kentucky. In 1983 Nancy Winstel became head coach at NKU. By the beginning of the 2006–07 season she had won 499 games at NKU and lost only 168. She led her team to the national championship in 1999–2000, the school's first in any sport. Although the national championship season is the obvious highlight of her coaching career, the year-after-year excellence of her teams is the best measure of her success. In addition to being the Division II National Coach of the Year in 2000, she has been GLVC Coach of the Year in 6 different seasons. Her teams have made 17 NCAA appearances, have been nationally ranked in 16 seasons, and have made the NCAA Final Four in 4 seasons (1987, 1999, 2000, and 2003).

Basketball has given Nancy Winstel something more than power on the court. She has made the game her passion, her vocation, her primary way of bringing pleasure to others and of shaping young lives. The 12 young women she is shaping in this book are the members of her 2006–07 team. Like most coaches, she wants to unlock the power in her players that will prepare them for life beyond the court through what they achieve on the court. Like many great teachers, she wants to do for her student-athletes what was done for her.

Nancy Winstel's greatest goal, she told me, after saying farewell to her seniors at the April 2007 awards ceremony, is to help her players be strong and self-reliant. "When they leave the program, I want them to be able to stand on their own. There is nothing wrong with getting married or having a relationship, but I want them to be able to stand up for themselves, to support themselves, and not let anybody tell them they can't do something if they truly want to do it. Young women today do not always realize the degree to which we still live in a white man's world. I say to them, 'Don't let yourself be dominated by anybody, and especially be careful of the white men, because they run the world, and if you think they don't, you need to pay attention.'" Playing for Winstel requires each player to find inner strength against external pressure within the solidarity of a team. Few have been challenged to be as personally assertive as their male counterparts. Many weddings in this area still feature the scripture in which the bride is commanded to be subservient to her husband "in all things."

The game does mean something different for Winstel's current players than for Winstel herself. No one prevented them from playing as young girls. Their skills have been nurtured and encouraged every step of the way. Success in sports is something to which they can naturally aspire. Yet this does not make it easy. The demands of the coach, the intensity of the competition week after week, the day-to-day drudgery of the offseason conditioning and the preseason workouts, the challenge of becoming an independent person while following the rules of the team and meeting the expectations of the coach, the responsibility of being a true student-athlete while also wanting to relax and have some fun—all these pressures make being a player for Winstel as intense, in some ways, as being Winstel herself.

I decided to write this book because of the pleasure of watching these players play. By February 2006 Winstel's team was playing with a joy and precision we had not seen in years. When this team went on to win the GLVC championship by upsetting Drury University—the number-two Division II team in the country, a team that had demolished us on our own court in December—it was clear that these players had a grit and determination as strong as their grace. They showed these same qualities in defeating Michigan Tech in the first round of the NCAA Great Lakes Regional, winning by one point on a basket with three seconds left.

Although NKU lost the next game to Grand Valley State, the eventual national champion, we would have all 12 players returning for the next season, whereas Grand Valley would be losing its senior All-American, Niki Reams. The season to come looked to be a writer's dream. So I put aside my other projects in order to follow this team. Once I got approval from the coach and the athletic director, I interviewed all 12 players in May 2006. I finished my exit interviews with each player in April 2007. In between, I saw every home game and many of the away ones. More important, I saw how the team prepared for these games throughout the summer months, during the preseason, and at practice sessions from October 15 through the NCAA Tournament in March. By observing all this— while also interviewing our coaches, rival coaches, and parents of our players along the way—I learned much more than I had previously imagined about what it takes to play basketball at the highest level of the women's Division II game.

Like the players, coaches, and most other fans, I had hoped and expected that the extraordinary achievement of the 2005–06 season would lead to even greater success in 2006–07. This did not happen in all the ways success is usually measured. In other ways, the players achieved even more than during the previous season, given the adversity they encountered and the way they worked through it. The strength these young women showed was physical, mental, and communal. They showed it on the court but also off the court and inside themselves. This book presents a detailed account of the 2006–07 season, preceded by enough of the three previous seasons to show how that year's seniors, and the program that challenged and nurtured them, got to where they are now. The conclusion chronicles the remarkable postseason accomplishments of the next year's team.

In the exit interviews I asked each senior what she most wanted readers to know about her team. One said simply, "The amount of time we put in." Another spoke of "how much time and effort goes into being a college athlete." Another stressed, in addition to the hard work and dedication, "our strong bonds and connections off the court." Another emphasized "the intricacies and uniqueness that everyone brings—there is more to us than who we are on the court." The fifth senior said this: "It is very rare that you are in a group where you like everyone that you're with."

INTRODUCTION

I asked each senior, now that her college basketball career was over, to choose the word or phrase that best expressed how she felt about it. The words they chose were "tremendous opportunity," "great experience," "learning experience," "successful," and "ups and downs." Most of these young women had played the game since they were six or seven years old, so I asked each to comment on the importance of basketball in her entire life so far. For Brittany Winner, basketball has been "defining, shaping every aspect of my life." For Karyn Creager, "it has shaped the person I am." For Karmen Graham, "it has shaped the kind of person I am." For Betsey Clark, who arrived with Karyn and Karmen as freshmen, "it *was* my life." For Katie Butler, a two-year transfer, basketball "has gotten me through college."

These impromptu answers give a small taste of what playing on the team has meant to these players. What has their play meant to me as a fan who has watched every Winstel team since she became head coach in 1983? I value the young women on this particular team because of their exceptional talent as individual players and their exceptional devotion to one another. I admire them for their style of play—for the strength and beauty with which they move the ball and the tenacity with which they defend. I enjoy the quality of the entertainment they provide their fans, but what I most admire is the way they show what women can do. The game they play, in the program in which they play it, builds character, strength, and solidarity in women as few activities in life can do. Their coach, Nancy Winstel, is as fine a teacher as any you can find on this expanding campus of more than 14,000 students.

Here is what *she* would like my readers to know about the players on her 2006–07 team: "There's a lot more to these young ladies than just the athlete. They're very bright, they're very driven, they have a lot on their plates. There's a lot that makes them who they are. There's not a person in the group that you wouldn't be proud to have as your friend, to have as your daughter, to have your son date. . . . I think they will all be very successful and very happy in their lives because of the way they go about doing what they do."

Their multidimensionality as persons is what first struck me when interviewing the players in May 2006. The way they expressed their tremendous ambition and drive is what first brought to mind Dickinson's "I took my power in my hand / And went against the world." Dickinson expressed her power by taking a pen in hand. These young women have done so with a basketball in hand. Most have done so since the third grade, training their hands to bounce, pass, catch, and shoot the ball with increasing sophistication and security. Yet it is in college that each has learned to make the way she plays the game express the full power of her own evolving personality—not only through the strength, the touch, and the quickness with which she handles and shoots the ball but also through the toughness of body and mind with which she meets challenges both external and internal.

Each player must develop her toughness of body and mind in the context of the group. The players as an organism must empower themselves as a unit, internalizing what the coaches have shown them until it becomes their own. They must become accountable primarily to themselves at the same time that they are playing for their coaches and fans. For Winstel, this is the ultimate stage in a healthy team dynamic. As she said to me more than once, the game ultimately belongs to "the players, not me." As one of the seniors put it in her exit interview, "Once the game starts and the whistle blows, there's only so much a coach can do. As a player, you do have to take the power into your hands. When you are out there on the court you have to feel that 'this is my game. I'm the one playing it.'"

I have written this book to reveal how 12 young women, empowered by their challenging yet nurturing coach, made themselves into a team worthy of deep pride and admiration whether they won the national championship or not. The players who completed their NKU basketball careers in March 2007 embodied, week after week and year after year, the kind of drive, dedication, honor, pride, and devotion to fair play to which many Americans continue to aspire. They came to campus as talented girls. They were leaving as seasoned young women.

1

WATCHING WOMEN'S BASKETBALL

My life had stood a loaded gun.
—*Emily Dickinson*

The pleasure with which they played was the defining quality of Winstel's teams in 2005–06 and 2006–07. Not only did they enjoy the game; they enjoyed one another. A small group of faculty fans saw this at the conference tournament in Evansville, Indiana, in March 2006. We had been invited to watch the team work out for its semifinal game with Quincy University. After the workout, sitting on the floor outside the locker room as they waited for the bus, all 12 players broke into spontaneous song, serenading one another until the bus arrived. One player later chose "random" as the single word that best defines the essence of her teammates. "It's hard to explain 'random' with us because it's so random."

The team as a whole made a more deliberate choice when they put together the sound track for their pregame warm-ups during the 2006–07 season. Their signature song was Fergie's "Fergalicious":

> I'm Fergalicious (so delicious)
> My body stay vicious
> I be up in the gym just working on my fitness
> He my witness (oooh we)

Nancy Winstel lived in a different era when she put on a basketball uniform for the first time in the same Regents Hall in 1974.

It is during the games themselves that these outstanding athletes convey their greatest pleasure. Playing basketball at their level requires complete concentration for the whole 40-minute game, and absolute coordination of body and mind. At its best, Division II women's college basketball epitomizes the ancient Greek ideal of "soundness of body, soundness of mind." The all-absorbing challenge of the game at this level at times produces such an absolute high that fans in the stands can be lifted as high as the players themselves. The rapturous transports of such elevated moments are universal. The sporting arenas in which they occur are intensely local.

Northern Kentucky is a contradiction in terms. Kentucky is thought of as a southern state; like many newcomers, I was surprised to find that its northern edge abuts Ohio. Most people identify Kentucky with the "Bluegrass" ethos of the horse farms and distilleries near Lexington, extending westward to Churchill Downs in Louisville on Derby Day. This captivating image of speed, ease, and adventure contrasts with the stereotypes of coal, poverty, and ignorance projected by the popular mind onto the rest of the state. When Nancy Winstel was born in northern Kentucky in the 1950s that region had few, if any, positive associations. Newport, her hometown in Campbell County, was known locally as "Sin City"; it was a thriving center of gambling and prostitution, the underground playground for straitlaced pleasure-seekers from across the river in Cincinnati. More recently, the Kentucky side of the Ohio River has become the southern suburb of Cincinnati.

Northern Kentucky is divided geographically by the Licking River. Politically, the area divides between Newport and Covington, on opposite sides of the Licking at its confluence with the Ohio. They and their adjacent river towns have traditionally been condescended to by the more affluent communities of Fort Thomas and Fort Mitchell on the rolling Kentucky hills above them. Northern Kentucky State College began as a two-year school in Covington in 1968. The opening of its new campus as a four-year college in Highland Heights in 1972 helped give the region its first sense of an integrated identity, either among its own fractured parts or in the legislative chambers downstate. Highland Heights is seven miles south of Cincinnati, high above the Licking River. A new site of community pride for all of northern Kentucky will be created by the completion of the new Bank of Kentucky Center, the 9,000-seat arena in which Winstel's team is scheduled to open its 2008–09 season.

I arrived in Highland Heights in August 1972 as a brand-new PhD from Columbia University in New York. The new campus then consisted of two concrete buildings near a cow pond. Nunn Hall was a five-story classroom building. Regents Hall was a basketball gymnasium in which the first graduating class received its degrees in May 1973. In some ways, things were dicey from the get-go. Our first college president had big dreams. He spoke of our becoming "the Harvard on the Licking." The locals were not yet impressed. To them, NKSC meant "No Knowledge State College."

In the three decades since becoming a university in 1976, NKU has achieved a national reputation as a metropolitan university that excels in undergraduate education. Situated in a rabid basketball state, however, for some time the school was known to the general public more for its hoop dreams than its educational aspirations. The men's team in the 1970s was blessed with an excellent former high school coach, Mote Hils. He led us to several outstanding seasons, including the 1977–78 team that went 20–8 and took us to our first-ever NCAA Tournament. His players, like the student body in general, included many first-generation college students. Now some of their own their children are filling the college ranks and excelling on the court. Two leading players on Mote's teams were Dan Doellman and Jeff Stowers. In March 2003 Jeff's son Brandon Stowers was the floor leader who took NKU into the NCAA Division II Tournament and made second-team All-American. In March 2006 Dan's son Justin Doellman scored the basket that put Xavier University into the NCAA Division I Tournament.

NKU's women's team was even more successful than the men's team in the 1970s—although they were not yet so well known on campus. I learned about the women's team during the 1974 fall semester because Nancy Winstel was a student in my American literature class. She was another of our first-generation college students. Neither of her parents had completed high school. She has often said that if the new college had not opened in 1972 she would never have received a college education. She was a very good student in spite of having two part-time jobs. I must have attended quite a few games when Nancy was a player, because I remember her blocking out under the boards. The men's teams drew larger crowds, but those who saw the women play knew they were seeing something special. Our team was on the cutting edge of the changes Title IX was bringing to the nation.

In advance of the 1976–77 season, Mel Webster created a booklet whose title celebrated NKU's "Golden Tradition in Women's Sports." In a "tradition" only two years old, the school's female athletes had already compiled a combined record of 91 wins and 27 losses. Webster was not afraid of invoking Knute Rockne and John Wooden as he speculated about how dynasties are born. Our pioneering women athletes "can never have one thing taken away from them—they were the first. Their magic moments have been recorded. Their greatest performances will be treasured." Webster's profile of Nancy Winstel as an exemplar of this budding tradition stressed that she had become one of "the best college players in Kentucky," even though she had never played the game in high school. Already Coach Scroggin Moore was praising her as a "communicator on the court," a post player providing the kind of leadership that more often comes from guards. I am sorry that I missed Winstel's senior year as a player because I was teaching as a Fulbright lecturer in Bilbao, Spain.

My first memory of becoming a serious fan of our women's team dates back to when our radio station, WNKU, affiliated with National Public Radio in 1985. In the morning after both basketball teams had played, I would turn on the station to hear the results. Only one score would be announced. NKU won by such and such a score, or lost by this or that score. "NKU" meant the men's team. The score of the women's team was usually not mentioned—either on our own radio station or on the local television news outlets. I enjoyed watching our women's team enough that year that I made a pest of myself by calling Maryanne Zeleznik, the morning host on WNKU, whenever she would announce the men's score and not the women's. It took a while for the spirit of Title IX to take hold with either the general public or the broadcasting fraternity.

We continue to have lapses even as I am writing in a new century. On Friday, March 11, 2006, Winstel's NKU team won the first round of the NCAA Great Lakes Regional by beating Michigan Tech 67–66 in Springfield, Missouri, scoring the winning basket on a beautiful feed from Nicole Chiodi to Karyn Creager 3.9 seconds before the buzzer. This dramatic victory gave us a 27–4 record in a surprising season in which our players had been christened the "delightful dozen" by Lonnie Wheeler in the *Cincinnati Post*. Even so, this exciting accomplishment in the early afternoon went unmentioned on that night's "Final Quarter," the 15-minute, late-night sports report on Cincinnati's Fox-TV, channel 19.

That Friday night broadcast, reported by the highly professional Dan Hoard, indulged in much speculation whether two hometown men's teams, Xavier and Cincinnati, would be selected on Sunday for the NCAA Division I Tournament. It failed to report, even in those running lines on the bottom of the screen, NKU's first-round NCAA Division II victory. I telephoned the station the moment the broadcast was over and asked if Dan was still there. He came right to the phone and said, as soon as I made my complaint, "We should have covered it." The next night, unfortunately, that year's run was over. NKU lost to Grand Valley State, setting the stage for the 2006–07 season in which our incoming seniors would complete their college careers and take what they gained into the world beyond.

Women's basketball at the college level began in 1892 when Senda Berenson created a team at Smith College in Northampton, Massachusetts, one year after James Naismith had invented the game of basketball for boys in nearby Springfield. As Pamela Grundy has shown in *Shattering the Glass: The Remarkable History of Women's Basketball*, the women's collegiate game had developed with considerable parity in relation to the men's game before World War II. After that war, social norms began to favor demure forms of "femininity" over female accomplishment. During the 1950s many colleges with women's programs actually cut them back, and few new programs were started. During this period of retrenchment the women's game was kept alive in the northern states not so much by the elite colleges that had founded it but by the gritty inner-city playgrounds of the larger metropolitan areas. In was at this point in the history of the game that Nancy Winstel came of age in the streets of Newport.

In one of our many interviews I asked whether she could remember when she first "hated to lose." Her answer began with the memory of being a five-year-old girl on the West Side of Newport and getting a doll for Christmas when she would have preferred a helmet or a machine gun. "To be honest, when I was little, I used to cry because I wanted to be a boy. I just thought boys had so much more fun than girls. My mom had to tie me down to put a dress on me. Tie me down."

Nancy started playing sports with her brother Bill, who was three years older. "I would wait for him to come home from school and we would go play. If that day was football, we'd play football. If it was baseball, we'd play baseball. Whatever the sport was, we would play. There was a playground and we would go and all the boys would be there and me. A lot of times when I was little, they would say, 'She's too little; she's a girl.' And my brother Bill would say, 'If she don't play, I don't play.' He would always make sure that I got chosen."

If the game was football, "he would say something like, 'Go out there and stand there by the goal line. I'm going to throw the ball as hard as I can right at your stomach, so as soon as it comes, you just grab it.' Nobody would guard me because I was little, I was young, I was a girl. So he'd throw it and I'd catch it and I got to be pretty good. Bill and I would play every sport. I was a tomboy. I thought there was something wrong with me because I enjoyed it so much."

At some point, "it got to where we could compete. We would start keeping score. In my side yard, we had shingles on both sides. If you hit the shingles with the Wiffle ball you were automatically out, first of all. And, secondly, my mom would have a fit, because if you broke the shingles on that house you were dead. So it taught you to hit the ball right up the middle. When we played in the alleys, there were certain neighbors that if you hit it in there, they wouldn't give the ball back, so that was an automatic out. And then you had to have enough guts to sneak in there and get the ball. If you hit it in there, you had to get it out."

Nancy and the other kids "ruled the neighborhood. That taught us leadership, because there were no adults to be found. You had to form your own games and you had to choose your own sides. When I was little, I was the last one to be picked, but of course my goal was to be the first one picked. I absolutely hated school because I didn't want to be in school. I wanted to be outside. We concreted our back-yard and put a basketball court in it. We would put the gear on, full football gear. We played tackle football in our backyard."

Nancy reached a new level of competitive intensity when her brother Bill began to play tennis. He really liked the game, "so he would talk me into going to play tennis with him. We would walk from the West End to the East End of Newport, where there were courts near the football stadium. In the summer we would leave at 8 or 9 in the morning and play tennis all day. Well, he was obvi-ously a lot better than me and he would beat me. And every time he would beat me I would take my tennis racquet and throw it over the fence to the football field. It was all locked up and he would have to climb the fence, go get it, and then come back. And eventually I think he just decided he was tired of climbing the fence and he would just let me win. I know I was being a pretty poor sport. But I would get so mad. I guess that's probably my earliest recollection of how I hate to lose. I was such a baby."

When Nancy's parents moved up the hill from Newport to Fort Thomas, she attended St. Thomas High School. She played on its volleyball team for girls. But in basketball its only team was for boys. That sport would have to wait until college, when Nancy joined the first women's team ever to play in Regents Hall. For the first time, she was able to channel her competitive instincts by play-ing organized ball with female peers at the intensity she desired. Now, for 24 years, she has coached her own team at NKU, hoping each new class of incoming players will develop a drive for success as deep and tenacious as her own.

The little girl who had wanted a machine gun rather than a doll for Christmas eventually found her identity on a court in competition with other women. Until she found that form of self-expression, her "life," like that of Emily Dickinson, "had stood a loaded gun." Dickinson died in Amherst, Massachusetts, in 1886, six years before Senda Berenson initiated women's college basketball in nearby Northampton. Dickinson had discovered her own form of self-expression by writing more than a thousand unpublished poems during the decade in which her nation fought its Civil War. In one of them, "My cocoon tightens, colors tease, / I'm feeling for the air." And "A dim capacity for wings / Degrades the dress I wear." And the emerging new self realizes that "A power of the butterfly must be / The aptitude to fly."

Dickinson's delicate poem of forceful transformation was first published in 1890, two years before Berenson created the first college basketball team for women. What Emily Dickinson and women's basketball have in common is the urge for female self-expression beyond the confines of an artificially feminine role.

Being somewhat intense about my teaching and research, I have always enjoyed watching basketball games in Regents Hall. When NKU joined the Great Lakes Valley Conference for the 1985–86 season, the pleasure of doing so doubled. Nearly all our conference games were scheduled as doubleheaders for the men's and women's teams. Our home games would be on Thursday evenings and Saturday afternoons, with the women's game preceding the men's. If I had a lot of grading to do, I would sometimes watch all of the women's game and part of the men's. The men's fans would give me dirty looks when I left to go home, even though no one had criticized them for showing up for only the last few minutes of the women's game. I always enjoyed keeping score of the women's games as they were being played—perhaps because it seemed too few were playing attention.

Attending games become especially exciting during the 1995–96 season. Our men's team, coached by Ken Shields (who had taught Nancy Winstel biology at St. Thomas High School), surprised everyone by reaching the finals of the NCAA Tournament. The Elite

Eight was played that year in Louisville, Kentucky, only 90 miles south of our campus. The enraptured group of fans who had come to love this team during the season took buses down to each game. In the quarter-final game NKU upset Cal State–Bakersfield. In the semifinal we upset Virginia Union and its star center Ben Wallace (now an NBA All-Star). We lost to Fort Hays State in the championship game.

The finals were in Louisville again the next year. Again NKU played in the national championship game. This year we lost to Cal State–Bakersfield by one point. These back-to-back national championship games put our basketball program on the map—and on national TV. But our first national championship in any sport was won by Winstel's women's team in 2000.

Our women had been to the nationals before. In March 1975 the very first team, of which Winstel was a member, had played the National College Division Tournament sponsored by the AIAW. NKU continued to play in the regional and national tournaments of the AIAW throughout the 1970s. When that organization was supplanted by the NCAA in the early 1980s, our women's program joined the NCAA as a Division II member; our athletic department helped sponsor the legislation that established the first NCAA basketball championships for women. By the time NKU began its first season as a member of the GLVC in 1985–86, Nancy Winstel was already the coach of the women's team on which she had played as a student.

After graduating from NKU in 1977, receiving her master's degree from Indiana University in 1978, and completing three years as head coach at Midway College in 1981, Winstel had returned to northern Kentucky to be with her mother, whose health was declining. She had no job when she returned to the area, but she was soon hired to coach three women's teams for the next year at NKU. In basketball she was the assistant to Jane Meier, who had succeeded Marilyn Scroggin Moore. She was also assistant volleyball coach and head softball coach. In 1983 Winstel became head basketball coach. Her first great season came in 1986–87, when NKU compiled a 25–5 record and reached the Final Four of the NCAA Tournament, losing in overtime to New Haven College, that year's national champion. The national championship team went 32–2 in 1999–2000, upsetting North Dakota State in overtime to win the title game in Pine Bluff, Arkansas. Michelle Cottrell, our sophomore forward, was chosen first-team All-American and national MVP at the end of the championship season.

Being a fan has certain idiosyncratic elements (such as my habitual need to keep unofficial score of every game I see), but it is also a collective experience of a special kind. We already had a small faculty section watching Winstel's team by the time they made that first trip to the NCAA Final Four in 1986–87. Our numbers began to grow during the men's back-to-back national finalist years in 1996 and 1997. Quite a few who came out in those years to see the men play began to take notice of what the women's team could do. Once Cottrell arrived on campus and began to show how a female All-American could play, increasingly with a team to match, the faculty section at the women's games became larger and more intense than ever, and so it has remained in subsequent years.

The success of a team with a tradition like ours cannot be separated from the emotions we share with our fellow fans during our most intense moments of joy or loss. We felt breathless disbelief when Cottrell, as a freshman, rose from nowhere to stick back what had seemed to be a game-ending miss by senior Shannon Smith to beat Michigan Tech by one point when we hosted the NCAA Regional tourney in 1999, sending us on to the Elite Eight. We instantly looked to one another to see if what we had seen was true before we swelled into a joyous burst of shouting and applause. Michelle's fluid, powerful move was stasis in motion, female force transfigured in form. She was suddenly Aphrodite arising from the foam, ending the fray with the powerful grace of her Poseidon-like lightning strike, in every way enough to take your breath away.

One year later Cottrell again scored a last-minute basket to beat Michigan Tech in the NCAA Regional at Regents Hall. After a more commanding victory over Northern Michigan the next night, we were off to the Elite Eight again (where we had lost in the semis the year before). The site in Arkansas was much too far to drive to without missing classes. Only the final game of the women's Division II national tournament was to be televised. So we listened to the first two games on the radio. First we upset the College of St. Rose, undefeated and ranked first in the country. Then we upset Western Washington to reach the finals against highly favored North Dakota State. My wife and I decided to rent a large-screen TV so we could host a party.

With 20 of our friends crowded into our living room and overflowing into the entrance hall, emotions were strong as the teams appeared on the screen and the announcers dismissed any chance NKU might have to win, saying our players looked like "gnats" in relation to the powerful North Dakota State team. The game was close, exciting, and, toward the end, excruciating. We were afraid it was all slipping away when we lost a four-point lead in the last two minutes and let North Dakota take us into overtime. It was now, however, that our young team went into overdrive, two early baskets by Cottrell being followed by freshman Amy Mobley's breathtaking touchdown pass over the top of the press, breaking the back of North Dakota with an authority we could never have expected, the overtime ending at 71–62.

Cottrell was the nation's MVP that year, but winning the championship had been an entire team effort. Junior guards Jessica Jensen, Heather Livingstone, and Michele Tuchfarber had controlled the perimeter on both offense and defense. Freshman wing players Bridget Flanagan, Kristin Polosky, and Amy Mobley had helped spark the successive victories over St. Rose, Western Washington, and North Dakota State.

One might think that we fans could never be that happy again unless we won another national championship. But it does not happen that way, at least not during the joy of the moment. We fans who had experienced the national championship were now ourselves a team for whom any joys experienced in the future would be intensified by those we had shared in the past.

Indianapolis—March 2003. Cottrell is gone but seniors Mobley, Flanagan, and Polosky have been joined by freshman Sharell Snardon. The Indianapolis Greyhounds are hosting the NCAA Regional because they are the top seed and are expected to win it. But in the semifinal game NKU plays with more intensity and skill than we have shown all season. We beat Indianapolis 66–57 in spite of an ugly incident in which Snardon is taken down while going up on a fast-break layup, losing two teeth to the hardwood as she crashes to the floor. She is not able to play in the Great Lakes Regional Championship two days later against Quincy, another team favored to beat us, after having knocked us out of the conference tournament a week earlier in Evansville. But Sharell does suit up. She watches the game from the bench, her mouth wrapped in bandages. And somehow her teammates, without their joyous, go-to power forward, find a way to reverse a 16-point second-half deficit and take over the game in the closing minutes. Amy Mobley plays the game of her career in what otherwise would have been the last of her career: 19 points, 9 rebounds, 5 assists, 5 steals.

Indy is only two hours away, so our core group of fans had been able to drive to this game even though it was on a Monday night. The second-half comeback was so dramatic and improbable, especially with Sharell not able to play, that I am sure each of us felt as excited at the end of this game as we had when winning the national tournament three years earlier. My own impromptu response at the end of this game was something I had never quite experienced before: I felt big, round, fully formed tears literally pop from my eyes in entirely unadulterated and unanticipated joy. Our team went on to win the first two games of the Elite Eight, far away in St. Joseph, Missouri. We lost to South Dakota State in the national championship game. That disappointment did nothing to erase the magic we fans had felt as we embraced in the mystery of that furious second-half finish on Indy's floor. Such moments of transcendent joy are complete in themselves and truly incomparable. They are what players, fans, and coaches live for.

Growing up in the state of Washington in the 1950s I had no opportunity to watch women play basketball. Everett, my hometown, is north of Seattle on Puget Sound. We had a lot of tall girls in town, but none of them played basketball because there was no team for them—not at North Junior High School in the late 1950s, not at Everett High School in the early 1960s. Decades later, when my wife from northern Kentucky went to one of my high school reunions with me, the first thing she said was, "The women are so tall!"

While I was learning the joys of playing basketball with my friends on our junior high team (I will never forget the agony of walking home on raw, blistered feet after our first serious practice), our female friends had no comparable outlet. Boys of unusual height were immediately sized up as potential ballplayers in our cozy little gym; girls in the same condition were too often singled out as wallflowers at the sock hops on that same cozy floor. Those roles and expectations continued throughout our high school years. The only difference for me was that I did not make our high school team. At 5-foot-11 in junior high, I was a shooting forward who could rebound. At the same height in high school, while many of my friends and competitors for the team had grown, I was suddenly a slow guard who could only make the junior varsity team. My varsity sport was golf.

I suppose that my own frustrations at never quite making the grade, as well as my retrospective thoughts about all those girls in Everett who never got a chance to play, contribute to the great pleasure I have in seeing the young women on Winstel's team playing together and playing so well. Those junior high sock hops would have been a lot more exciting if some of our taller girls had been able to show what some of today's girls can do out on the floor! Women who play basketball have done much to expand the concept of female beauty. A young woman no longer needs to fear being tall.

This was brought home sharply to me during one of the men's games in Regents Hall during the 2005–06 season. I was intently watching the court when one of my fellow fans suddenly announced, "Here come the queens!" When I asked what he meant, he pointed to five or six tall, elegant young women walking behind the scorer's table on the other side of the court. These were well-dressed women from Winstel's team whose unconscious grace and erect carriage had my friend thinking more of a fashion show than of basketball. If he had not pointed them out, I might not have recognized his queenly beings as members of our team.

Tall can now be beautiful, but whatever their height, the women who play the game embody a kind of beauty superior to that of the fashion models my fellow fan was comparing them to. The role of a model is to display someone else's fabrics to make a designer look good. The role of a player is to employ her own elastic limbs and tactile hands in the service of her own heart and mind in flowing self-expression. She does this in the face of constraints from the opponent as well as in the flow of her own team, altogether a more sophisticated and satisfying form of self-actualization.

As a viewer, one can focus on a single player for much of the game, on the five who happen to be on the floor at a given moment, or on our five in continuous interplay with the other five, if one can manage to take all that in. But however narrow or broad the focus, the result, at its best, is the same—kinetic beauty in human form. There are timeless moments of arrested motion that approach the divine stasis of Greek sculpture—with the difference that in the continuous action of the game, those split-second epiphanies usually pass so fast they can only be caught and held with the lens of a camera. (See the frozen motion of Nicole Chiodi driving past Molly Carter in Tim Downer's photo from the December 2005 loss to Drury University.)

So much has changed since my high school days. Yet much has remained the same. I learned this most memorably from a job candidate who had arrived from a distant state to interview for a position in the English Department in which I teach. Although he had misspelled the name of our department chair in his application letter, the rest of us on the search committee liked his credentials and felt we should interview him anyway. It was one of those interviews that got off to a bad start and never improved. I had to take him back to the airport for a flight quite a bit later that evening. I told him we had a great women's basketball team that was playing a 5:30 game and asked if he would like to watch the first half with me while we waited for his plane. To which he replied, "I dislike tall, sweaty women." I did my duty before, rather than after, the first half and saw another good one.

Whatever the pleasure of watching college women play, there are still some men out there, as radio personality Don Imus made clear in his comments about the Rutgers University team in March 2007, who are threatened by women of such power and grace. Even among the faithful, opinions about female appearance can vary sharply. My sociologist wife and I had different reactions to the "razorback" design our players chose for their new black uniforms in 2006–07. To my eye the cutaway jerseys, exposing the shoulders and upper arms, highlighted the wonderful strength and conditioning of our female athletes. She saw the new style as an athletic variation on a dinner-dance dress.

Of all the courtside pleasures at NKU, one of the greatest is watching Winstel coach. The players on the floor may change year after year, but their coach is a constant, always getting the most from her players with an activist style her fans will never forget. Over the years it seems her gestures have gotten larger, her voice stronger, her patience with officials smaller, her love for her team warmer. We can easily hear her from across the court 12 rows up as she shouts at a referee for a bad call or barks instructions to her team. She has a large repertoire of gestures for expressing displeasure to a referee—from pointing to the spot on the floor where the infraction occurred, to acting out a blocking foul with her body, to standing hands on hips in disbelief. What longtime fans have come to appreciate most, however, is her comings and goings with her players on the bench.

From across the court we cannot hear what she says to them as she puts them in or takes them out but we can see how she says it: sending a new player in with a pat of encouragement, bringing one out with a scowl of displeasure, yet at the same time draping that arm around her as she explains what went wrong or needs to be improved. The intensity of her caring is so visible in these courtside encounters that we fans will often miss a bit of the game itself as we watch the sideline action. Here is where the most personal coaching and teaching take place, one on one, moment by moment, in the heat of the game, as Winstel lets each player know exactly what she needs from her as she puts her in or takes her out of a particular game. Some games are more dramatic than others due to the nature of the opponent or the closeness of the score, but the drama on the sidelines is a continuous present, every matchup and situation presenting some new teaching moment for the coach and a player, some new, vicarious pleasure for the seasoned Winstel watcher.

College teachers love their best students not so much for the final grades they earn as for the progress they show throughout a single semester or a college career, often of a life-changing kind. Watching a talented team coached by a master teacher is to see the educational process made visible, week after week and year after year, as it seldom is in the classroom. Some excellent classroom students remain quiet all semester, no one but the teacher knowing what they have achieved. On the court the opposite is true. Everything that is learned—or not learned—is exposed, visible to the eye. So is the body language of the teacher-coach through the course of each game. How many teachers, students, or readers of this book could endure the public scrutiny felt by coaches and players as we watch them learning before our very eyes? Title IX has opened this kind of learning to women as well as men.

NKU president Jim Votruba sees Title IX as "one of the most important events in postsecondary education in the last century because of the opportunities it has provided to women in all areas of university life, not just athletics." He values the women's athletic program on his own campus because it is "so centrally aligned with the educational mission of the university." Because our student-athletes are playing for their own education, not for a future professional career, this "takes off the table the kind of false dreams that some coaches create for athletes who in fact have no hope of playing after their college years." Moreover, the women who play for Nancy Winstel have a coach who is "entirely devoted to the well-being of her players." Votruba sees the "three loves" she describes in the afterword to this book—a coach's love for her players, for the game she coaches, and for the process of becoming a team—as directly analogous to the love that great teachers have for their students, for the subjects they teach, and for the learning process. Nancy Winstel is "a great guardian and steward of the game itself."

This does not mean it is always a pleasure to watch Winstel coach. Her intensity is occasionally so strong that fans worry about her or her players. Sometimes she rides a referee so hard as to hazard retaliation. Not all seasons are not as happy or healthy as those

I am writing about here. A few years before the national championship season, one of Winstel's players, a talented transfer from a Division I school, became unhappy with her playing time and accused the coach of treating her unfairly. In addition to trying to undermine Winstel's authority from within the team, she threatened legal action against the coach for allegedly discriminating against her because of the player's sexual orientation. We fans in the stands could sense the rift that was developing on the bench, even without knowing its exact cause. During the season itself we had to watch Winstel coach under this exasperating pressure, itself intensified by the legalistic aftermath in the newspapers.

Having endured this kind of agony, even indirectly from the stands, has made every season since then all the more of a pleasure. I remember one summer after Cottrell's first season when I stopped at a stop light near the campus. In the lane to my immediate right were Nancy and "Cott" in a convertible. I had never seen Nancy so relaxed and happy. The light changed quickly, but the image remains.

We fans, being fans, sometimes second-guess even a coach as fine as Winstel. But we have done so much less since she coached that seemingly impossible victory over Quincy at Indy in 2003. During the next season a new imperative command was started by John in our faculty section: "Listen to what Nancy says!" Several months before we began chanting this phrase from the stands in November, Karmen Graham, Karyn Creager, and Betsey Clark were learning what it meant to listen to Winstel as incoming freshmen.

2

LEARNING THE SYSTEM

We play at paste
Till qualified, for pearl . . .
And our new hands
Learned gem-tactics
Practicing sands.
—*Emily Dickinson*

Having played in the national championship game in March 2003 raised the bar even higher for the 2003–04 season. It had been exciting enough to upset Indianapolis and Quincy to win the NCAA Great Lakes Regional and make the Elite Eight. Then to go on to beat Washburn University (Kansas) and California University (Pennsylvania) before losing to South Dakota State in the final was even more of a thrill. That team had not been considered one of Winstel's strongest. They had been unranked during much of the regular season, and few had given them any chance to beat Indianapolis, much less Quincy, in the NCAA Regional. Washburn and California both came to the Elite Eight with records far superior to that of Northern Kentucky, yet Winstel had found a way to beat them both. For associate athletic director Scott Eaton, who had arrived at NKU several years before, the 2003 postseason showed, more than any, Winstel's uncanny ability to win NCAA Tournament games that her team "should not have been able to win."

The dramatic achievements of seniors Amy Mobley, Kristin Polosky, and Bridget Flanagan during the 2003 postseason rivaled those with which they, as freshmen, had helped win the national championship in 2000. But their departure now left gaping holes to fill for the 2003–04 season. Winstel endeavored to fill them with some heavy recruiting across the river in Ohio, not only in nearby Cincinnati but also farther north in Dayton and in the upper northwest reaches of the state. Three recruits she brought in as freshmen in the fall of 2003 were to be four-year stalwarts during an intense and often difficult rebuilding period. Guard Betsey Clark was from McNicholas High School in Cincinnati. Center Karmen Graham was from Fairmont High School in Kettering, near Dayton. Forward Karyn Creager was from Patrick Henry High School up north near Leipsic, Ohio. All three were outstanding recruits from whom much could be expected.

Karyn Creager was Patrick Henry's all-time leading scorer and a second-team Division II All-State player in Ohio. She was recruited by several Division I schools and visited the Central Michigan campus, where she found the weather too cold. Many expected Karyn to go to Findlay University in northern Ohio, where her father, Dale, had been a basketball All-American. She was close to her family but she also "wanted to get away and experience something else and not be the norm." As a farm girl, she also liked the idea of living near a big city. So she chose Northern Kentucky and the Greater Cincinnati area.

Karmen Graham was an outstanding scorer and rebounder who earned All-Greater Western Ohio Conference honors as both a junior and a senior. She was also recruited by Division I schools. She had never heard of NKU before Brian Neal, Winstel's assistant, contacted her. Once she visited the campus and learned about the winning tradition, she knew this was where she wanted to play. She was highly competitive and had always been disappointed that her high school team could never get past Battle Creek and its 6-foot-7 center Alison Bales in the postseason; Bales would be playing for Duke University in the fall.

Betsey Clark was a four-year letter winner in both basketball and track; she led her basketball team to the 2001 Division II Ohio State Championship. Her older sister Ashley played basketball for both Kent State and Indiana State, and Betsey had always thought she would go away to college too. When the time came for a decision, however, she realized that she wanted to stay closer to home. She also wanted to play on a team with championship aspirations. This made NKU the obvious choice. She decided to live on campus in the dorms, but it was reassuring to have her parents just across the river.

Karmen and Karyn had both been extremely shy in high school, their parents say, though you would never know it now. They arrived in Highland Heights on the same day for freshman orientation. Karmen's mother remembers her daughter asking, when they saw Karyn across the room, "Is that the other girl that's going to play basketball?" Before the day was over they were such good friends they asked Coach Winstel if they could room together. She agreed, and they remained roommates throughout their college years. Karmen's mother "could not believe how much Karmen had blossomed in just that one day."

The friendship helped them survive a freshman season that was far different from what either had hoped for or expected. For Karmen the difficulty began the first time her dad drove her down from Dayton for an open gym workout with the team. This was not long after the team had played in the national championship game, and they were in great condition. All these college players seemed so strong and so fast that Karmen told her dad on the way home, "I don't know if I can play here. I don't know if I am good enough." She was afraid the coach would take her scholarship away.

She did not feel much better when she and Karyn came down in the summer for voluntary workouts with next year's team. Karyn would drive down from Leipsic and pick up Karmen in Kettering. She would stay overnight on the way back so they could commiserate over what they had gotten themselves into. Their all-star skills from high school were a long way from what was needed to compete at the highest level of the Division II college game. Some moments were downright humiliating. There had been no shot clock in high school, and Karmen would be teased mercilessly each time she stood there holding the ball as the buzzer went off.

The summer was tough, but nothing compared to what they faced when the school year began. Now the coaches were coaching

(NCAA rules had prevented them from doing so in the summer). From the first day of class on August 25 until the first official practice on October 15, they had weight and conditioning sessions and individual workouts that pushed them far beyond anything in their previous experience. From the first practice until the first game on November 20, they practiced for two and a half hours a day, six days a week, with a coach who seemed impossible to please. Betsey Clark recalls these practices as "incredibly intense, very difficult. We all knew what the coach's expectations were, and we all knew that we were not able to meet them, and it always seemed like we couldn't make her happy."

For Karmen the first weeks of school were "overwhelming" because so much was going on. "You had your conditioning three days a week, you had your class schedule, you had your individual drills and team meetings, and you had study table four hours a week. You are always running back and forth from the gym, to your class, to your dorm." It got worse when the official practices started on October 15. "Learning all the plays was very difficult. It was so complex." Then, when the season begins, "you go from this person who was expected to do everything on the team in high school to one who, if you don't play, it doesn't matter, because the others are so much more experienced."

For Karyn everything was absolute "confusion" at first. "In high school I was used to being the leader. I understood our program and I would help the younger players. But when I came here I felt lost. Every day at practice was a struggle." It was especially a struggle on defense. Karyn had always been a shooter. She had never played any man-to-man defense; her high school team had played only zone. "So when I came here and we started defensive drills, Coach Winstel said I was 'just awful.' She said I'd have to score *34* points a game if I played defense like that. So I spent 99 percent of my effort working on my defense. It was a hard transition from high school just because the game was so much faster in reaction time."

Betsey was sharing a suite in the dorm with Karyn and Karmen and they all remember nights when they got back from practice and "we'd just want to cry." It got so bad, Karmen's mother told me, "they even thought of running away together." According to Karmen, "that was only a joke." But it lasted all year. It began the night Betsey's mother invited them over for some homemade chili. To give the evening a more festive feel, she put some Mexican hats on the table. The girls were all complaining so bitterly about practice that someone put on a hat and said, "Let's run away to Mexico." After that, whenever one of them messed up in practice, the others would say, "We'll send you to Mexico." For the rest of the year "we joked about going to Mexico or lying on the beach in California, but we never actually thought about leaving."

Karmen and Karyn adjusted well enough to Winstel's expectations that they averaged 19.8 and 18.7 minutes per game, respectively, during their freshman season. While they were adapting to Winstel's demands on the practice court, Betsey was struggling with the coach in her office. "I kind of put myself in a hole because I had a job and Coach did not agree with me. She told me, 'You are on a full ride. You don't need to be working.' We kind of butted heads on that and that put me in the doghouse. So I didn't really play at all my freshman year. I was very angry and I didn't understand it."

Betsey got some good advice from Liz Burrows, a junior guard who had had similar difficulties as a freshman. "She kept telling me that 'Coach believes players are made in the summer. So do everything you can to get better in the summer. And it's all going to work out.'"

We fans who came out for "Meet the Norse Night" in October 2003 knew very little about how tough or easy the practices could be, for freshmen or anyone else. We were especially happy to see Sharell Snardon on the court again, the 5-foot-11 post player who, as a freshman, had powered last year's team all the way to the national championship game. Sharell had made the All-Tournament teams in the GLVC, in the Great Lakes Regional, and in the NCAA Elite Eight. At the beginning of her sophomore year she was already a legitimate candidate for All-American. Her incredible strength and her generous, winning personality seemed enough to assure an exciting and memorable season. I was so drawn to her as a player that

LEARNING THE SYSTEM

I decided to document her season by addressing a journal entry to her after every game we played, creating a fairly substantial folder I could present to her as a surprise at the end of the season.

It was also wonderful to see junior Connie Myers back on "Meet the Norse Night." She was a 5-foot-10 pivot player who had perfected a nearly out-of-control spin move that gave her the space she needed to get a shot up no matter who was guarding her. This muscular move always reminded me of Degas' sculpted ballet dancers. Supplementing Snardon and Myers on the outside were Liz Burrows, our 5-foot-9 junior point guard; Jessica Brock, a 5-foot-11 senior wing player in the mode of Jessica Jensen; and Nikki Perkins, a 5-foot-4 junior transfer from Cleveland State who was expected to be a major offensive threat.

The above five players started nearly all our games for the first half of the season, a season that started out very well. By the time we beat a powerful Southern Indiana team in Regents Hall on January 10 our record was 10–3. We certainly seemed on the way to another 20-victory season. But that was not to be. For the rest of the season we were 7–8, finishing 17–11 overall, 12–8 in the GLVC. In the GLVC Tournament we lost in the first round to Indianapolis. That loss had appeared to cost us a place in the NCAA Regional, but we did sneak in as the eighth seed among eight teams. We lost in the first round to Quincy, the number-one seed, on their own court. But we did nearly upset them, 51–49.

It had been a very uneven season. Our freshmen had to adjust to the intensity of the GLVC competition as well as to that of their own practices. There were 11 teams in the league and we played each of our conference opponents twice, home and away. The Thursday-Saturday scheduling required five two-game road trips, alternating with five two-game home stands. All the road trips were by bus. The two closer ones took us to Bellarmine and Kentucky Wesleyan in Kentucky and to Indianapolis and St. Joseph's in Indiana. The longer trips took us to Southern Indiana in Evansville and the University of Missouri at St. Louis; to Southern Illinois at Edwardsville and Quincy University in Illinois; and to the University of Wisconsin at Parkside and Lewis University, near Chicago.

The turning point in this season came on February 5. A month

35

after beating Southern Indiana 83–74 on our court, we lost to them 93–66 on their court. Many of our difficulties in the second half of the season related to difficulties experienced by Sharell, whose family in Louisville had been victimized by a traumatic crime, causing her to miss several games. Subsequent family concerns further reduced her playing time. Her struggles were heartbreaking for all who knew her. For a while we were hoping she would be able to return to school, and to the team, for the following season, but it was not to be. I was never able to give her that game-by-game journal I had addressed to her, and I do not know if the athletic department was able to pass it along. Losing Sharell was all the more painful in that she was the first African American superstar in women's basketball at a university whose predominantly white student body reflected the demographics of northern Kentucky since the time of the Civil War.

During this up-and-down season, Karmen Graham and Karyn Creager had made very strong impressions as freshmen. Karmen started in 12 of 28 games. Many of her starts were in the absence of Sharell during the closing weeks of the season. Karmen also got a lot of playing time because of the freewheeling style of Connie Myers, who fouled out of seven games. Karmen averaged 6.5 points and 3.8 rebounds in under 20 minutes a game. She shot for exceptional percentages, making 58.6 percent of her field goals (68 for 116) and 57.9 of her three-pointers (11 of 19). She always brought great energy and focus whenever she was on the court. Even so, she does not feel she really arrived until her sophomore season. What she most remembers about her first year is how "you are a little freshman and you play against these seniors who have been here for four years. They were pushing me around and I just wanted to get to the point where I am pushing someone else around. Coach would keep telling me, 'You need to be in contact with people.'"

Karyn started seven games and she also averaged 6.5 points a game. She immediately established herself as a three-point threat by making 18 of 45 attempts as a freshman (40 percent). She was truly exceptional on the free-throw line, where she made 61 of 70 attempts (87.1 percent). Two games were especially memorable for her that year. In the third game of the season she started against

Findlay, her father's school. The next game was at home against the University of Missouri–St. Louis. "It was a close game and we were down. I scored maybe 16 points, a lot of them toward the end, and we won. It was kind of a relief. I felt I was starting to understand the system."

Although Betsey had much less playing time than Karmen or Karyn, she did have one memorable game as a freshman. It was the home game against St. Joseph's in late January. Betsey claims that the only reason she got in is that "the whole team was struggling. Coach finally came down to her last option and she threw me in there and I put up something like eight points in a few minutes and it changed the game around." Betsey's eight points sparked a 30–6 run in a game that NKU won by nine. This lifted our record to 12–5 at a time when we were still ranked number 22 in the NCAA Division II poll. The toughest part of this season was the very end, when we lost four of our last five.

No matter how well a player plays as a freshman, the transition is tough. It can be tough on parents as well. Players seldom come from high school with either the skills or the work habits they are going to need; Winstel immediately lets them know what needs to change. Karmen's parents remember that she would come home early that first season and say she "did not want to go back." She also wondered how the coach could scream at her on the practice floor but act so friendly to her in public. Dale and Kathy Creager both remember how Karyn and Karmen "shed tears together. Without each other they might not have got through it." But these tough times were also preparing their daughter for "a real world where everything is not handed to you." The Creagers were the first of many parents to tell me that "if they can play for Nancy, they can handle any situation life is going to give them."

Betsey's parents also felt concerned for their daughter during that first year. But they also appreciated the special kind of education that she and her teammates were getting. "Coaches have to say things that students who are not athletes might never hear. They have to tell their players when they are not doing a good job. Without that, some students might just go through life and never know it. Players have to listen to being criticized, and they always have to improve themselves. That's a wonderful lesson, whether you like it or not." The Clarks found one additional advantage to the coach's intense interaction with their daughter. "We kind of looked at Coach Winstel as the 'parent' who is on the scene, and involved, and able to speak her mind like we can't, once our kids go off to campus. So now we have that person here on campus who is the eyes and ears. As a parent, that's comforting."

After the awards ceremony in April 2007, looking back on the friendship that Karyn and Karmen had begun on orientation day four years earlier, I asked Coach Winstel what she remembered most about them during their freshman year. "They were followers," she answered immediately. "And they worked very hard." It is hard to imagine Karmen and Karyn as followers, given the leaders that they, and Betsey too, had become by the time their playing days were over.

The absence of Snardon for the 2004–05 season left a huge gap in the coach's plans and in the hearts of both players and fans. Myers was here for her senior year, but Graham would have to step up fast underneath. More help was needed inside, and Winstel was hoping to find some of it in Angela Healy, an incoming freshman from Highlands High School in nearby Fort Thomas.

Angela had been an outstanding goalie on the Highlands soccer team. Her dream had always been to play soccer for the University of North Carolina at Wilmington, near the Atlantic Ocean. That school offered a scholarship but she had also been exploring her options in basketball. She made a recruiting visit to Belmont University, a Division I school in Tennessee. She even considered playing both sports at Transylvania University in Kentucky. The turning point came when Belmont informed her that it had signed someone else for the post position. This opened the way for Winstel, who was just finding out that Snardon was unlikely to return for her junior year. Angela had never given much thought to NKU because she had always wanted to go away to school. But when she visited the campus and learned about the program, she knew this was where she wanted to play. With senior Connie Myers and sophomore Karmen Graham the only returning post players, she would be certain to get some playing time in her first year.

For the three starting positions on the perimeter, Burrows and Perkins were back as seniors and Creager had proved herself a capable wing player. Returning senior Sarah Woods also provided experience out front. Still, depth was needed at all three positions. One of the most talented recruits for the new season was Nicole Chiodi from nearby Newport Catholic High School. She had been a prolific scorer in high school, averaging 18.5 points a game in her senior year and making second-team All-State in Kentucky. In her four-year career at Newport Catholic she was the school's all-time leader in points (2,124), assists (486), and steals (429). Nicole had serious offers from Division I schools but she is very close to her family and had decided to stay within two hours' driving time of northern Kentucky. This decision eventually led her to accept a scholarship from NKU, a one-minute drive from her home.

On the day Angela and Nicole came for their first open gym, they arrived at the same time, but no one else was there (they had not gotten the word that the starting time had been delayed an hour). This was a bit awkward for them because their high school teams had been bitter rivals—so much so that friends at their respective schools had "freaked out" when they heard both would be playing for NKU. When Nicole walked in and saw only Angela there, she thought, "Uh-oh, something's not right." Angela remembers saying something like, "Hi, I guess we're supposed to meet each other." At first they wondered if someone had pulled a prank on them. But they got along well enough in that first hour that they soon became the best of friends, sharing all the tribulations of their freshman year and then becoming roommates for the rest of their college careers. After the graduation of Karmen and Karyn, they would become the leaders for the 2007–08 season.

Two other recruits at the guard position in 2004–05 were sophomore transfers whom Winstel had tried to sign the year before. Brittany Winner had been a track, cross-country, and basketball star up in Minster, Ohio, midway between Kettering and Leipsic. She had come very close to committing to NKU but instead had accepted an offer from Elon University, a Division I program in North Carolina. (Her friends on the boys' team at Minster had celebrated her decision by spelling out *Elon* with their bodies at her games.) Her first collegiate game had been against Duke University in the Cameron Indoor Stadium; "they put me right out there to guard Alana Beard, the Player of the Year." But as the season progressed Brittany became less and less satisfied with the program and began to regret that she had turned down NKU. Winstel had said to "give me a call" if she ever changed her mind, so Brittany did. She returned to the campus, worked out with the team, and was accepted as a sophomore transfer. She was listed in the 2004–05 media guide as a "good shooter and versatile player" who "will challenge for significant playing time."

The other transfer at the guard position was Keri Finnell. Keri had been a high school standout at Purcell Marian in Cincinnati, where she averaged 22 points a game as a senior and was Greater Girls' Cincinnati League Player of the Year. She had attended Nancy Winstel's summer camps since the fourth grade and had always been interested in NKU, but she decided instead to accept a basketball scholarship at the U.S. Military Academy Preparatory School. She suffered a season-ending injury at the very beginning of her freshman season, two days before coming home for Thanksgiving. Thirty seconds into the game she had stolen the ball and was going for a layup when an opponent undercut her. The result was a torn anterior cruciate ligament (ACL) and serious damage to the meniscus, both requiring surgery at West Point on January 8, 2004. The injury was not only season-ending but also life-changing. Keri still wanted to be a West Point cadet, but she knew her knee would not be ready for the military training that would begin in the summer. So she, too, got back in touch with Coach Winstel. Now she, too, was one of the guards competing for playing time during the 2004–05 season.

These four new players—Healy, Chiodi, Winner, and Finnell—were the added ingredients for the upcoming season. Winstel would have to blend them in with the three returning sophomores—Graham, Creager, and Clark—and the four returning seniors—Myers, Burrows, Perkins, and Woods. Another newcomer this year was assistant coach Matt Schmidt. He replaced Brian Neal, who had become head coach of the women's team at nearby Thomas More College. Schmidt had been assistant coach of the women's team at Findlay College in northern Ohio for three years. His connections in that geographical region were to be especially helpful in future recruiting.

It is always exciting to see the new team on "Meet the Norse Night" in October. This year the absence of Snardon was very hard to assimilate. But Myers and Graham gave us two strong starters in the post. Freshman Healy impressed us that first night with her strength, her alertness, and her athleticism. On the perimeter Burrows was secure in her knowledge of the system at point guard, and Creager was already looking like a long-term fixture on the wing. Among the newcomers at guard, Chiodi immediately caught the attention of the faculty section with her brilliant passing and all-around finesse. She has the kind of athleticism you love to see on the court. We had every reason to expect a very good, if not exceptional, season. Certainly none of us expected the worst start an NKU team had ever had—five straight losses.

The first two losses were at home in Regents Hall. Georgetown College, a National Association of Intercollegiate Athletes (NAIA) team from Georgetown, Kentucky, beat us in the opener by an extremely embarrassing 85–64 score. Guard Kim Ingle scored 27 points off their bench, exploiting a weakness in our perimeter defense that would be an issue all year. Our second loss at home was to Central State (Ohio), 73–63. The next three losses were on the road. Each was a conference game with a GLVC opponent, putting us in a huge hole for the rest of the season. The first, and worst, of these was a 63–48 loss to Kentucky Wesleyan in Owensboro. Kentucky Wesleyan's men's team had always been a powerhouse. Its women's team had always been one of the weakest in the conference; this was only our fourth loss to them in 45 games. Our next two road losses were to teams with much stronger traditions. Bellarmine University beat us by 11 in Louisville; at the University of Indianapolis we lost by 3.

If the players could do little to please Winstel at practice during the previous season, when they won 12 of their first 15 games, one can only imagine what practice was like as the losing streak was growing to five. It was hard enough just to listen to the road losses over the radio. At least we did beat St. Joseph's in Rensselaer two days after the loss to Indianapolis. And then, once the team got back home, they began to find their rhythm.

During the rest of the season NKU won 9 of its 10 home-court conference games, revenging itself on Kentucky Wesleyan, Bellarmine, and Indianapolis. Overall, the team won 16 of its last 23 games, finishing the season at 16–12, only one game worse than the 17–11 of the year before. We did make the first round of the GLVC Tournament, where we lost to Bellarmine. We were not invited to the NCAA Great Lakes Regional. This was the first time a Winstel team had failed to make it since 1997.

The 16–12 record was the worst ever for a Winstel team at NKU. Yet in some ways this season was better than the previous one. That year's team had started 12–3 and then gone 5–8 the rest of the way. This year's team began 0–5 but then won 16 of its last 23. This year's conference record of 13–7 was better than the previous year's 12–8, even though we began at 0–3. Quincy University led the conference standings both years with records of 17–3 and 16–4. In 2004–05 our 13–7 record put us fifth in the conference, one game behind both Bellarmine and Parkside. One more victory probably would have put us in the NCAA Tournament.

What had allowed this team to turn the 2004–05 season around? One constant all year was the play of Myers and Graham in the post. Connie averaged 16.5 points and 8.6 rebounds for the season and was our leading scorer in 14 of 28 games. She made the first-team GLVC All-Conference team. Karmen averaged 11.2 points and 5.7 rebounds a game and was our leading scorer six times. She made honorable mention All-Conference in her sophomore year. Angela Healy supported both these post players extremely well as a freshman, averaging 18 minutes, 5.1 points, and 3.7 rebounds a game.

On the perimeter Creager was our only consistent scorer, averaging 9.7 points a game as a starter on the wing. Burrows provided stability as a senior point guard who knew Winstel's system; she had more minutes on the floor than anyone else, scoring 5.4 points a game. The biggest change at the guard position during this season was the play of Brittany Winner, who increasingly challenged Nikki Perkins. Brittany started 13 games as opposed to 8 for Perkins, averaging 22 minutes and 6.8 points a game.

Three players had disappointing seasons for very different reasons. Keri Finnell, after all the rehab she had done to get her knee back in shape after the surgery at West Point in January, reinjured the knee during her first preseason at NKU. The injury was not enough to require further surgery, but it was enough for her to be redshirted for her first season in the program. She could practice with the team as her condition allowed, but she could not suit up to play.

Betsey Clark, after working hard all summer to get back in Winstel's good graces, had been proud to break into the starting lineup in the game at Bellarmine on November 28. Three weeks later, playing in our holiday tournament at Regents Hall, she suffered a season-altering injury while trying to fight through a screen: her shoulder caught that of her opponent and popped out of its socket. She decided to postpone surgery until the end of the season in March so she could contribute as much as possible in a supporting role. Even without the full use of her arm, she was a great help to a team struggling with its perimeter defense. This was the season in which our faculty section began calling her "Spark" for the spark she brought in off the bench.

Nicole Chiodi's playing time was limited by the presence of Burrows, a senior point guard who thoroughly understood Winstel's system. The system is hard enough to learn for any freshman, but even more so for a point guard, who needs to understand all five positions, not only her own. Nicole did get into enough games, usually in the closing minutes, that her fans in the stands wanted to see more of her. Her passing remained as brilliant as it had been on "Meet the Norse Night," but this year we saw very little of the form that had made her Newport Catholic's all-time leading scorer.

What do the above players remember, now, about the 2004–05 season? The first thing they all remember is the 0–5 start, a trauma they never want to relive. This became, in retrospect, a huge motivation for the two highly successful seasons that followed.

Individually, Karmen Graham began to feel she was finding her place in her sophomore year. "You begin to realize that you have your role to play and you bring to the table things that no one else can. You have to find that special thing that you can do to help contribute." Karmen was already showing the exceptional desire and fierce competitiveness that would make her the heart and soul of next year's team. She was also developing a new kind of confidence in herself as an athlete. The individual game she most remembers from her sophomore season is "when I hit kind of a big shot against Parkside at home. In high school I was always taking the last-second shot but I would never make it; we'd always lose and I would be so mad." The shot she made against Wisconsin–Parkside on January 22 gave her team a 53–50 victory and its sixth straight win. Karmen had scored 20 points on 8 of 11 field goals, along with 9 rebounds and 4 blocks. Opponents who were keying on Myers down low were now paying for it.

After the loss of Sharell and the 0–5 start, what Karyn Creager most remembers about her sophomore year is "how we came together. We only lost one game in January. We had that win streak. We felt if we can do this, we can to a lot more. We were developing a good inside force, with Connie and Karmen and Angela." Yet it was a big blow to lose in the first round of the conference tournament and not make the NCAA. That was another strong motivator for the next year. Individually, Karyn set two school records as a sophomore: one when she made 27 free throws in a row; the other when she made 88.5 percent of her free-throw attempts for the season (77 of 87). On defense, she was no longer the liability she had been as an incoming freshman. Working hard in practice gave her confidence during the games. She was beginning to develop her own personal mantra as a defender: "To get after someone the way you hate to be defended; what they do, that you hate, do that to them." When did Karyn look most like an awkward sophomore? When she tried to drive around a defender who was overplaying her to deny her the three and would be muscled aside or stripped of the ball.

Angela Healy does not remember experiencing the degree of confusion and bewilderment during her freshman season that some of her teammates felt. She had always wanted a coach who would push her hard, so Winstel was no problem in that way. As for the games, "They threw me in there and I just played. As a freshman you don't feel so much pressure. You just play and if you make a mistake it's because you're a freshman. Just working with Connie and Karmen was a great learning experience." Angela's biggest problem in practice was that "we only had three post players, so we had to bring in Coach Schmidt to play against" (he had been a post player in his younger days). Occasionally, Michelle Cottrell filled in for the missing post. "She was incredibly strong. And her shots—you don't even think they are going to hit anything and they go in."

Brittany Winner felt like she was having a second freshman season. She had to fit in with a whole new team and "there was a whole new system to learn, which was very different from Elon's. It was a season of ups and downs. I got really down on myself and just thought I should be playing better." When she got really depressed, she went to the coach to talk about it. Winstel reassured her by saying, in effect, "I wouldn't trade you for anybody. I waited a year for you to come here and I know you are worth it. I know that you deserve this scholarship and I wouldn't recruit you if I didn't think you could play in our system."

Reassurance came to Betsey Clark in a different way. Following Burrows's advice, she had "worked my butt off over the summer." The payoff came in something Winstel said during one of the individual drills early in the school year. "We were doing a defensive drill and I was doing so well that the Coach just said, 'Well, Betsey's sick of sitting on the bench.' And I said, 'Yes, I am. Let's go.'" Before long she had made the starting lineup against Bellarmine. Even after the shoulder separation took away her offense, Betsey's ability to bring tough defense in off the bench kept her on the floor.

Nicole Chiodi's first shock as a freshman had come "on the first day of lifting." Her lifting partner was Liz Burrows, and she was surprised at how strong a guard needed to be: with Nicole's speed and finesse, strength had not been an issue in high school. Once the season began, Nicole realized that the coach had her sitting on the bench so she could "watch and learn the system. But I was rearing to get in there, instead of working on things only in practice. It was hard. 'Hard' is a small word, but it was crazy." Especially for the freshman who had been the outstanding high school player in northern Kentucky the season before. One faculty member began referring to her, sympathetically, as "our brooding Byron" on the bench.

For Keri Finnell, hurting her knee again after everything she had gone through the year before was extremely frustrating. Sitting out as a redshirt made a lot of sense, but it was putting her way behind. Next fall she would still be a freshman in eligibility while already being a junior academically. One silver lining during her redshirt year—her parents came over from Cincinnati for every one of the home games even though she could not suit up and was unable to play.

Another member of the program having to make first-year adjustments during the 2004–05 season was assistant coach Matt Schmidt. Losing those first five games during his first year working for Winstel was certainly a trial by fire. He had coached women's basketball for nine previous years in three different programs, but Winstel had a system and an attitude different from any he had encountered before. He was quite pleased when the team rallied to finish at a respectable 16–12—until he realized how absolutely unacceptable that was to a head coach who had never had a record that "bad." He had known "a lot of teams that would kill to win 16 ball games." NKU would be graduating four seniors this year and had no juniors during the current season, but he still had much to look forward to. This year's sophomores and freshmen had shown impressive skill, fight, and heart in the course of the season. Whether they realized it or not, they were laying the foundation for the exceptional season to come.

How did Winstel respond to the five losses in a row that began this season? Had she felt that things would work out well enough once the newer players adjusted to the system? "No," she told me, "I was ready to jump off a bridge. When the going gets tough, I tend to dig in and become more stubborn. So I would say to them, 'This is going to change. It's going to change whether you change it or I change it. It is going to change because this is unacceptable.'" The changes were made at practice. "There are some things you have no control over," she told her players. "But you *do* have control over how you come to practice. You have control over whether you're prepared." She has always felt that the best way to be prepared for game day is to play quality basketball every minute of every day in practice. "But most kids don't see that. They see the game. They live for the game."

Because kids live for the game, losses can provide some of the best, if most painful, teaching moments. The five losses that began the 2004–05 season were an obvious wake-up call. But the worst single loss during the entire season was probably the one to Southern Indiana in Regents Hall on February 3, our only conference loss at home. We lost by one point, 60–59, even though two successive three-pointers by Karyn Creager had given us a six-point lead, 58–52, with four minutes remaining. Southern Indiana was able to outscore us 8–1 for the rest of the game because we made three turnovers in four minutes—and allowed them an offensive rebound for the game-winning shot. We had beaten this same team by 26 points on their court one month earlier. But here at home we had come out flat and let them take a 12-point halftime lead. As freshman Angela Healy said in a postgame interview, "I really don't think it was them. I think it was us. We really didn't come prepared to play in the first half, so we beat ourselves, I guess."

Comments such as the one above showed Angela to be unusually mature for a freshman. Later I was surprised to learn that she is a year younger than her classmates because she skipped the third grade. She was so far ahead of the other students that the teachers were confident she could move on to the fourth grade. The only resistance came from the school administrators, who asked her parents, "Don't you want her to have one more year as an athlete?" Her parents had answered, "No, we would rather have her not be bored in school."

What exactly is the Winstel "system" that her sophomores and freshmen were trying to learn during these two seasons? Part of it involves a variety of offensive and defensive alignments designed by a coach who builds her offense around a high-low post, a point guard, and two players on the wing; who has a strong preference for man-to-man defense over the zone; and who relies on half-court defense much more than on the press. As much as players have to learn about all the plays in the playbook, however, the most difficult element of Winstel's system is the intensity of effort she demands, in practice as well as in the game.

In college basketball each team has five players on the floor for 40 minutes. That makes a total of 200 minutes for the players on each team. I have come to believe that the supreme quality that Winstel wants from her team is 200 minutes of intensity, whoever the five rotating players happen to be. Her preseason practices are usually scheduled for two and a half hours, six days a week. If she has 12 players practicing for 150 minutes a day, this means she is looking for about 1,800 minutes of intensity a day. Do that six times a week and you have about 10,800 aggregate minutes per week. That is all she wants.

Admittedly, that adds up to a lot of intensity. But that is the approximate number of minutes that she and her players are working together every week. So why not make them as intense and productive as you can?

3

MAGICAL SEASON

As if no soul the solstice passed
That maketh all things new.
—*Emily Dickinson*

Winstel's team remade itself during the 2005–06 season. It did indeed pass the solstice that "maketh all things new." In the record book that change is measured in one of the most remarkable turnarounds any Winstel team had ever made from one season to the next—from a 16–12 record to 27–5. As the season unfolded, the change occurred incrementally, one game after another, until something extraordinary happened—the team had suddenly transcended itself more fully than anyone could have expected. When that happened, the solstice was passed not for any single soul but for all 12 players on the team. They will never lose the sense of having been part of something remarkable and blessed. Their defining day was March 5, 2006, in the 30th game of a 32-game season.

For assistant coach Matt Schmidt, preparation for this moment had begun one year earlier, on March 4, 2005, when Bellarmine eliminated NKU in the first round of the GLVC Tournament, ending any hope of making the NCAA Tournament. That defeat ended the difficult season that had begun with five losses in a row. Seven weeks remained in the spring semester, and Winstel and Schmidt made the most of them. Looking ahead, they saw major "deficiencies" that had to be addressed immediately. "We pushed the returning players very hard for the rest of that semester, from 6 A.M.

conditioning to individual workouts, and probably some of them thought we were crazy. We pushed them about as hard as they could be pushed in that postseason. I give Nancy a lot of credit for sticking to her guns. And it was a good thing."

Failing to make the NCAA Tournament meant that Winstel's players got a spring vacation like the rest of the university. Karyn Creager recalls that a team meeting had been called "for the first day after the break. We were told to bring workout gear, but we didn't think much about it; we thought we were going to talk and then lift weights or something. As soon as we walked into the gym, it was like, 'Get on the line. We're doing conditioning.' I was thankful that I'd stayed in shape by practicing with my former high school team during the break, because from the first day back we were conditioning and working out hard. The 0 and 5 start and not making the NCAA was a great motivator for the next season and that really helped us. Whenever you were tired, or just didn't feel the urge to continue with the workout, you just thought back on that and it gave you the extra to go that much farther."

In addition to the conditioning and the individual workouts, each returning player has a one-on-one meeting with Coach Winstel in her office. In this "exit" exam from the recent season, Winstel asks each player to evaluate her performance with an emphasis on areas for further improvement. These can be make-or-break sessions, with all the cards on the table. A player might say, "Coach, I don't know if I can play on this team." Or the coach might ask, "Are you sure you really want to be here?" Simple statements lead to strong challenges. If a player says she wants to get better, Winstel might ask, "What are you going to do to get better?" And not only that, but "Are you willing to do it?" If the player says, "Yeah, I want to get faster and I want to get stronger," Winstel will ask, "But what are you going to do to get stronger?" And "when are you going to do that?" Winstel's blunt questions force her players to "make a commitment. They have to see that it's not my team, it's their team, and they have to take over." The best thing about the postseason meetings in 2005 is that "the players were as upset about their season as I was. I was impressed by the fact that they were mad, too."

Winstel's blunt method of interrogating her players resembles the way her mother had challenged her 30 years earlier—when Nancy had announced that she wanted to go to Indiana University for a master's degree immediately after getting her degree from NKU. "Don't you think you need to get a job?" her mother asked. *"What were you doing* going to college?"

When Nancy explained that she wanted to earn a master's degree so she could become a women's basketball coach, her mother demanded, "You want to do *what*? You'll never make a living as a basketball coach." Nancy agreed that it might be hard to make a living. "But once I convinced my mother that this was something I really wanted to do, my parents were very supportive."

In hindsight, Winstel sees "a kind of fascination in doing something like that. It took a lot of guts to do it because it was not something that was done. A daughter just didn't go away. But I always felt that to come back and do what I wanted to do, I had to leave."

At the end of the 2005 spring semester the players and coaches had something entirely new to look forward to. After graduation ceremonies for the seniors the team flew to Australia for two games in Sydney and one in Cairns. This was the second time Winstel had taken a team overseas. A few years earlier, as a way of improving team chemistry and rewarding players for their hard work, she had arranged a trip to France for the team that included Cottrell, Tuchfarber, Mobley, Polosky, and Flanagan. This year's excursion to Australia included four graduating seniors and seven returning underclassmen. Each player had to raise the money for her trip. And each had to come to 10 days of practice for the games they would play—even the seniors who had graduated at the May 7 commencement.

Nicole Chiodi remembers those practices "as being a big point in my career, because the coach had taken a couple of us aside and said that this was an opportunity for us because the point guard position was now open. The seniors were with us for practice but they were kind of laid back; they taught me a lot and showed me a lot and I got to play point for one of the teams. Once we got to

Australia I got to play quite a bit, but at the same time, Liz was still there, so we all kind of adjusted and switched in and out." The graduating seniors who made the trip were Burrows, Myers, Perkins, and Woods. The returning players were Graham, Creager, Clark, Winner, Healy, Chiodi, and Finnell.

Keri Finnell had also looked forward to being part of the competition for the guard position now that her redshirt season was over and her knee was much better. But bad luck struck again just two days before the trip to Australia. A ball jammed the thumb of her right hand and made it swell so badly that she could not catch or dribble the ball. She did enjoy the trip as a chance to bond with her teammates. So did Betsey Clark, still very early in the eight-month rehab from her shoulder surgery in March.

One highlight of the Australia trip for Coach Schmidt is that Coach Winstel encouraged him to bring his 82-year-old grandfather Herb along (a welcome recognition of the inevitable sacrifice assistant coaches make in their family lives during the regular season). Eleven players and assorted family members made for a traveling party of 24. Schmidt will never forget that number because he was responsible for counting heads whenever they would board the bus for some diversion, practice, or game. After the 18-hour flight had landed them in Australia, the players spent their free time watching kangaroos and holding koalas, snorkeling on the Great Barrier Reef, dancing into the wee hours, and posing for pictures against the sea, the city, and the sky. They won each of the three games they played, but this trip was more about bonding. You see evidence of this in the small-group photos as well as in the team photos they all brought home.

Athletic director Jane Meier attributes much of the team's subsequent success and chemistry to the Australia trip. "Nancy's focus earlier in her career was more on the Xs and Os. Her focus now is more on team dynamics. She has always cared deeply about her players, but now she is more personable. She has gotten to know her players better as people and persons, and because she knows them better, she can motivate them better." In Australia some of her players were away from home and their parents for the first time. They could therefore attach to others in ways they had not done before. Those whose parents did make the trip related to their parents or coaches in new ways. As one player put it, "You can't avoid talking to some people on an 18-hour flight."

Winstel, too, thinks the Australia trip was crucial for the chemistry that developed on this team. Raising the money for the trip was a huge challenge for the players and their families, but everyone who went got the kind of adventure they will never forget. "Our players traveled together and they had a ball. They didn't go crazy, but they went out at night too. They're cute girls and they like to have fun." Not wanting to be looking over their shoulders, she gave Coach Schmidt the responsibility of chaperoning on the night they went dancing in Sydney. He remembers that "the girls took a long time to get ready and it was probably about midnight by the time we left. Coach Winstel wanted them back by 2:30, but when 2:30 came I knew I didn't have a chance, so I didn't even try. When 3:00 came I told them we 'all have to start to move along.' At 3:30 I simply had to say, 'It's time to go. You don't have a choice.'"

The game in Cairns was against an Australian club team. What Schmidt remembers most is that the home team "played loud music" the entire game. "I think the kids liked it because they could not hear Coach and me screaming at them. They would say, 'Oh, I couldn't hear you, Coach.'" The flight home began at 4:30 the next morning, so Winstel decided she might as well let the players stay up all night as long as they were ready for the bus to the airport. This created more chaperone duty for Schmidt, whose only memory of the final leg of the flight home is that he fell asleep before takeoff and did not wake up "until the plane landed."

After returning from Australia the members of the next year's team continued to bond with one another in a somewhat more strenuous way—early-morning workouts throughout the summer with the team's new strength and conditioning coach. Schmidt remembers being with Winstel one day on a local recruiting trip. They were talking about the players' need to become stronger and faster, and he mentioned that some of the larger schools have coaches specifically devoted to strength and conditioning. He was surprised by how quickly Nancy found a volunteer willing to work with their players during the upcoming summer.

Livey Birkenhauer had been a freshman guard at NKU during Winstel's senior season (1976–77). Like Winstel, she is one of the few NKU athletes to earn varsity letters in three sports (hers being basketball, volleyball, and softball; Winstel's third sport was tennis). An informal history of the women's basketball program written by David Phillips in 1985 notes that Livey Birkenhauer "was one of the first female collegians at Northern to see the benefits of weight training." She had transformed herself from "a skinny college freshman" into "an aggressive, somewhat flashy" force on the court. After 20 years of a business career in sales with Xerox, Birkenhauer had decided to become a personal trainer. She was certified by the National Strength Conditioning Association. She was delighted to be able to work with Winstel's players in return for becoming the program's official strength and conditioning coach.

Birkenhauer met early in the morning three times a week during the summer of 2005 with those returning players who were in town and wished to establish a workout routine. Although most fans of the team did not know that this extra conditioning was going on over the summer, we could see an immediate difference at "Meet the Norse Night" in October. The difference was not so much in size as in muscle tone, speed, and stamina. When the fall semester began on August 23, the seven veteran players on the team could begin working out with five new recruits. Two were transfers and three were incoming freshmen. All were from Ohio.

Katie Butler was a junior transfer from the University of Dayton. She was a 6-foot-1 post player who had been a prodigious scorer at Liberty-Benton High School in Findlay, averaging 25.3 points per game as a senior. Coach Schmidt had heard through his connections in Findlay that Katie was unhappy at Dayton and was looking to transfer to another Division I program; he got her to NKU for a campus visit a day before she was going to sign transfer papers to another school.

Angela Estes was a sophomore transfer from East Tennessee State. She was a 6-foot-1 post player from Cincinnati who had helped lead Mount Notre Dame High School to the 2004 Division I state championship. Angela had planned to return to East Tennessee State but found herself telling her father in August that she had not enjoyed playing there. She decided at the very last minute to stay in Cincinnati and play at NKU.

Cassie Brannen, an incoming freshman, was yet another 6-foot-1 post player. She had been a younger teammate of Angela Estes at Mount Notre Dame. Angela remembers that Cassie had blocked her first shot at her first open gym there. "Next time at open gym I blocked her shot." They became "best friends" then, even though they were competing for the same position on the team. Now they were back together at NKU. Cassie's older brother, Bobby Brannen, had been a post player for Bobby Huggins at the University of Cincinnati, where his teammates had included Danny Fortson, Kenyon Martin, and Ruben Patterson.

Winstel's other two incoming freshmen were guards. Five-foot-nine Karen Brackman had been a younger teammate of Brittany Winner at Minster High School, where she too had excelled in track as well as basketball. She helped lead Minster to the Division IV state championship in basketball the year after Brittany graduated.

Five-foot-six Danyelle Echoles was a scoring guard from Colerain High School in Cincinnati, where she scored 1,228 career points and was named first-team All-Greater Miami Conference as a senior. In her younger years she had played with Keri Finnell at both the Friar's Club in Cincinnati and Winstel's summer camp. The Friar's Club was about to close when Danyelle arrived at NKU; she would like to run an athletic club for inner-city kids when she graduates.

One of the challenges for the new season would be to blend the five new players with the seven veteran ones. Until official practice began on October 15, all players were limited to a certain number of hours of strength and conditioning per week. They were also limited to a certain number of individual workout hours with the coaches. This is always a difficult period of individual effort without any opportunity to play as a group, so Winstel decided to do something new. She created a weekly leadership seminar to which she invited her returning juniors and sophomores. They met once a week for six weeks. They studied various materials on leadership and motivation. They took turns making presentations to one another. This was another way in which Winstel could encourage her players to internalize more of the team-building responsibility among themselves. Karyn Creager found that "by getting everyone's views, you kind of see what kind of a person they are, and what they want out of a leader."

One result of these meetings was a list of goals for the season that the players generated among themselves and posted in the locker room. Three of these were very specific goals that no player on the team had ever accomplished: "Beat Indy at Indy," "Beat Bellarmine at Bellarmine," and "Beat Quincy at Quincy." Another was "Make it to the NCAA Tournament." The players in the leadership seminar also initiated a poster-making session for the whole team. Each player received a poster on which each of her teammates wrote a phrase of praise for what she contributes to the team. These hung in each player's locker throughout the season and expressed these young women's admiration and affection for one another in unforgettable ways. "Always uplifting and knows what to say." "Ankles of iron." "So versatile you can do everything." "Uses really long arm power to swat people's crap." "You have the speed of a cheetah."

During the period of the leadership meetings, the team elected Creager, Graham, and Winner as cocaptains. Earlier in her career Winstel had sometimes chosen the captains or cocaptains herself. In more recent years she often lets the players do it. It was unusual to have three cocaptains, but when the vote came out this way she accepted and embraced it. This result was a huge vote of confidence for Brittany, a relative newcomer in relation to both Karmen and Karyn. This would be yet another way to distribute the leadership responsibility broadly throughout the team. All these special group dynamics during the offseason and the preseason—the trip to Australia, the summer conditioning, the leadership sessions, the three cocaptains—were helping to build leadership and motivation on a team with no returning seniors.

Earlier in her career Winstel had been much more reluctant to share authority. "When you are a young coach, you want to be in charge. You want to show you are in control. As you get older and you have more confidence in yourself, you can allow others to contribute." In those earlier years, "I hated to admit I was wrong. Now, I want to win more than I want to be right. I want to win so bad that I will change. I've not mellowed so much as I've figured out a better way to get what I want."

What Winstel ultimately wants is for her players to want what she wants as much as she does. She is now increasingly aware that "it's not about me. I am part of the process, but it's not my team. We are all part of the whole and I want them to realize that it's *their* team, it's *their* dreams. It's about them. It's not about me winning. My job is, while they are here, to help them fulfill their dreams, help them have the successes we can have, but also help them prepare for life beyond."

For Betsey Clark the 2005–06 season began when she got permission from her doctor to work out in October, the eighth month of her rehabilitation from shoulder surgery in early March. She had heard about some of the new players but did not realize the difference they would make until she tried to drive through them to the basket. "They had said in the locker room about how much people were getting blocked and everything, but I hadn't actually played yet, so I just would go in there and get blocked left and right—I mean, you've got Angela Estes, you've got Cassie, Angela Healy, and Karmen. You've got all these arms up there, and then you've got Nicole, who's a 6-foot point guard. And Katie Butler too. And it's not only that we have the height. They're all real thin and put together and they can run the floor, so they're going to get up and down. That helps, when our posts can outrun the other team's posts and get ahead of them on a fast break."

The new players who impressed Betsey were having their own reactions to being on this new team. Transferring from the University of Dayton, Katie Butler felt she was getting a new lease on life. During her freshman season her Dayton team had won 3 and lost 25, setting a school record for the most consecutive losses. "I'll never forget the first NKU practice in which we split into two teams and played a 40-minute game. The coaches refereed and we were getting so mad if our team was losing. Our team came back in the second half and we won. We were so ecstatic. And the other team, the other girls, were so mad at us. It was so good because I had missed that for two years—people not having the drive to win."

Cassie Brannen had a more typical freshman initiation. "The first couple of practices I was just in shock. Coach comes off as a real sweetie, and then when she's on the court, she'll yell at you. I just wasn't expecting that and I didn't know how to take it. So I learned from all the older people how to act and what I would need to do." Her parents remember one day when she came home and said, "I love school, but I hate basketball." Cassie was thrilled when Angela Estes, her old high school friend from Mount Notre Dame, transferred in just before the semester began. Winstel pushed them both very hard to be more aggressive offensively. Once Angela told Cassie she was afraid she could not do anything right. Cassie told her, "I don't know if *I* could go through this without *you*." They pulled each other through the first year like Karmen and Karyn, and then Angela and Nicole, had done.

The arrival of a second Angela on the team created a need to distinguish between them. So Winstel asked Healy to come up with a new name she could call her by. Angela suggested, in jest, "A-Unit." (This was her variation on "G-Unit," nickname of rapper Fifty Cent.) The name stuck, and Angela helped christen some of the other members of the team. Nicole was always "Ed" but she could also be "Paki" or "Nappy." Brittany had always been "B-Dubs," all the way back to high school. Karmen was "Grammy" and Karyn was "Creags" and Betsey was "Becky" (a name Winstel had called her by mistake one day during Betsey's freshman year, making the coach furious when Betsey failed to respond and kept walking in the other direction). It did not take long for Katie Butler to become known as "K-But." Keri was "K-Dog," Danyelle became "D," and Brackman became "Bracky." The other Angela, whose arrival had forced the issue for "A-Unit," became "E-Man."

Fans got to see the new team on "Meet the Norse Night," October 24. The most obvious difference was in personnel. Four players had graduated, seven were returning, and five were new. It took some time to distinguish among the three new 6-foot-1 post players and the multitude of guards. But even the players we knew from before were different this year. Part of this, though we did not know it, was the summer conditioning. Creager was still long and lean, but her muscle tone was more smooth and supple. Chiodi was an even sleeker greyhound as she went up and down the court. Healy was more of a presence in the post than before, in part because Myers had graduated, but also because of the strength and conditioning work she and her teammates had done over the summer.

As striking as the physical changes were the internal ones. Graham and Creager, with no more seniors to follow, were becoming leaders themselves. They assumed their positions on the floor with more confidence and authority than they had shown before. Winner, after struggling to find her place as a sophomore transfer, was now being looked to for leadership. And Chiodi was suddenly at the center of the team, rather than on the periphery, distributing the ball in a way we had not seen from the point in years. And Healy suddenly had much more company in the post.

All the returning players seemed freer and more assured than we remembered. They were all a year older, of course. They had all come closer together in Australia and during the summer conditioning. But it was also clear that they enjoyed playing with the new transfers and freshman recruits. The chemistry had changed. The coach was still tough, the demands were still high, but so were the solidarity and the skill level. We had more talent, height, and athleticism on the floor than we had seen in a long time. If it all came together, we fans would have an enjoyable year. The team looked eager for whatever the season would bring.

For those who scheduled our games, the 2005–06 season presented a major new challenge because of the reconfiguration of the Great Lakes Valley Conference. The GLVC had expanded from 11 to 14 teams by adding three Missouri schools: Drury University, Rockhurst University, and the University of Missouri–Rolla. Instead of playing every conference team twice, home and away, we were now split into two divisions. NKU was in the Eastern Division with Bellarmine, Kentucky Wesleyan, Indianapolis, St. Joseph's, Lewis, and the University of Wisconsin–Parkside. The Western Division included the three new Missouri schools and four of our old rivals:

Quincy, Southern Indiana, Southern Illinois at Edwardsville (SIUE), and the University of Missouri–St. Louis (UMSL). We still played each team in the Eastern Division both home and away, but we would play each Western opponent only once a year, alternating each year between home and away.

This season would be the first one in which we did not play Quincy, SIUE, or UMSL at home. Instead we had home games with two of the new teams, Drury and Rockhurst. The addition of the new Missouri teams extended the geographical range of the conference and the length of our bus trips. Because most conference games are female-male doubleheaders, the women's and men's teams usually ride together to both destinations on a road trip; this makes for an extremely full bus with all the equipment. For the longer trips into Missouri they would have to leave on Wednesday and return on Sunday.

In the preseason poll for 2005–06 (voted by the coaches) NKU was ranked third in the Eastern Division, behind Lewis and Bellarmine. This was probably justified in view of our 16–12 record the year before, our first-round elimination from the GLVC Tournament, and our failure to qualify for the NCAA Tournament. We had two excellent starters back in Graham and Creager, but it was not yet clear how deep we would be in the post or how good we would be out front, especially at point guard. Lewis, in Romeoville, southwest of Chicago, would be led by three exceptionally gifted returning players: Mary Moskal, Darcee Schmidt, and Shante Glenn. Bellarmine, our longtime nemesis from Louisville, also had a stronger team returning, on paper, than did we. They had the additional distinction of having beaten us badly in the first round of the 2005 GLVC Tournament.

Drury was the odds-on favorite to win the Western Division in their first year in the league. In the two previous seasons they had compiled the best overall record in the nation, 65–4. In 2004 they had played in the national championship game. This year they had most of their key players returning, including All-America candidate Amanda Newton, now a senior center. Quincy was picked second in the Western Division as the defending GLVC champion; they had an extremely talented senior center of their own, Deana Mc-Cormick. In the scheduling for 2005–06 we were relatively lucky to draw Drury at home, relatively unlucky to play Quincy only on their court.

The first conference games came early in the season, when we hosted Rockhurst and Drury on December 1 and 3. But we had three nonconference games first. The season started with home-game victories over Wilberforce University and Northwood University and an away victory over Wayne State. The latter two teams were members of the Great Lakes Intercollegiate Athletic Conference (GLIAC), the sister conference of the GLVC, so our games with them would influence our regional ranking at the end of the season. At the beginning of the 2005–06 season we were not among the eight teams considered most likely to make the NCAA Regional in March.

As I watched the season unfold, I had no idea how much work behind the scenes was required for what my fellow fans and I were enjoying week after week. That kind of knowledge would have to wait until the next season, after I had decided to write this book and follow much more than the games themselves. I did sense early on that this season was something special, though. I began writing a little summary of the game on each score sheet I kept, trying to capture the essence of what I had seen. These recorded a season in which we never knew who our offensive leader would be—and in which strong defense was a constant, no matter which team we played.

The defense made a statement in the home opener, holding Wilberforce (Ohio) to 10 points in the first half of a 71–40 victory. Chiodi was our leading scorer with 11 points in her debut as point guard. She also had six rebounds and six assists and turned the ball over only once. Creager was the leading scorer in our 81–55 victory over Northwood (Michigan), scoring 17 points on 6 of 8 from the field, including 3 of 3 three-pointers. Chiodi was again impressive, recording a "double-double" with 10 points and 10 assists.

In our victory over Wayne State in Detroit during Thanksgiving vacation, Graham scored 17 points with her patented inside game; she made three field goals while drawing enough fouls to go 11 of 14 from the line. Creager continued to shoot extremely well, making 3 of 4 three-pointers and 5 of 6 free throws. Butler showed what she could do off the bench, with 13 points in 15 minutes on 4 of 5 from the field and 5 of 5 from the line. All 11 players scored in the 76–48 victory, with only Keri Finnell unable to play. She had badly strained her nonsurgical knee in the first full scrimmage and would not be able to enter a game for three more weeks.

Although we won the first three games by large margins, these games also showed how tough the women's collegiate game can be on the body. Near the end of the opener, Chiodi had tried to split two defenders on a drive and had hit the floor directly with her chin, scaring her fans as she lay dazed, bleeding on the floor, not yet knowing what had hit her. She was back at the point, a bandage on her chin, for the Northwood game, in which she dished out 10 assists. Karmen Graham was fouled so often while putting up her 17 points against Wayne State that she left the game with a slight concussion. She had to miss the conference opener with Rockhurst but was back on the court when Drury came to town.

Butler started for Graham in the Rockhurst game and she played well. But we trailed 29–28 at halftime. In this game Cassie Brannen, the freshman from Mount Notre Dame, came in off the bench and saved the day. She had 14 points and 13 rebounds and was unstoppable in the second half as we surged to a 70–57 victory. Cassie is a tall, thin, temperamentally shy young woman. On the court she is quick, agile, and strong.

We knew Drury would be tough two days later. We were undefeated so far, but so were they. They were ranked second in the nation; we were unranked. They beat us soundly, 56–45. But the game was not nearly as close as the score. Their press forced us into 22 turnovers in the first half, and we were never able to establish our half-court offense with any authority. Graham was back in the lineup and had a strong game with 15 points, 9 rebounds, and 2 blocks. But no one else was in double figures. Drury was famous for its full-court press, and now we could see why. Their three outstanding guards—Regier, Rutledge, and Carter—were all over Chiodi and everyone else in our backcourt. For the first time this season our sophomore point guard was overwhelmed, and we found no way to help her out.

It was a humiliating defeat because of all the turnovers, but it could have been worse. We held Drury to 56 points in spite of giving them the ball so many times. Newton, their All-American center, was averaging 19.4 points per game, but we held her to 8; Healy and her teammates allowed her no points in the second half. We did fight back from an eight-point halftime deficit to close the gap to 38–36 on a three-pointer by Winner with 7:24 to play, but Drury went on a 10–2 run and put us away.

This game showed we were vulnerable to the press and could not depend on Chiodi alone to get the ball up under pressure. It showed that Graham could hold her own against an All-American like Newton but that we needed to diversify our offense the way Drury had against us (all three of their guards scored in double figures and combined for 13 steals). "This was a tough game," I wrote on my score sheet that evening, "but a good one to have at this point of the season. Drury is strong, tough, and experienced. Their press and defensive pressure did us in. But there were strengths. . . . It will be a different story if we play them in March."

It was one thing to lose to Drury. It was another to lose to St. Joseph's on their court in Rensselaer, Indiana. Yes, it is a weird court to play on—a small, overheated former airplane hangar. Yet we did not expect to lose to a team that had a 4–23 record in 2004–05 and had lost its first three GLVC games in the new season. The 50–47 win by St. Joseph's on December 8 was its first victory over our team in 12 years. Brittany Winner had a good all-around game, with 12 points, 5 rebounds, 3 steals, and 2 blocks. But no one else scored in double figures, and we shot only 35 percent from the field and 14 percent from three-point range. Chiodi may have still been rattled from the Drury game, as she had only two points and two assists and shot 1 of 7 from the floor.

With our conference record suddenly at 1–2, we needed a victory at Indianapolis on Saturday before returning to Highland

Heights for final exam week. Nicoson Hall had been the site of our upset victories over Indianapolis and Quincy in the 2003 NCAA Regional, but none of our current players were on the team at that time. Winstel decided to challenge her juniors to show their leadership. She called them into her hotel room and said, "You five, I'm going to start you. This is your team. You have to take ownership of your team." So she started Clark in place of Chiodi and Butler in place of Healy.

This game was close all the way. Indy led by one at the end of the first half; neither team led by more than four in the second half. NKU pulled the game out in spite of another very poor shooting game. The three cocaptains, Graham, Winner, and Creager, scored 16, 14, and 10 points, but no one else scored more than 5. This game came down to which team could play best in the closing minutes. NKU took the lead with 1:24 left when Healy scored on an assist from Chiodi. Graham increased the lead to 56–52 on an assist from Winner. Single free throws by Creager and Clark helped us hold on to a 58–56 victory.

"We didn't play great," Winstel said after the game, "but we played hard, and we stepped it up and made some plays at the end." Later she would look back on this game as a "moment of truth" for her juniors, "especially for Betsey and Karmen and Karyn, who had been in the program since their freshman year. They always wanted to be leaders, but you have to experience it, or kind of be thrown into that situation. The time had come for them. It was their moment of truth, and they embraced it."

Winstel waited until the game was over to tell her players that this was her birthday—and to thank them for giving her such a good present. A 5–2 record before final exams was much better than 4–3. And 2–2 in the conference was much better than 1–3.

As usual, our players were very busy while other students had a Christmas break. They played four games between final exams and New Year's Day. On December 19 and 20 they hosted West Virginia Wesleyan and Hillsdale College in our annual Holiday Tournament. The West Virginia Wesleyan game was dominated by Karmen Graham, who scored a career-high 31 points on 12 of 13 shooting from the field. NKU won easily, 68–48. Winstel was able to give a lot of players playing time, including Keri Finnell, who made 3 of 4 free throws during her first five minutes on the court this season.

Hillsdale College (Michigan) was one of the leading teams in the GLIAC. They came into our game with a 9–2 record after beating Virginia Union in the first game of the tournament. This was a very disciplined and well-coached team with mostly juniors and seniors, and they did what they needed to keep the game out of our reach. In the first half they forced 14 turnovers. In the second half they hit three-pointers when they needed them while taking away our perimeter offense. They beat us 56–52 in spite of 17 points by Graham. To beat a team like Hillsdale we would have to play with the same intensity they showed all 40 minutes. In Winstel's words, "Their experience beat us. We did not yet understand the things we need to do to beat a team that good."

Two days after losing to Hillsdale we hosted Loyola of Chicago, a Division I team from the Horizon League. We won 74–55. Loyola came in having lost all nine games, but we trailed 22–20 after 15 minutes, playing poorly. Then we woke up, scoring 15 unanswered points as Graham and Healy dominated the inside, finishing with 31 points between them. In my postgame note I began to see a new kind of energy from this team: "In the second quarter we started being alert and in motion at both ends of the court. We played hard & well, and Cassie & Brittany really gave us a lift off the bench. . . . Karmen, Angela, & Cassie are getting to be a real trio under the boards."

On December 29 we beat Brescia College, an NAIA team, by a similar margin, 63–42. Healy and Graham were again our leading scorers. Betsey Clark played well at a starting guard position, with eight points and five assists. But Winstel was not pleased. As a team, we failed to sustain the intensity she needs to see no matter who the opponent is. And Chiodi began an inexplicable free-throw funk, missing 6 of 7. The team headed into the New Year with an 8–3 record but with a coach wanting much more than she had seen so far.

Apart from the issues of intensity and concentration, two recurrent problems in the first 11 games had been turnovers and free throws. Winstel was already addressing these in practice with contrasting incentives. After any game with more than 14 turnovers, the entire team had to run laps for every additional turnover. After a game in which they had fewer than 10 turnovers, however, they would have a day off from practice (something they were not close to achieving at this point of the season). With free throws, if they made at least 75 percent in a game, they would get to eat Graeter's ice cream as they watched the film of their next opponent. If they shot under 65 percent (which this team was doing too often), they had to shoot 100 free throws apiece at their subsequent practices until their numbers improved. All the players remember shooting a ton of free throws over Christmas break. Their percentages against Loyola and Brescia had been 56 and 48 percent.

Between Christmas and New Year's, Winstel recalls, "we had three or four days of practice where we were very focused. Our team accepted the fact that they needed to improve and they allowed our coaching staff to do our job. We broke down our offense and took time to *teach* the offense. It was a major teaching time. We would practice for two and a half hours, from 9 to 11:30 in the morning, and then we would shoot free throws for half an hour, until everyone made 250 shots. Then I would take them to lunch." The new calendar year would get off to a quick start, with home games against two conference opponents before the first week of class.

What a coach like Winstel wants is a sequence of opponents that can bring out the best in her players as they continue to grow. This can be hard to attain in the early part of the season because of the variable talents of the teams on the schedule. A blowout against an inferior team pleases absolutely no one if the victorious coach is unhappy. One of the glories of the GLVC in the last five years has been the increasing level of play overall—and the diminishing talent gap between those at the top and the bottom of the standings. The conference schedule in January and February 2006 gave Winstel and her players just what they needed: a sequence of opponents week after week they were capable of beating, but who could beat them if they were not at their best.

The first teams to come to Regents Hall in 2006 were Kentucky Wesleyan and Southern Indiana. We beat the one by 62–47 on January 5 and the other by 62–42 on January 7. Kentucky Wesleyan played us close in the first half. NKU led by only 21–18 at halftime. Wesleyan defenders were fighting through our screens and stifling our offense. As Winstel explained in the postgame interview, "We decided to go to a cutting and moving offense in the second half, as opposed to screening." The motion offense opened up Graham to score 20 of her 22 points in the second half. Winner was back in the starting lineup and she showed her versatility during 38 quality minutes: she had 12 points and 8 rebounds while also helping to spell Chiodi at point guard. Winstel was making long-term adjustments.

Last year Southern Indiana had given us that 1-point loss at home that had hurt our postseason chances, so it was satisfying to avenge that loss with a 19-point victory. Equally satisfying was to hold this opponent to only 42 points. Our offense was well balanced, with 12, 10, and 10 from Healy, Graham, and Chiodi. Ten players contributed to the scoring. Our free-throw shooting finally improved, as we made 31 of 39 for 79.5 percent, with Creager and Graham each making 6 of 6.

When the spring semester started on Monday, January 9, it was good to have the two wins from the week before under our belt. On Wednesday, however, the team had to leave for one of its longest road trips of the year, riding six hours to St. Louis for a Thursday game with UMSL, and then farther into Missouri for a game with Rolla on Saturday, after which they would watch our men's team play before joining them for the eight-hour bus ride home.

The UMSL Riverwomen are always tough for us up front. During this game in their Mark Twain Building, they outrebounded us 37–28. One reason for this was the presence of Jennifer Martin, a 6-foot-1 transfer in the post. Another was the absence of Angela Healy, who fouled out after only 14 minutes of play. The game was tied at 50 with 2:46 remaining. After Martin put UMSL ahead with a layup, Katie Butler immediately countered with a three-pointer from the corner. Graham was fouled during Butler's shot; her two free throws gave us a five-point play and a three-point lead. When Butler made another three-pointer with one minute remaining, UMSL had no choice but to foul. NKU made eight free throws in a row to close out a 66–57 victory.

Our game at Rolla was billed as a GLVC showdown, as they entered the game 11–2 overall and 5–1 in the conference (against our record of 11–3 and 5–2). This was expected to be our toughest road game of the season so far. But we dominated Rolla 62–50, giving them their first-ever GLVC home-game loss. Our defense held them to 29 percent shooting in the first half and 32 percent in the second. Our offense was again well-balanced. We made 80 percent of our free throws, and Chiodi had a strong floor game with seven rebounds, four steals, and four assists. It was a pleasure to hear us play so well in a game with so much at stake. As I wrote on my score sheet next to the radio: "Excellent game to listen to. We played extremely well against a strong team & shut them down on their own court. Karmen was fantastic, as usual, lately, & it was a real team effort. . . . Our defense is getting harder and harder to beat. Lewis next week should be a great game."

Recalling this road trip six months later, Winstel remembered Rolla as "the first game in the season where I thought we were very impressive." And she told me something I had not known about Butler's first three-pointer against UMSL. "We had been getting an open baseline three all night long but no one could make it—not Betsey, not Karyn, not B-Dubs. So we put Katie in as a shooting forward and we said, 'Kate, you're going to get that shot.' So here we come running down the floor and the kid's running the baseline and she shoots the ball. I swear to God the ball hits the rim and it must have bounced 20 feet in the air. And while it is up in the air, that's when Grammy got absolutely shoved so that, as the ball went through the net, Grammy went flying. She was airborne. Fortunately, they called the foul. And Grammy made the shots. A five-point turnaround. It was a backbreaker for them. And then that doggone Kate comes down a second time and makes another three from the right elbow, a good two feet behind the line."

Such are the breaks of the game. A whole season can pivot on one split second in a 40-minute game, a missed shot dropping through the net as a teammate flies through the air.

While NKU's 995 faculty members and 14,000 students were settling into the second week of the new semester, Winstel and her 12 players were gearing up for Lewis at 5:30 on Thursday evening. The Lewis Flyers had been a strong favorite to win the GLVC East. Their leading scorers, Moskal, Schmidt, and Glenn, were currently averaging 15, 15, and 13 points per game. (Only Graham was in double figures for NKU.) Lewis arrived in Regents Hall with a 6–1 conference record and a five-game win streak. We were only a half game behind at 6–2 and had now won six in a row. Our 62–51 victory, like the one at Rolla the week before, was more commanding than one could have expected, increasing the feeling that this team was becoming something special.

In the postgame interview Winstel used a new word for this year's team. "I thought in the first half, in some ways, we were unstoppable." Brannen had come off the bench to score six points and grab six rebounds in the first-half surge. Clark scored five straight points to open the lead to 12 at the half. Things tightened up in the second half when, in the coach's words, "we stopped executing." Lewis cut the lead to four with 1:52 remaining, but NKU answered with 9 of 10 free throws for the 11-point win. Winstel tends not to dwell on statistics, but she did note in the postgame interview that we had only 11 turnovers. "We have to be thrilled about that; it's the first time we've been anywhere near that total. That's focus and taking care of the ball." Chiodi had no turnovers, against five for her counterpart Shante Glenn.

The Saturday game against Wisconsin–Parkside showed how tough the GLVC had become. Parkside entered the game with a 1–7 record in the conference. They were at the bottom of the Eastern Division and we were now at the top. We started off with a 10–0 run, but they hit one three-pointer after another to close the gap. In the second half Parkside rallied to tie the score at 51 with 6:42 to play. But they could not stop Angela Healy, who scored 15 of her 21 points in the second half as we held on for a 68–62 victory. Karen Brackman and Katie Butler helped us with 8 and 9 points off the bench. Again we took care of the ball. We had only 9 turnovers compared with 21 for Parkside. Our players had finally earned that day off from practice—though when they would get it was unclear, as we had a Tuesday game against Georgetown followed by a Thursday game against Bellarmine.

Against Georgetown our returning players were still smarting from the 85–64 whipping they had given us at the beginning of the previous season. This year they came to Regents Hall with a seven-game win streak and a 16–4 record. This time we derailed *them*, 57–51. Georgetown was still up by 45–40 with 8:22 remaining when NKU went on a 10-point run. We ended the game with 7 of 10 from the line to seal the victory. Our defense held Georgetown to 27 percent from the field for the entire game. We were especially tough on Kim Ingle, who had burned us with 27 points last year. This time she scored only 10 points on 3 of 17 from the floor. In the postgame interview Winstel praised Creager, Clark, and Brackman for the way they challenged Ingle's shot and denied her the ball.

The game against Bellarmine two days later was one of the defining moments of the season. They had beaten us badly to knock us out of last year's GLVC Tournament. This year's Homecoming Game in Regents Hall was a nail-biter to the end. Brittany Winner scored the winning basket on a 12-footer with only 13 seconds to play for a 66–64 victory. In her postgame interview Winner said she had never hit a game-winning basket like this one—not at Minster, not at Elon, not at NKU. Winstel in *her* postgame interview "joked" that it was good that Brittany had made that last shot because she "had let her player hit the three-pointer that had tied the game."

While our fans were nervous in the closing minutes, Winner was calm. Bellarmine had led for most of the second half until Winner tied the game with a jumper with 2:02 remaining. She then made a second jumper to give us a lead with 1:26 remaining, leading finally to the game-winner at the end. As I wrote on my score sheet, "Bellarmine played tough but we hung in there and played an incredibly strong last five minutes to pull it out. Winner's 3 straight 12-footers were so cool & sure. The point distribution—with 5 players between 11 & 14 points—was a dream. We had to play tough under adversity & we did it."

Our next trip was another long one, driving due west for a Thursday doubleheader at Southern Illinois at Edwardsville, across from St. Louis on the Mississippi River, then following the river upstream to Quincy.

Our game at Edwardsville was one of the first conference games that we won by a fairly comfortable margin, 72–55. We were up by 8 points nine minutes into the game and we led by 9 at the half. We increased the lead to 17 at the nine-minute mark in the second half (on a rare three-pointer by Healy) and held it there for the rest of the game. This was another game with admirable depth. Creager, Chiodi, and Healy scored 14, 13, and 12. We outrebounded Edwardsville 40 to 23, with five players getting six or more. Our shooting was impressive in all categories, as we hit 50 percent from the field, 41 percent of our threes, and 79 percent from the line.

In this game Creager and Chiodi gave us the offensive spurt we had not always had from our guards. Creager made four three-pointers and Chiodi shot 5 of 7 from the field and 3 of 4 from the line. Winstel in her postgame interview called this Chiodi's "best offensive game as a college player." In addition to 13 points on almost perfect shooting, Nicole had 6 rebounds, 5 assists, 2 steals, and a block against only 1 turnover. She was the only starter who had not made much of an impact in the victory over Bellarmine, and it was good to see her getting back on track.

Edwardsville had been near the bottom of the GLVC West, but Quincy was right up at the top under Drury (which had not yet lost a conference game). Quincy was the GLVC defending champion from both 2004 and 2005. We had not beaten them on their own court since February 2003, the season before Graham, Creager, and Clark had arrived at NKU. For all these reasons, one of our team's goals was to "Beat Quincy at Quincy." It took excellent play by the entire team to win this upset victory on the road, 73–70.

NKU played a strong and commanding first half, opening up a 7-point lead in the first four minutes and leading by 5 at halftime, as Graham scored all of her 15 points and Butler had 7 off the bench. In the second half, too, we held a 7-point lead for much of the half. But center Deana McCormick, who had been held to 2 points in the first half, exploded for 18 in the second, fouling Healy out of the game. McCormick scored 6 points in the last two minutes to cut our lead to 70–69 with 0:53 remaining. But freshman Cassie Brannen matched her by scoring 6 points and grabbing 3 rebounds in the last two minutes to preserve the victory.

Overall, we had another fine shooting game, hitting 52 percent of our field goals and 91 percent of our free throws. Although Mc-Cormick hurt us badly inside, we kept Quincy's starting guards, Wisser and Crawford, from having breakout games, holding them in check with good perimeter defense. Graham, Butler, and Chiodi led our scoring with 15, 15, and 13. We had strong play inside and out, from our starters and off the bench. This was a thrilling game to hear on the radio. As soon as it was over I wrote on my home-made score sheet, "Excellent game to beat Quincy on their floor. Cassie was the star of the game, in clutch scoring & rebounding. Karmen and Katie had great first halves. Nicole was strong in both halves, with another fine scoring and floor game. We answered very well when Quincy came back at the end (& when some fouls went the wrong way). This continues to be a very special season." We had now won 12 in a row.

Our last home games of the season were against Indianapolis on February 9 and St. Joseph's on February 11. (The Saturday game would have been "Senior Day," except that we had no seniors on the team.) After beating Indianapolis by 2 points on their court in December, we beat them by 19 on our court. We opened up an 11-point lead in the first half and never looked back, winning 81–62. Butler and Brannen had 9 and 10 points off the bench in the first half alone. Seven players scored between 9 and 14 points. As a team, we shot 49 percent from the field, 57 percent from three-point range, and 81 percent from the line.

More than the statistics, this game was about effort, fluidity, and flow. In the words of the Dickinson poem, the team that had been learning "gem-tactics" a year ago was now becoming "qualified for pearl." As I wrote on my stat sheet, this was "a beautiful game to watch. The whole team played with precision & passion.

Balanced scoring . . . matched by strong play all over the floor for 40 minutes. Offense is now catching up with defense. Cassie & Katie were incredible off the bench. Nicole is now a college point guard. Our junior co-captains are all Winstel players now & are showing the underclassmen how to do it. Drury, watch out. We'll be ready."

In December St. Joseph's had upset us by 3 points on the road. We now beat them by 25 in February. With an 18-point halftime lead, Winstel was able to play her entire bench. All 12 players were on the floor for at least five minutes, and they all contributed to a major achievement in this game: only nine turnovers. The final score was 76–51, extending our season record to 20–3. My postgame note recorded: "Another very impressive game. First half about as good as we've seen in Regents Hall since the national championship season. Again the scoring was extremely well-balanced and the defense extremely effective. . . . Cassie's 2 blocks in a row, Katie's scoring off the bench again, Brittany's overall game, which is now showing so much finesse in addition to alertness. . . . Our four upcoming road games will be a good challenge. Will help season us for Conference and Regional tournaments and maybe more."

We could expect difficult games on the road against Bellarmine and Kentucky Wesleyan. Each was now immediately below NKU and Lewis in the GLVC East and battling for a spot in the conference tournament. Our last-second victory over Bellarmine in Regents Hall three weeks earlier seemed to ensure an extremely tough game on their court in Louisville, where NKU had not won since January 30, 1999. "Beating Bellarmine at Bellarmine" had been another of the goals the team had posted during the preseason. On Valentine's Day 2006 they did this in decisive fashion, 82–70. We played punishing offense and defense from the opening whistle, leading by 37–8 only 12 minutes into the first half. A furious rush by Bellarmine cut the lead to 6 points halfway through the second half, but we rallied on three consecutive baskets by Brittany Winner to regain the 12-point margin that we held to the end of the game. This was a breakout game for both Winner and Brannen, who had career-high totals of 16 and 19 points, respectively. Brittany shot 7 of 8 from the field and had 4 rebounds and 3 assists; Cassie shot 6 of 8 from the field and 6 of 6 from the line and had 7 rebounds and 3 assists. The team as a whole continued its torrid shooting, making 56 percent of its field goals, 56 percent of its three-pointers, and 85 percent of its free throws.

This game, however, was not all sweetness and light. We committed too many turnovers after building up our huge lead, allowing Bellarmine to creep back. And Healy was having trouble against Bellarmine's strong center, Ashley Lewallen. Healy remembers Winstel trying to fire her up at halftime by saying, "Number 45's owning you. She owns you." Winstel remembers telling Angela something more: "*I recruited you over her,* and she owns you." The A-Unit did play better in the second half, but this was not one of her better games. She played only 15 minutes compared with 28 from Cassie, who rose to the occasion the way few freshmen can do. I did not know until much later that Angela had played much of her freshman season with serious back pain. As a sophomore the bursitis in her shoulder was so bad that "I would feel like my arm was going to fall off" after each pair of Thursday-Saturday games, "although it never hurt when I was playing." Such is the life of a college post player.

We no longer took Kentucky Wesleyan for granted when we arrived at the Owensboro Sportscenter on February 18. We remembered how badly they had beaten us there during our 0–5 start the season before. This time NKU led by six with four minutes remaining, but LaTasha Henry made five consecutive points to give the Panthers a one-point lead with only one minute left. In a replay of our home game with Bellarmine, Brittany Winner scored the winning jumper with six seconds remaining, giving us a 62–60 victory. Our Knight-killer was now a Panther-killer too.

As soon as our players returned home from Owensboro, it seemed, they had to get back on the bus for the long trip to play Parkside in Wisconsin, near Kenosha, and then Lewis, near Chicago. This trip has always been tough for Winstel's teams. Last February we had lost at both Parkside and Lewis even though we were then playing very well elsewhere in the conference. This year Parkside, in spite of playing us so close in Regents Hall a few weeks earlier, was still only 3–13 in the GLVC when we arrived in their DeSimone Gymnasium. Yet they beat us badly, 70–62. This was one of our worst defensive games of the year. We could not stop senior Carrie Schieve, who scored 27 points. They challenged us to shoot three-pointers over their two-three zone, and we missed 10 of the 12 we shot. We outrebounded Parkside 34–23 but committed 19 turnovers compared with their 7. This was the first game we had lost since Hillsdale beat us on December 20, and it ended our win streak at 16.

The loss to Parkside set up what would have been a huge game against Lewis on Saturday. But Bellarmine did us a favor by beating Lewis on Thursday while we were losing to Parkside. We would now receive the first seed from the East in the GLVC Tournament whether we beat Lewis or not. But we did beat them—as decisively as we had at home, 75–65. We led by a comfortable margin throughout the entire second half. We had broken open a tie game with 7:52 remaining in the first half—with two straight threes by Katie Butler and five straight points by Cassie Brannen. They came off the bench to take the game away.

To win the GLVC East outright after being ranked below Lewis and Bellarmine in the preseason poll was a major achievement. So was our record of 23–4 overall and 16–3 in the conference. Now we would see how far we could go in the conference tournament. In 2005 we had been eliminated in the first round by Bellarmine. In 2004 we had been eliminated in the first round by Indianapolis. We had a lot to prove to our conference opponents as well as ourselves.

Our exploits in January and February had not gone unnoticed. During the second week of February we had entered the national rankings at number 24 in the NCAA Division II poll. One week after that, on the day our win streak reached 16, Lonnie Wheeler published a tribute to Winstel and her "delightful dozen" in the *Cincinnati Post*. He was much taken with 6-foot point guard Chiodi who, combined with Creager, gave the team "12 feet of basketball skills" out front. Winstel told Wheeler that she "likes size on the perimeter" because "it gives you a whole level of versatility," allowing a coach more creativity. "Then you have somebody like Brittany Winner, who's a

5-10 forward but is really a power guard." And Betsey Clark, who is also about 5-foot-10 but "could guard a post player if she had to. So could Brittany. But then our post kids, like Karmen Graham, could play on the perimeter if they had to."

What had finally brought all this versatility into play had been the improved play of Chiodi. Winstel gave Nicole a lot of credit for how well she was beginning to understand everything required of a point guard even while still learning the system. "The poor kid has a coach who has been coaching for 25 years and expects her to think as fast as I do, to read and react as fast as me, and I'm standing over here on the sidelines without somebody in my face. You have to have a point guard with thick skin. When the post player is out of position, I usually get on the point guard. Nicole's not there quite, as far as bossing people around, but she's moving in that direction. A point guard has to be the heart and soul of a team. Our winning streak has just been a matter of us evolving as a team, and her evolution is a big part of that."

Winstel's words in Wheeler's story were a welcome confirmation of what was becoming increasingly evident on the court: that she and Nicole were becoming more compatible than ever before. How far they had come together was shown by a painful moment Winstel recalled during an interview with me a few months after Wheeler published his tribute. That moment is the one that begins this book. Nicole was the player to whom Winstel had said, in exasperation, "You're crying because you're not guarding anybody." And Winstel was the coach for whom Nicole had hustled hard when she got back into that game. That game was one of those that the team had played halfway around the world in Australia. That painful moment for both player and coach was one of the countless steps in the evolution of the entire team that Wheeler was now calling, nine months later, the "delightful dozen." The sand, they say, makes the pearl.

Winstel needs to clear the decks emotionally to coach effectively. Her frankness with her players, and their courage in meeting her forceful challenges, produced the growth and cohesion the team was now showing. In Nicole's case, any challenges from her coach had brought only deeper support from her teammates. Winstel never had any doubt that "the players feel that Nicole's their point guard."

The GLVC Tournament begins the week after the regular season ends. In 2006 it was again held in Roberts Stadium in Evansville, Indiana, a capacious arena that dwarfs the courts on which most teams play during the regular season. Drury, with a 26–1 record, was the top seed from the Western Division, followed by Quincy, Missouri–Rolla, and Missouri–St. Louis. NKU, with a 23–4 record, was the top seed in the East, followed by Lewis, Bellarmine, and Kentucky Wesleyan. Our first-round game was against Missouri–St. Louis on the afternoon of Thursday, March 2. Three of my faculty friends and I decided to make the drive to Evansville even though we had classes on Thursday that would cause us to miss NKU's opening game in this single-elimination tournament. We listened to the first half of that game in my office before jumping into the car for the four-hour drive during which the radio signal faded only during the last two minutes of the game.

NKU got off to a fast start against Missouri–St. Louis and led by seven at halftime. We held Jennifer Martin scoreless in the first half, but she exploded for 13 points in the second half and got all our post players in foul trouble. Healy and Brannen both fouled out, and Graham and Butler each had four fouls by the end of the game. Fortunately, Graham was able to match Martin on our end of the court, scoring 16 of her own 20 points in the second half as we held on for a 72–62 victory. Angela Estes played a key role in the closing minutes, after Healy and Brannen had fouled out.

"Come here!" Winstel said, on the bench. "Can you guard that girl without letting her score?"

"Yes, I can," Estes said. So Winstel put her in to protect Karmen from getting her fifth foul. "The first time down, I just boxed out and got a huge rebound." This memorable moment was the highlight of the season for Angela, who got very little playing time behind our four strong posts.

The second-round game was against Quincy, which had eliminated Bellarmine in the first round. No women's games were scheduled for Friday because that was the first round of the GLVC men's tournament in Roberts Stadium. The four surviving women's teams—Drury, Quincy, Rolla, and NKU—each had a one-hour workout across town in Southern Indiana's P. A. C. Arena. Our small faculty group was invited to attend. This was the first time I had ever seen Winstel conduct a practice. As our second team simulated Quincy's offensive sets, our starters worked at various adjustments by which we could try to stop "No. 50," Deana McCormick, who had hurt us so badly on Quincy's court a month earlier. It was after this practice that our players broke out in spontaneous song while waiting for the bus to take them back to the hotel.

In the Saturday game against Quincy our team reached a new level of coordinated, intense, joyous basketball. We played both ends of the court against an outstanding opponent in such a way as to transcend our previous level of play. The transcendence came primarily in the second half. The first half was close, as one would expect. Chiodi drove the length of the court for a layup with just two seconds remaining to give us a four-point lead. In the second half NKU scored 40 points to Quincy's 26, for a 67–49 victory.

The entire game was a defensive clinic by NKU. Quincy as a team made only 26 percent of its shots. We held McCormick scoreless for the first half and almost shotless for the game. She made only 1 of 2 field goals for a two-point total. As Winstel emphasized in the postgame interview, "Angela Healy and Cassie Brannen were outstanding at defending her in the post." In addition, NKU set a GLVC Tournament record with 10 blocks. The 10 blocks were made by seven different players (we also had nine steals, also made by seven different players). Winstel attributed the blocks to "our help-side defense. And it's a tribute to our size and length. We did a good job of protecting the ball on offense and we're growing up as a team. They have grown a great deal since we started practice on October 15."

Offensively, Graham led us with 18 in her typical fashion—5 of 9 from the field, 8 of 8 from the line. She seemed unaffected by the one scary moment in the second half when Healy accidentally stepped on her head while grabbing a rebound. As a team we made 24 of 28 free throws. And again we kept the turnovers under control—only 11 against Quincy's excellent guards. As I wrote in the open space of my score sheet: "This was an incredible game. . . . Our second half was awesome. . . . Everyone played great and dominated a very good Quincy team in every element of the game, offensively and defensively. . . . The team is reaching a new level of group achievement at the right time in the year. We are now, I am confident of saying, a national contender."

Nothing proved that more than our next game, for the conference championship, against Drury, the team that had humiliated us on our own court back in December. They entered the tournament ranked number 3 in the nation. We were currently number 22. We put together two full halves like the second half against Quincy. We took a 39–30 lead into the locker room and never let them back in, winning 86–73. Drury had come out ready to shut down Karmen Graham, the only player who had hurt them back in December, when she had scored 15 of our 45 points. They were not prepared for Brittany Winner, who broke out for 30 points in the game of her life, 20 of them in the first half, while also skillfully protecting the ball against the Drury press. For the entire game we had only 10 turnovers compared with their 16—and compared with our 30 turnovers when they had beat us in December.

Graham had an off day and got in foul trouble too, scoring only two points for the entire game. But Winner made up for that, and so did her teammates—especially in the second half, when Winner's 10 additional points were matched by 10 from Chiodi, 10 from Creager, and 9 from Butler as we extended a 9-point halftime lead into a 13-point victory. This kind of balance from four different players in the second half of the most important game of the season was what our coach had been hoping to create after we had lost to Drury three months earlier, when Karmen was our only go-to player. Throughout the second half we showed the same combination of passion and precision we had shown in the second half against Quincy, but now the stakes were even higher and the opponent was even tougher—a team considered much superior to us. Winner's 30 points were nearly matched by 28 from Drury's sophomore guard Molly Carter, but she did not have nearly so much inspired help from her teammates.

With three minutes left the game was still close enough to lose, but Chiodi got a little opening and drilled a three, putting the game out of reach as long as we could make foul shots. This we did to perfection, making 14 of 14 to close out the game (and giving us 31 of 34 for the game as a whole). Drury's free-throw shooting was almost as good—24 of 29 for the game—but this time we outplayed them on the floor and took the game with authority. The pure joy of the players as they held up the conference trophy thrilled the fans in the stands as much as the national championship victory in 2000 or the magical upset over Quincy in 2003. This was the moment when this year's team had passed that solstice "that maketh all things new." They had earned a permanent place in the heart and memory of any fan who had seen this game. They had crystallized all their growth since their loss to Drury three months before, showing that they were, indeed, "qualified for pearl."

As momentous as this victory was, the single moment our players are most likely to recall from this game is something that happened on the sidelines. During a time-out following one of the crucial baskets Katie Butler scored off the bench, Grammy gave K-But a powerful chest bump that sent Katie flat on her back. Despite the tension of the game, the whole team, coach included, could only laugh. Karmen later told me about a tense moment with the coach shortly before she delivered the infamous chest bump. Winstel had pointed to Katie out on the floor and said, "See her out there. That's supposed to be you, but you're sitting here in foul trouble." And Karmen snapped back something like, "Well, she's doing a good job," sending the coach away in a huff. She remembers this as the first time she had ever talked back to Coach Winstel on the bench, perhaps adding an unconscious charge to the emphatic bump.

Another bump that neither team will forget had occurred in the heat of battle out on the floor. We had been breaking the Drury press quite effectively, but Molly Carter was still sticking a bit too close to Nicole each time they sped up the floor, and the refs were doing nothing about it. So Healy stepped in by setting one of her rock-solid backcourt screens. Carter bounced right off it onto the floor. Angela will do this only when necessary, but she does confess that "it's fun to lay out those little guards who don't know what's coming." Carter had scrambled right up and gotten after Nicole again, keeping Drury in the game throughout the second half until Nicole drilled that key three-pointer.

As Drury was making its last desperate attempt to close the gap, another body hit the floor. It was Cassie, and she was not moving. The game was stopped. Noriko Masamoto, our trainer, came out, and for quite a while Cassie remained motionless. It turned out she had gotten an elbow in the gut that knocked the wind out of her. She was not able to reenter the game, but she was okay by the time of our postgame celebration. She was even allowed to climb the ladder to cut her piece of the cord as the team took down the net through which they had made all those free throws.

No one wanted to leave even after the net was cut down. Not the players on the floor, not the fans in the stands. Our players finally did start filing back to the locker room. All that we fans had left to watch now was Brittany, wearing a big set of headphones at the press desk below us. She was having the postgame interview every player dreams of, trying to explain how it feels to have the game of your life in the game that mattered most.

Brittany's 30 points had come on 10 of 13 field goals and 9 of 9 free throws. The points had nearly doubled her previous single-game high. But beginning in the Bellarmine game at home we had already seen her ability to rise to the occasion in ways unexpected. This game was especially welcome because she had not played particularly well in the two previous tournament games against Missouri–St. Louis and Quincy. I asked Coach Winstel a few months later if she had done anything to inspire, or provoke, Brittany's breakout game against Drury. Her answer was a quick overview of a relationship in which she holds Brittany "to a very high standard." Because "she is so inconsistent at times. . . . I really get on her and I challenge her in a way that I think she really wants. But I also think I drive her crazy too. And then, she's hard on herself, so I have to be careful about that. So then I have to take a step back and relax a bit."

With the whole team, "you're constantly teetering on this line of influencing without antagonizing. But you can't just be the nice one all the time. So you have that line, and Brittany and I are on that line all the time. We teeter probably more than with any of them, but it happens with all of them. With Brittany and me, I don't think you could say it's a love-hate relationship, but I'm going to challenge her to play at a higher level than she has ever been challenged because I see that she can do it and I think she likes the challenge. I would rather be too tough on them than not tough enough." As a result, Brittany had become, in the Drury game, our living gyroscope, always spinning, always in balance.

When I asked Karyn Creager why she thought we were able to play so exceptionally well against Drury, she said, "It's just something that everyone wanted, and I think you could just see it in our eyes, that there was nothing that was going to stop us from doing it." She also said that she and the other juniors were determined not to let Drury, no matter how good they were, win the conference championship during their first year in the league. Betsey remembers this too. "They just can't win the GLVC their first year. No, that's not happening."

After beating Drury, NKU was six games away from a national championship. We had every reason to feel we had as good a shot at it as anyone else. In spite of its shocking loss to NKU, Drury remained the top seed in the Great Lakes Region and hosted the NCAA Tournament in Springfield, Missouri (a nine-hour drive from our campus, much too far for our faculty group to go without missing classes). The number-two seed was Grand Valley State from Allendale, Michigan, impressive winners of the GLIAC Tournament. NKU was seeded third. Our first-round opponent was Michigan Tech, a GLIAC team with a 19–8 record this year and a memorable place in NKU's NCAA history. In March 1999 Michelle Cottrell's stick-back at the buzzer in the Great Lakes Regional at Regents Hall had given us a 65–63 victory over Michigan Tech and a trip to the Elite Eight, where we lost to Arkansas Tech in the semifinals. One year later we had played Michigan Tech again in Regents Hall in the Great Lakes Regional, winning 60–59 on a shot by Cottrell with six seconds left, on the way to the national championship. This year we won another close one with Michigan Tech, 67–66, Karyn Creager scoring the winning basket with 3.9 seconds remaining.

The first half was extremely close, with 11 lead changes. The lead continued to alternate in the second half until NKU surged ahead 60–54 with 4:59 remaining on a shot by Healy. After two three-pointers by Michigan Tech tied the game at 60, Creager answered with a three to regain the lead. With only eight seconds remaining, Michigan Tech inched ahead, 66–65, on a layup by Amanda Sieja. With the game on the line, and no time-out taken by the coach, Chiodi pushed the ball up the floor, saw Creager cutting for the basket, and delivered the pass that Karyn converted for the game-winning layup. They did this almost too quickly, as Michigan Tech was left with time for a desperation shot, which missed.

That final basket was a fine example of how this team had learned to improvise and internalize, to take advantage of what the situation offers—in this case, without any input from the coach or the bench. Chiodi and Creager knew enough about each other's skills and instincts for everything to happen at lightning speed, before anyone on either team could plan, think, or react. This was a close, well-played game. One big difference in the outcome was the productivity of the NKU bench, which outscored its Michigan Tech counterparts 27–8, 19 of those points coming from Brannen and Butler.

As we were squeaking by Michigan Tech, Grand Valley State was pounding Ashland, 85–59. They beat us nearly as badly, 91–70. This was an extremely tough game to listen to, as they were up 51–34 at the half and we were never in it. We simply could not stop them from shooting, and they hardly ever missed. They made 11 of their first 13 shots and shot 73 percent for the first half. Our only hope for reversing their momentum was the tornado warning that stopped the game for 15 minutes in the first half. But Grand Valley came back from that too, with the same hot hands and superior play.

We scored quite well in this game, with 17 from Graham, 13 from Winner, 12 from Chiodi, and 11 from Healy. But these totals could not begin to match the 25 from Ryskamp, 23 from Reams, 17 from Cyplik, and 15 from Zick. Niki Reams, a Division I transfer from the University of Michigan and the Great Lakes Region Player of the Year, was a senior in her last season. But all their other leading players would be back next year. So our players, for all they had achieved during this season, knew how much better they still needed to become. It was some consolation that Grand Valley beat Drury by a similar score to advance to the Elite Eight, and then went on to sweep through those three games to win the national championship. But it is always tough to be beaten so soundly by a superior team.

The tornadoes did not end with the first half of the Grand Valley game. Tournament funding from the NCAA allowed the team to fly home the next day rather than take the nine-hour bus ride. Winstel had to divide her players between a morning and an afternoon flight. She did so alphabetically, which made Keri Finnell feel good until she realized how many Bs and Cs come before F on this team. While the second group was waiting at the airport, a tornado warning caused everyone to be evacuated in cabs. Keri ended up in the last cab, crammed in the backseat with assistant coaches Matt Schmidt and Travece Turner, trainer Noriko Masamoto, and assorted bags (team manager Zach Cook and Coach Schmidt's bag were up front with the driver). "The guy starts driving, and he's driving really fast, and I'm looking out the window and the window wipers are not moving fast enough." The one time Keri could see out the window the cab was over the yellow line. Even after they arrived safely at the hotel, she continued to shake and say to Travece, "The wipers weren't moving fast enough."

Telling me this story several months later, Keri said, "Our record was great this year, but years will pass and I will never forget my experience in Missouri with the tornadoes."

After the team returned from Missouri in mid-March, six weeks remained in the spring semester before final exams in early May. In addition to catching up with their classes, these student-athletes played open gym twice a week, worked out three days a week, and had their oral exit exams with Coach Winstel. On Saturday, April 22, they were greeted by many of their fans at NKU's 16th Annual Walk for Women's Athletics. On Sunday, April 30, they held their annual awards ceremony. This year's group had much to celebrate and little to mourn, as there were no graduating seniors. The players themselves had chosen the recipients of the four major awards. Karmen Graham was the Outstanding Offensive Player and Karyn

Creager the Outstanding Defensive Player. Nicole Chiodi was the Most Improved Player and Brittany Winner received the Hustle Award. This team had chosen not to vote for a Most Valuable Player, believing that every player was necessary for the success of the team.

These 12 players had more to celebrate than any Winstel team since the one that made the finals of the NCAA Tournament in 2003. This team's 27–5 record was superior to that team's 26–8. It was the third best record in Winstel's 23 seasons as head coach at NKU. The awards ceremony provided a welcome opportunity for wearing something other than basketball uniforms. The highlight of the event was a DVD that Coach Schmidt put together of highlights from the 2005–06 season. Combining still photos from the games with informal shots contributed by some of the players, he set a delightful sequence of images over some of the players' favorite songs. The video captured the balance between the intense pleasure in the game and the relaxed pleasure with one another that this team had shared the whole season. One lighthearted highlight showed the whole team sitting as "coneheads" in Roberts Stadium after the victory over Quincy. Each player had followed Angela Estes in making a cone of her head by wrapping her hair around a water bottle. They were enjoying themselves so much that some of their GLVC competitors had come over to chill out with them.

One touching moment for Coach Schmidt at this year's ceremony was when Katie Butler came up, gave him a hug, and said, "Thanks for bringing me here." Then her mom and dad came up and said, "Thanks for giving us our daughter back." Katie had lost her pleasure in the game while playing at the University of Dayton; now her personality had come back, along with her game. She had taken a bold step in transferring from the Atlantic Ten Conference to a Division II program, and it was gratifying to know that it had worked out as well for Katie and her parents as it had for her teammates, coaches, and fans. Her mother had been to many of the games during the season, but she had to ask Katie to identify some of her teammates, saying, "I just can't recognize these girls without their basketball uniforms and their hair up and their red faces."

Two weeks earlier, at the awards ceremony for the Literature and Language Department, Keri Finnell had received the award for the outstanding essay written at NKU in an advanced writing class. Her prize-winning essay addressed how long it had taken the U.S. Senate to officially acknowledge the thousands of African Americans who had been lynched in the southern states between Reconstruction and World War II. She "almost had a heart attack" when she heard her name screamed out as she walked up to receive the award. The screaming was done by her teammates Chiodi and Healy, who were sitting with coaches Winstel, Schmidt, and Turner toward the back of the room. Even before this moment, Keri had been the scholarship queen of the team; her minority and science scholarships were so large that Winstel was able to give her basketball scholarship to another player.

When the grades came in at the end of the semester, the team grade point average for the 2005–06 season was 3.524, the highest in the history of the program. Nine of our players made the GLVC All-Academic Team (Cassie Brannen, Nicole Chiodi, Karyn Creager, Danyelle Echoles, Angela Estes, Keri Finnell, Karmen Graham, Angela Healy, and Brittany Winner). The team as a whole was fifth in the nation when the rankings were published in July. In the GLVC basketball honors for the season, Karmen Graham made first-team All-Conference, Karyn Creager received honorable mention, and Nancy Winstel was Coach of the Year. Karmen was also first-team Great Lakes Region and honorable mention All-American.

Karmen Graham is so modest that when anyone praised her for being an All-American as a junior she would point out that she was only honorable mention. But she had completed an extraordinary season. She had averaged 14.5 points and 5.5 rebounds a game. She had made 54.2 percent of her field goals and 84.3 percent of her free throws. Her free-throw percentage ranked 30th in the nation. But she led the nation in both free throws attempted, 210, and free throws made, 177. The 210 that she shot are a direct measure of her courageous play against post players who were often taller and larger than she. The 177 she made show her exceptional shot-making concentration immediately after being pushed around.

In spite of Karmen's exceptional year, it was fitting that this group of players had decided not to give an MVP award. All 12 players who experienced this season *were* essential to the team. Danyelle Echoles had not gotten to play much during her freshman season. But she already had the excitement of being on an NCAA Tournament team, something most players never achieve in all four years of college. The hardest thing for Danyelle in the course of the season had been "catching on to what Coach wants" in practice. "After you learn what she wants you to do, it's not so bad." Mainly what she wants is "intensity every day. Sometimes you don't have intensity every day, but she's going to go after you to find it." By the end of her first season Danyelle was realizing that this coach's "system" is "an ongoing process. I think you learn the system the whole time you are in school. Next year the system will be a little more intense because the bar has been raised by what we did this year."

Danyelle and her teammates had experienced a season of hard work and inspired play in which they had exceeded most people's expectations—and maybe their own. They had done so by learning to find that "intensity every day," individually and as a team. In the process, these 12 young women had continued to love one another while competing fiercely. "We are friends," Betsey Clark recalled a year later, "but when you are playing for a starting position or for more playing time, the claws come out. Everyone's individual determination comes alive then. No one wants to be on the bench. And you see that a lot in practice. That alone is so amazing to watch and be a part of."

The magical ride that Danyelle, Betsey, and their teammates had taken together during the 2005–06 season will always be behind them. Next year they would all be coming back for a season they hoped would be even better. They were part of a nurturing, challenging sisterhood that left them, even after being flattened by Grand Valley, looking up from higher than they had ever been, individually or as a team.

4

OFFSEASON DEVOTION

One most perilous and long voyage ended, only begins a second; and a second ended, only begins a third.
—*Herman Melville*, Moby-Dick

Psychologically, the offseason began soon after Grand Valley defeated us on Drury's court. At the team dinner after the game,
Coach Winstel announced that Grand Valley would be one of the
teams coming to Regents Hall for our Christmas tournament in
December. This announcement raised the bar not only for the upcoming season but also for the summer.

That December date became all the more challenging—and exciting—when Grand Valley went on to roll over Drury in the regional final and win three in a row for the national championship.
Playing them in December would be a great way to see how far we
had come in the summer and how far we might go in the spring.

As soon as final exams were over, each player's responsibilities
to the team were officially suspended until the beginning of the fall
semester on August 21. So were Winstel's opportunities to coach
her players: NCAA regulations forbid coaches to coach their teams
between the spring and fall semesters. Even so, the players remained
devoted to the team—and to one another—throughout the summer
months.

As student-athletes, most of them took courses during one or
more of the summer terms. Being here for summer school allowed
them to get together voluntarily to do whatever they could to be-

come better in the upcoming season. With strong encouragement from their coaches, they chose to do a lot.

After the three-week intersession in May, when some of the players from more distant Ohio towns got a chance to go home, the team as a whole set up a weekly schedule to which they adhered as a group throughout June, July, and early August:

7:30–9:00 A.M. every Monday, Wednesday, and Friday: Voluntary workouts with strength and conditioning coach Livey Birkenhauer, Albright Health Center.

Between 6 and 10 P.M. every Thursday: Two separate games against teams of other college players in the Greater Cincinnati Women's League, Open Division, Conner Convocation Center, Thomas More College.

7:00–8:30 P.M. every Sunday: NKU players host other college players in open gym competition, Regents Hall.

In addition to the above, most of the players also assisted Winstel in running a series of summer basketball summer camps in Regents Hall (the kind that Danyelle Echoles and Keri Finnell had attended when they were younger). These typically run four days a week from 9 A.M. to 4 P.M. and are spread through June and July.

It is often said that basketball teams are made in the summer. In 2006 our team was certainly trying to make that true for themselves. The strength and conditioning would make them fitter. The competition in the summer league and open gym would refine their skills. Both kinds of activities would deepen the group dynamic that has become such a priority during Winstel's evolution as a coach. The fact that the players themselves were setting their workout schedules and coaching their summertime games would help give them more ownership of their performance in the upcoming season. When I asked athletic director Jane Meier in July to comment on the level of dedication she was seeing from Winstel's current players, the first thing she said was, "They're here. They're working out together. They're lifting together."

Winstel's players, in their summer devotion, were not alone. Competing teams in the GLVC and throughout the country were working to "make" themselves over the summer, often with a special emphasis on becoming bigger, stronger, and faster, qualities currently epitomized by Grand Valley State.

The offseason for the players was the preseason for me as the author of this book. I began to think about writing such a book after seeing the victory over Drury in Evansville. After Coach Winstel approved the idea, she gave me a few minutes to speak to the players as they warmed up for one of the last practices of the spring semester. Some seemed quite surprised that I wanted to write a book about them. But they all seemed willing to help, and each wrote her contact information in a spiral notebook I passed around so I could schedule some interviews.

During the month of May I interviewed each player on the team. Doing so has been one of the great pleasures of working on this book. Before, I had known each player only by what she did on the court. Now I could begin to learn more about who they were and how their love of the game had developed. I began with Karmen, Karyn, and Brittany, the three cocaptain seniors-to-be. After speaking with each of them, I had a new and immediate understanding of why the team had done so well in the season recently completed. Each young woman had a will to win as strong as you could find in any player on any team in any sport.

In conversation, their styles contrasted as strongly as their play on the court. Karmen had that same infectious energy and enthusiasm she showed in every move on the floor. Karyn was quick and responsive: each answer was immediate, thoughtful, complete, and concise. Brittany was quite independent in thought and expression, yet full of gratitude for everyone who had helped her along the way. What they most had in common was their passion for the game. Brittany had decided she would become a basketball player during the summer between first and second grade in Minster. Karyn began dribbling the ball when she was five; she learned to play the game in a former church on her grandfather's farm in Leipsic that her father converted into her personal gym. When Karmen was five she "loved to play the game with my dad and brother, out in the driveway." The game was "not so much fun" when she played on a first-grade team, but it became her passion after she had a "growth spurt" in middle school.

Every player on the team had her story of coming to love the game. Angela Healy played on a YMCA team when she was five; in the second grade she played on her school's fourth-grade team. Nicole Chiodi's parents remember that "she was in a gym from the time that she could walk." She remembers what "torture" it was to sit on the bench of her older sister's team without being able to play. Cassie Brannen was one of eight children who all began playing in the second or third grade; she started out as a guard—until she grew four inches in the eighth grade. Betsey Clark cannot remember a time she was not running or playing ball; her father came from a family of coaches and taught her the fundamentals "in the backyard." Keri Finnell played both basketball and soccer in grade school, but it started long before that. Her father remembers that as a baby she always had a ball in her hands, what kind of ball did not matter.

These young women not only began playing as young girls; they were already intensely competitive. Brittany's parents remember her being "a fighter" in the third or fourth grade; "she really wanted to win, all the time." The Healys remember the time an aunt came down from Chicago and was surprised that Angela was "mad all day" because her team had lost a Little League soccer game. Nicole's parents remember that she was "an extremely competitive person who hated to lose in anything"; she would play her grandmother one-on-one in the basement and then come up and proudly announce, "I won 20 to 1," sneaking over to whisper to her mother, "I let her score." When Cassie's parents took her to play in a Saturday morning league as a fourth grader she would usually sleep on the bleachers before the game began; when she got in the game to "guard the middle" she would enrage the other team because "when the ball came in she just took it every time, like five times in a row, because she's quick."

One recurrent theme as I interviewed these young women was how close basketball had brought them to their fathers. Karyn's father, Dale, had taught her to shoot in the converted church on the family farm. He started her just in front of the basket so she could develop a smooth stroke, moving her out as she got older and older. She would shoot shot after shot and he would rebound and rebound until she finally became so good he would not let her end the practice until she had made 90 percent of her free throws. They both remember that "not a day went by" that they did not work on her shot. Even on vacation, if it was a summer trip to the Smokies, "we would find a gym to shoot in."

Katie Butler had a similar relationship with her father (who, conveniently, was the athletic director at her high school). "Whenever I would ask, 'Dad, can we shoot? Will you rebound for me?' he would take me to the gym and he would always rebound for me as long as I wanted." Betsey Clark's parents coached her in CYO basketball and soccer before turning her over to the coaches at school, and her father continued to give her backyard tutorials even after she began playing for Winstel.

Karmen's father, John, taught her "all the fundamentals" of basketball—"boxing out, how to shoot, how to defend." He always encouraged her in any kind of sport and gave her plenty of space to come back to basketball when she was finally ready. He no doubt influenced her daredevil style of play. He was a semiprofessional baseball player and once played through a terrible blow to his thigh only to find out the next day he had been playing with a blood clot.

Nicole remembers going to watch her dad when he was playing in a recreation league; she would "just dribble on the sideline trying to learn." When he began to teach her, "he always told me to keep my head up when I dribble—and to dribble with my left hand because I was naturally right-handed." From *her* father, Angela Estes learned a "baby hook shot" that served her very well in high school; Winstel discouraged it in college, though, wanting Angela to develop that drop step that would take her right up into the basket.

Keri's father not only coached her soccer and basketball teams when she was in grade school; he also took her to the Friar's Club every day for a personal workout that was "all worked out" in his mind. When she was 10 he began taking her to Winstel's summer camps. At home he gave her and her brothers calisthenics every morning. By the time Keri left high school she was ready for both West Point and Winstel.

Beyond actually developing their daughters' games, all these fathers (and many of the mothers, too) drove them to and from not only their practices and games in grade school, middle school, and high school but also their Amateur Athletic Union (AAU) games in their home states and adjacent ones. The level of bonding between fathers and daughters in particular was such a constant theme in the interviews that Stefanie Harrison, the English major who transcribed them for me, began to take notice as well. "Basketball," she wrote in her own commentary, "has allowed these daughters and fathers to overcome gender barriers, and they have united through this common interest."

Sitting with my faculty group in Regents Hall during the three previous years, I had not realized that Dale and Kathy Creager had been driving down to every single game from Leipsic, a six-hour round-trip; or that John and Kay Graham had been driving down to every single game from Kettering, a two-hour round-trip; or that Joe and Sondra Clark were coming over to every single game from across the river in Cincinnati. Most of the parents sat across from us on the other side of the gym behind the team bench. As new players were recruited, the Creagers, Grahams, and Clarks were augmented by the Winners, Finnells, Healys, and Chiodis in the second year, and then by the Butler, Brannen, Brackman, Estes, and Echoles families.

After getting to know their daughters, I was eager to interview the parents as well. This was not hard to arrange during the upcoming season since nearly all the parents came to nearly all the home games. I was especially interested in hearing what the fathers would say about how basketball had contributed to their relationships with their daughters. Joe Clark spoke for many fathers when he said that basketball gave him "something in common" with both his daughters "that I probably would never have had with a girl." For others, the game deepened a bond that had begun much earlier.

The bond between Dale and Karyn Creager began when she was born in the month of January. He was a farmer and had little to do until spring, so he spent most of the winter holding her.

The bond between John and Karmen Graham got stronger the day she fell headfirst off the dressing table into the diaper bin. John came from a large family and was initially more comfortable around the baby than his wife was, so he became a hands-on daddy early on.

Bill Finnell feels that "girls are always close to their daddies." He is in the construction business and had taken Keri to the lumberyard and taught her to set tile before he began to coach her in basketball and soccer.

Dean Butler, a high school athletic director, treasures a picture of Katie "sound asleep two years old on a bench in a district finals boys' game." From that time on, her deepening involvement in the game "has given me more good times than any one father should ever have from one child."

Another revelation for me during the interviews was the range and intensity of each young woman's career aspirations beyond basketball. Each is deeply committed to the game. But each sees it as a vehicle for her education—and her education as a vehicle for her career. Each is willing to work so hard at the game, even throughout the summer, because this will prepare her all the more intensely for life beyond the college walls. Stefanie observed that these players gave "extremely ambitious" answers when asked about their future plans. "Although some of the players have expressed interest in continuing their involvement with basketball after college, they all have life goals that extend outside the basketball realm." Stefanie could sense that the "life lessons" these players learn through basketball—"the discipline, the responsibility, and the teamwork"— would serve them well, whatever they do. So would what they have learned about "how to both win and lose gracefully."

I was impressed, when conducting the interviews, to see the extent to which the players' own desires and motivations seemed to mirror those of their coach. Winstel had learned in earlier years that players who receive full college scholarships to play basketball can sometimes give lip service to a coach's goals without really feeling them or living them out. She therefore seeks to recruit players who share her own goals or are capable of embracing them as their own. Her current players spoke of the need to be challenged and to be pushed—by themselves as well as by the coach. They spoke eloquently and often of the importance of every player to the team as a whole—whether they themselves were reserves or starters. Stefanie was impressed with the players' appreciation of the "depth and versatility" of their team, of how "any number of players can step up during a game." She noted, "All of the players verbally express[ed] their drive to win. Their motivation comes primarily from themselves rather than from outside sources. This internal motivation leads to intensity on the court," but it will also extend to "all aspects of their lives."

All the players expressed affection for their teammates and delight at the fun they have together. The chemistry of the team, its capacity for joy, was as palpable in the interviews as on the court. This is something a coach can wish for but can hardly create herself. Each player had her favorite moment of craziness or unexpected elation. Stefanie felt that these "lighthearted" moments conveyed a "power of positive energy." Yet she felt that the "closeness" of these players went much deeper. "I think every female desires a group of close-knit female friends in which to confide and share herself. This team has clearly achieved this often daunting task. Women can be so cruel and judgmental toward one another; ironically, they can also be one another's saving grace. Honest and authentic relationships, such as the ones displayed by NKU's women's basketball team, allow women to be themselves, which helps to build confidence. These players are fortunate to have each other. It is certainly encouraging to see such support among peers." Stefanie, by the way, had never seen these fellow students play a game. All her impressions were based on what she had sensed from transcribing the interviews.

As I interviewed these young women in an office whose shelves are filled with 19th-century novels, I thought more than once of Isabel Archer in Henry James's *Portrait of a Lady*. Isabel has it all—beauty, smarts, poise, and, most of all, a sense of self that captures the imagination of others without betraying her own inner essence. What Isabel is going to make of herself matters to all who know her. Living in the 1870s, however, the most positive thing she can do for herself is to turn down one unsatisfactory marriage proposal after another until she tragically accepts the wrong one. She is smart but has no formal education. She is talented but has no female peers. Her potential surpasses her society's expectations of what a young woman should be.

The young women I spoke with in May 2006 collectively embodied the condition of women and the potential of society in a multifaceted way that would have been rare 30 years ago, not to mention 130. The self-possession they have acquired by developing their basketball skills, combined with the discipline and community that arise from being on this team, enriched by the pursuit of a college degree that is crystallizing each one's sense of what she wants to do with her life in the wider world after she graduates—all this is powerful to contemplate. None of these young women will be exempt from the difficult choices all students face as they enter life beyond college. But each will make her choices from a broader range of experience—and actual accomplishment—than many of her female contemporaries. In no case has her athletic experience in any way detracted from the personal charm that will make us care for her as she goes out to "affront her destiny" (in James's phrase).

May 2, 2006. Today I interviewed assistant coach Travece Turner. Turner is a 2003 graduate of Morehead State University in Kentucky, where she averaged 15.1 points and made first-team All-Ohio Valley Conference. The 2005–06 season was her first as an assistant coach at NKU. She enjoyed the year but has decided to go back to school to become an English teacher. I interviewed her on one of her last days on the job, two months after she and Keri had survived the cab ride through the Missouri tornadoes.

As a first-year assistant, Turner had been responsible for monitoring the study table. She was not sure what to expect. The hardest part was to schedule four hours a week when all 12 players could meet in the designated area of the Steely Library. Once the schedule was set, no one ever missed. She never had to make sure they were actually doing their work. Turner had never seen such a capable or motivated group of student-athletes.

One of *her* biggest challenges was to adjust to Winstel's coaching style at practice. "I'm a pretty quiet person when you first meet me. So Coach would say to me, 'Now, you've really got to make sure you get onto them when they are doing something wrong.' It was hard for me at first, but I learned how to do it."

Turner admires Winstel for what she demands from her players and for how much she can see on the court in the course of a game. She was especially impressed with the way she "invited the kids in, and talked to them, and let them talk to her. She would let them express how they were feeling, what they felt they might need to improve, and how they could improve upon it." Because she "believes in them as persons," she gets more out of them as players.

Has she ever seen anyone work as hard as Karmen Graham? No, nowhere, ever. "She is one of those players that if you get one player like that in your career, you're lucky."

Does this team have the toughness to deal with the high expectations they have created for their next season? "Yes. I think so. We will have those five seniors and we will be a mature team. This team won't get too nervous or too overly confident. They will be able to handle the pressure and the expectations."

May 18, 2006. I have another interview with Coach Winstel. My first interviews with the coach were in April, before I had met with the team or began to interview the players. Her strongest concern as we spoke on April 17 was to "have the players take ownership, to hold each other accountable" on the court. She was happy to report that next year's seniors were making plans to live in a house together (as Nancy and her teammates had done 30 years earlier). Karmen, Karyn, Betsey, Brittany, and Katie had found a five-bedroom house that would be available for rent in early August. It was almost as close to campus as Chiodi's parents' house. Looking ahead to the upcoming season, Winstel was trying to schedule a couple of challenging games in Florida so she could give her players a day at the beach during Christmas break. As for the season itself, she declared that the only goal for any season is "to continue to be better, to be the best you are capable of being." Winning is important, but you cannot always control that, so she will be satisfied as long as they continue to grow and improve.

Later in April I learned a lot more about how busy Winstel had been when she was a student in my American literature class in 1974, during the semester she joined the basketball team as a walk-on. "I would have basketball practice from 1 to 3 and volleyball practice from 3 to 5 and then I would go to one of my jobs. By the end of the week I would fall into bed, I was so tired. It was crazy but I loved it. After my first year, I got a little scholarship money and our team moved into the house on John's Hill Road. One winter it got so cold we had to burn some of the furniture in the fireplace to stay warm."

On May 18 I interviewed Winstel in my office, where I had already spoken with most of her players. She spoke about the need for players to "live for the moment" on the court—not to be too worried about a past mistake or get too caught up in the future. She used her current point guard to illustrate a paradox: "You have to stay a little bit ahead, but you can't be too far ahead or else you can't play *in* the moment. Look at Nicole. The process, as fast as it goes, has to be slow in your head, so you can see the picture of it developing." Nicole had expressed a similar paradox a week earlier when discussing the need to push the ball up the court as fast as possible and then suddenly slow everything down to set up a play. "You have to be able to think on your toes. It's a lot of thinking in a small amount of time."

That kind of complex consciousness is something Winstel desires to extend to the whole team. "You have to speed up the game for the kids, even though they may be rushing. Last year there were times in practice when we were speeding the game up, and it almost felt like I was rushing them, but I needed them to. I would say, 'Ladies, picture us driving side by side down the road and my car is going 45 miles an hour, and your car is going 20, and I am under control. You have to speed things up but stay calm. Be quick but don't rush.' You have to get them eventually to where they are moving quickly and thinking quickly but they are also thinking ahead of where they are. It's like a controlled intensity. It's a calm intensity. You're quick and it goes fast but you're not overwhelmed."

When I asked about all the work her players would be doing over the summer to improve their game, she stressed the need for players to be "self-motivated" in the summer when coaches are "not allowed to be around them. You have to recruit highly motivated people who are mature enough to be able to do things on their own.

And they've got to want what you want. What I want is for them to go to college, and get an education, and get a degree—and also to be the best basketball players they are capable of becoming. If *I* want you to become a good basketball player more than *you* do, we've got a problem. And that's what is so nice about this group. They want it too. That sounds so simple, but it's a complex simplicity." One special incentive for this particular summer: "Grand Valley and Michigan Tech made our kids realize they've got to get stronger."

Working hard over the summer is especially important at the higher levels of Division II because "in Division II if you get the outstanding athletes, you're fortunate. The best-case scenario is to have a great athlete who is also great fundamentally. But we are more likely to have players that are great fundamentally but maybe they don't have the athleticism. Or maybe you are going to have a great athlete who is maybe not so great fundamentally. So you hope you can catch them up in whatever deficiency they may have. And a lot of it is whether they are willing to work at fixing what they need to fix. When I look at my team this year, we're not the fastest and quickest in perimeter players particularly, so we've got to be tenacious, we have to be stubborn, we have to be smart. You can get stronger, you can get faster, but you can't wish quick. You can't get quicker than you innately are."

Throughout the summer her players would be working to overcome their latent limitations while also perfecting their acquired skills. "Right now," she told me, "I don't know who will be my starting five."

Sunday, June 11, 7 P.M. This is the first open gym of the summer. Karyn Creager is one of the first to emerge from the locker room, but she cannot play because she accidentally cut her left thumb while slicing an apple with a paring knife. Tonight she has stitches and a bandage and the thumb is sore, but she hopes to be playing in a week or two. Our main opponent tonight, and for the rest of the summer, will be Xavier University, a Division I team (and Atlantic Ten member) from across the river in Cincinnati. As our team waits for theirs to arrive, we play a game against ourselves and a few others who have come to play. Games are to 10 points, with a 2-point basket counting as 1 and a 3-pointer as 2. The team that wins stays on the court until it loses. Our players divide into alternating teams in the open gym so that everyone gets an equal chance to play. The team that wins our first game loses to Xavier when they arrive, and Xavier stays on the floor for much of the evening until our players beat them once or twice near the end. Healy, Winner, and Estes are not here tonight. Healy is on a 10-day missionary trip to Belize. Winner is helping her father on the farm in Minster; she will return for the second five weeks of summer school. Estes has a work schedule that conflicts with open gym.

It is a pleasure to see our players out on the court again. Karmen is a powerful presence with her efficient rebounding and sweet shooting (this is the first time she has been allowed to play in quite a while after the healing of a stress fracture). Katie shoots well, as usual, and surprises a Xavier player by blocking a shot. Cassie is fun to watch, surprising at least two Xavier players with unexpected blocks and making one of those wonderful wriggling up-and-in power moves to the basket. Danyelle plays quite well, showing that smooth touch with at least three sweet threes. Karen Brackman is quick and alert and has some really good moments. Betsey moves well and looks really good on defense and on any offensive opportunity she gets. Nicole has some good moments and cuts off one drive beautifully on the baseline. Keri moves well and her legs look strong.

It is interesting to watch our players against Xavier. Those who chat with me when not on the court openly admire these Division I players. Two of Xavier's players look a cut above us in this workout—a short, quick guard who seems able to lay back and drain a three pretty much at will, and a lean 6-foot-4 forward who can slash and drive to the hoop in a way we can hardly stop (although I think she is the one Nicole impressively stopped that one time). Cassie and Karmen were holding their own pretty much under the boards, and our players played well the whole evening. When one of our teams finally beat Xavier by a pretty good score in the last game, they had been on the court continuously, winning about four games in a row and playing with a single team (and only a few subs) rather than alternating whole teams, as we had been doing.

Tomorrow, June 12, Coach Winstel begins her first four-day

summer camp for girls, grades 4 through 12. Nearly all our players will be working at this and subsequent camps, scheduling their hours around their classes. They are paid by the hour for their time, as this work is entirely voluntary, not something their scholarships oblige them to do.

Friday, June 17, 7 P.M. I am in a concert hall in St. Petersburg, Russia, with Rudy, John, and Bill—the same fans with whom I attended the GLVC Tournament in Evansville in March. We are here to hear 2005 NKU alumna Anna Polusmiak play Prokofiev's Piano Concerto No. 2 with the St. Petersburg Philharmonic, her prize for winning the first annual Louisiana International Piano Competition. Is it a coincidence that we four fans of Nancy's team are fans of Anna too? There are certain similarities. We have watched Anna's pianism mature on the stage of the Greaves Concert Hall, just as we have watched the athleticism of Winstel's players mature on the court in Regents Hall. Anna's pianism is as powerful and refined as the athleticism of Winstel's players. The combination of "passion and precision" that Winstel's team had begun to show by midseason of last year is what has always characterized Anna's playing. By winning an international piano competition at the age of 22 and playing as commandingly as we heard her play in St. Petersburg on June 17, Anna, too, could quite literally say with Emily Dickinson, "I took my power in my hand / And went against the world." A few days before the trip to Russia I saw Anna in a different corner of the weight room from where our basketball players were working out, refining the strength required for pianistic beauty.

Thursday, July 6, 7:40 and 8:30 P.M. I watch our players in back-to-back games in the third week of the Greater Cincinnati Women's League at Thomas More College. Our team plays under two different sponsors in this nine-team league; they wear Personal Best jerseys for one game, Campus Book and Supply for the other. As during the open gym, our players substitute and rotate freely, so that everyone gets to play. These are real games—with 20-minute halves, two referees, and an electronic scoreboard. Our players usually substitute about every five minutes. The level of the competition ranges widely—from two local small-college teams to teams made up of current Division I stars, former All-Americans, and even a former

WNBA player. We play one of the all-star teams tonight, sponsored by Legends Bar and Grill. We stay close for about 18 minutes, but Legends pulls away for a 45–38 victory when Tara Boothe takes over the game.

Boothe had just completed her career as Xavier University's all-time leading scorer, graduating as a leading player in the Atlantic Ten Conference and an honorable mention All-American. Her teammates tonight include other former stars from Xavier and the University of Cincinnati, plus Jamie Walz from Western Kentucky University. Walz had been Miss Kentucky Basketball in 1996 and was Angela Healy's basketball coach at Highlands in Fort Thomas (where Boothe had also played high school ball). Although Winstel is not allowed to coach in summer league games, she is allowed to watch. She will sometimes come to check on her team's intensity—and to let her players know she is interested.

There are no seats at these games; spectators lean over the rail of a track that runs high above the court. Winstel is here for this game and she invites me to stand with her by the rail—which I do when she is not pacing away in disgust at this or that. She is generally quite relaxed, talking on her cell phone now and then, but she gets absolutely livid when one of our players allows two uncontested threes in a row. That, to be sure, is filed away in her memory bank.

I was quite impressed with how our team played against these assembled all-star talents. This was the first time I could really see what Keri Finnell could do when she was healthy; she made two great drives for layups, took a charge against Boothe, and played well on defense. Karmen had a tough time underneath because everyone was collapsing inside and no one could hit any threes to free her up. Karyn looked happy to be playing now that her thumb was healed; she hit two threes at the end and clearly wanted to shoot. Katie was not shooting well tonight but otherwise played hard and well. Angela Healy was back on the court after treatment for bursitis in her shoulder, but guarding Boothe was no way to ease back in. Nicole kept fouling during the last minute, hoping we could get back in it.

This game was the first time I had seen our one new recruit for the 2006–07 season. Rachel Lantry is a 5-foot-10 guard from Holy Cross High School in northern Kentucky. She moves well and works hard and did not seem intimidated by any of our legendary opponents. Although she is not allowed to receive any coaching over the summer as a first-year recruit, she is able to participate in the voluntary summer league and open gym activities. After the excitement of this first game I was looking forward to seeing the second scheduled game, but the other team did not show.

Friday, July 7, 7:30 A.M. I meet with the team and Livey Birkenhauer to observe a regular Friday morning strength and conditioning session. Inside the weight room the players begin working immediately in groups of two or three. They all know exactly what to do, and they each have a personal book in which to record the morning's activities. Two pairs of two begin on the bench presses, one lifting weights while another spots for her. Three others are doing dumbbell squats—lifting light weights as they press a medicine ball behind them against the wall. Guards tend to be with guards and post players with post players, but everyone rotates through the same series of activities. I learn from Livey that the push press with barbells is good for explosiveness, and the reverse flex is good for the upper body. She prefers dumbbells over machines when players are working with both arms because a machine makes it too easy to favor one side or the other. When I ask how someone would know whether she needs to cut back on a certain activity on a certain day, she answers, "When the form gets bad."

Birkenhauer had kept the sessions "relatively light" in May. That is what she calls the "recovery period" or the "unloading cycle" at the end of a season. She then increases both the weight training and the conditioning gradually throughout the summer months so the players will be ready for the workouts coaches Winstel and Schmidt will supervise during the preseason in the fall. Livey uses the mile-and-a-half run as one benchmark for the team's overall progress in conditioning, and this year she is happy to see that their "postseason testing was faster than they were preseason for last year."

Because it was Friday and the team had played in the summer league the night before, she kept this workout a little lighter than normal. In addition to the exercises required of all players, some were adapted to individual needs. Betsey did little stretches with weights while facedown on the bench, recommended by Noriko for her shoulder. Angela Healy told Livey what the trainer and doctor had said about *her* shoulder and spent part of this workout on a machine that helped her work the triceps without lifting anything overhead. The players all worked in a quiet and relaxed way, enjoying one another's company as much as one can this early in the morning. Livey obviously enjoys working with these young women. After the weight work was done, she sent them outdoors to do their running without any further supervision, telling one of the cocaptains exactly what she wanted them to do. This left me free to interview her in a more direct way about her work with Winstel's team.

Like Winstel, she said that the loss to Grand Valley State helped each player realize how important strength and conditioning would be to next year's success. She explained the importance of conditioning not only for performance but also for preventing injuries, something that had not been fully appreciated when she played for NKU in the late 1970s. Then, she feels, players who had never lifted weights sometimes overdid it in college and made themselves liable to injuries; she had to sit out her own senior year with a knee injury. In addition to lifting for strength, a lot of today's activity is preventative—strengthening the knees and the hamstrings, building up resistance against shin splints and other debilitating conditions, being sure not to overcondition with too much running and jumping. We have a much better understanding of the damage done to the body by the "pounding of the joints" than when she was in school. Another improvement these days is that the conditioning is designed to "emulate the kind of movement you have in the sport. Basketball is sprint, stop, sprint, jump, sprint, backpedal, and side to side. So you match your conditioning to that motion."

The purpose of the weight training in this program is to "add strength, not size." The exercises therefore emphasize "repetitions more than heavy weight." Our post players, rather than getting heavier, are going to get "faster and stronger so they can run up and down the court with the guards." I had always wondered whether the legendary intensity of Winstel's practice sessions could increase the chance of injuries occurring, but Birkenhauer thinks the opposite is true. Injuries are more likely to occur, she says, in those programs whose practices are *less* intense than the actual games. Livey feels that working hard at both practice and conditioning has a double function. In addition to "helping you not to get hurt in either a practice or a game, it also gives you confidence in your playing level." Karyn Creager expresses that kind of confidence in these words: "When I've worked hard, I feel I deserve to be out on the court. Now it's time to lay it all out, to give it all I've got."

When I asked Livey whether any of our players seemed to worry that working with weights might compromise her femininity in any way, she thought not. This had been a concern for earlier generations of players, but she does not see it as a problem for the women on Winstel's current team. I certainly had to agree, based on what I had seen of these players on the court, in the weight room, and during the interviews in May. I am guessing that most of them would be quite comfortable with Herman Melville's declaration in *Moby-Dick* that "real strength never impairs beauty, but it often bestows it; and in everything imposingly beautiful, strength has much to do with the magic." In that passage Melville is celebrating the strength of the whale's tail, a quality that results in its delicacy and elasticity as well as its pure power.

Keri Finnell has known some young women who are "afraid to develop their own strength" because someone might think they would "look like a man." But for her it comes down to this: "I feel I'm not going to look like a man because I'm not a man." Many players mentioned in our interviews, as Katie Butler did, how much they and their teammates enjoy dressing up and going out on the town together: "We can be 'girlie-girls' as well as athletes." In Karen Brackman's words, the team has "two different faces. We can be athletic out on the court and sweaty and all that stuff, and all the people look up to us. And then, on the other side, we can be pretty ladies and have a fun time just being girls." Angela Estes expressed the same feeling this way: "We have a very pretty team. But it's fun to get all nasty, too, when you are working hard and having fun on the basketball court." Angela Healy enjoyed telling me how her teammates like to call her "the 'Hulk' just because my biceps tend to swell even when I'm pressing small weights." They also like to say, "the Unit's turning green." When the players wrote those phrases of praise on one another's posters, they celebrated their teammates' strength as much as their speed or their shooting. Next to "lifts houses" on one poster was "squats Landrum" (the building I teach in).

One measure of how things have changed since I was in school came in the words of the parents who said how pleased they were that their daughter "carried her height so well" in high school; "she didn't try to make herself shorter than she really was." They admire her "air of confidence" and the way "she carries it when she walks," qualities of both inner and outer strength that she has gained from playing basketball. It is perhaps not surprising that the team that had once inspired my fellow fan to blurt out "Here come the queens!" became somewhat active on the pages of Facebook and MySpace when those sites became popular with college students in 2006. When Coach Schmidt heard from a colleague that players on our team had posted some pages that were not entirely fit for public scrutiny, he arranged a team meeting and conveyed the seriousness of his concern. "I had two of them sprinting out the door to get to their computers. Like a bat out of hell."

A week before my interview with Livey Birkenhauer I met Noriko Masamoto, the team's sports medicine specialist. Noriko is a native of Japan who worked at Western Oregon College before coming to NKU. Last year was her first with the women's basketball team. Once the official season began on October 15, she attended every three-hour practice, every home game, and half of the away games (for these she alternates with the trainer for the men's team). Noriko is the one who attended to Nicole's chin and Karmen's concussion early in the season and to Cassie when she took an elbow to the gut in the championship game with Drury. She arrives an hour early for every three-hour practice to tape the players' ankles, and she stays for half an hour afterward to help with whirlpool or icing. She is very impressed with how hard this team works throughout the year ("they only have one day off a week") and with how hard Coach Winstel pushes everyone at practice ("it doesn't matter if you are a starter or a bench person").

Coming from Japan, Noriko is "somewhat jealous that American girls could get a scholarship that would give them a college education because they were an athlete." In addition to the "discipline," she is impressed with how being an athlete gives a young woman independence and "helps her develop her own identity." For her, the best example of the "closeness" of this particular team is that "they don't talk about each other." In the trainer's room she often hears players from some of the other teams complain about their teammates, but she has never heard that from this team. Noriko finds this especially impressive because "women are often critical of each other."

Sunday, July 16, 7 P.M. Open gym, again with Xavier. Arriving early, I have a chance to talk briefly with coaches Winstel and Schmidt before they leave the gym. They have each returned from separate scouting trips. When I ask how these trips went, they each say, separately, "It's always hit and miss." A top Division II program is "always going after people who are going to be hard to get but for whom you have to try." You never know when some extra effort is going to pay off—as when Schmidt, through his Findlay connections, heard that Katie Butler was going to leave the University of Dayton and arranged for her to visit NKU the day before she would have transferred to another school.

Tonight Tara Boothe, the All-American alumna, comes to play with Xavier's team. This ups the ante. But we have Brittany back, which helps our side. And now Angela Healy has been cleared by her doctor to play. And Karyn is no longer bothered by the sore thumb. This time, however, Cassie Brannen and Karen Brackman are not here, nor is Angela Estes. Danyelle Echoles is present but unable to play. She has just been in an auto accident. Her car got hit from behind. She thinks she is okay but Winstel wants to make sure before she plays again.

In the first game tonight Karmen, Karyn, Brittany, Angela, and Nicole are all on the floor, with Katie in reserve. We beat Xavier's team, with Boothe, by 10–8, and we look good doing it. Brittany makes a big difference. She is doing a lot of the playmaking out front and on breaks, looking very quick and strong. Karyn makes a couple of good baskets. Angela has good moments against both

Boothe and their strong center, scoring on one great turnaround move. Nicole makes one great save and backward pass on a fast break. Karmen moves and scores smoothly.

The best thing about this game is that when Xavier begins to pay attention to the score and tries to turn it on, we deny them. We play good defense and shoot well under pressure at the end to win. I wish I could have stayed longer to see how the rest of the evening played out. It had been good to see last year's starters out on the floor together, playing so well against a strong Division I team.

Thursday, July 20, 6 and 6:50 P.M. Tonight our two games at Thomas More College are back-to-back. The first is a good old summertime blowout. The other team is entirely outmanned. We win 77–12. We manage to keep our intensity the whole game, especially on defense. After allowing 10 points in the first half, we allow only 2 in the second! Two players who are here are not able to play. Danyelle is still not fully recovered from the auto accident. Karyn bumped her head in a scrimmage and is staying out as a precaution. Of the seven who do play, incoming freshman Rachel Lantry is the standout. She is all over the floor in steals, assists, and rebounds—in addition to scoring about 25 of our 77 points.

The crowd is much bigger for the second game because we are playing Noll, one of the top summer teams. Their players include Nicole Levandusky, a Xavier standout who had played in the WNBA; Erica Hallman, a local product who had a strong career at the University of Kansas; and Megan Fletcher, another local product who had impressed us with her play for Kentucky Wesleyan against Drury in the conference tournament. Coaches Winstel and Schmidt are in the crowd along the track above the floor. So is Brian Neal, Winstel's former assistant, now head coach of the women's team at Thomas More.

We start slowly this game, falling behind 12–6. Winstel has to walk away from the rail a couple of times, as we are shooting threes, poorly, instead of working the ball inside. We play much better during the next 10 minutes and tie the game at 24 before the half. Our defense made the difference; we held them at 18 points for about 6 minutes, it seemed.

In the second half we open up a good lead and keep pulling

away with strong offense and defense, winning 67–47. Winstel becomes a lot more relaxed. She begins talking, very affectionately and jestingly, with one of Brian Neal's young daughters: "I hear your daddy wants to have seven kids; how would you like be to the oldest of seven?"

In this game Keri shows a lot of hustle and scores well. Lantry continues to play aggressively. But we do have some bad news. Coaches Winstel and Schmidt have just learned that Angela Estes has decided not to return for next year. She cannot get the courses she needs in speech pathology at NKU, so she has decided to transfer to the University of Cincinnati. Both coaches understand Angela's decision and fully support it.

Now the addition of Rachel will keep us at 12 rather than raise us to 13. We can no longer say "we have everyone coming back." Practices will not be the same underneath. Someone else will have to be the conehead queen.

Sunday, July 23, 7 P.M. Another open gym with Xavier. Because Xavier has become our constant opponent on Sunday nights, I have learned a bit about them and who their players are. Their Web site reveals that they have the 10th-ranked incoming freshman class in D-I women's basketball. No wonder they have been looking so good. I will have to start matching up some names and faces. Their team, like ours, has some variation in who comes from week to week. This week we are missing Nicole, who is on vacation; Cassie, out with a sore foot; and Danyelle, not yet cleared to play after the auto accident. But Karyn is back now, after the light concussion. And Betsey's sister Ashley Clark is playing with us, having completed an excellent career at Indiana State. I watch five games this evening and we win three of them.

The first game sets the tone for the evening. We start Karyn, Karmen, Betsey, Katie, and Keri, with Angela coming in. We play tough all the way and hold a good lead to the end, 10–7. Karmen looks great all night, making four of our baskets in this game. Angela, Karyn, and Katie all shoot well, and Betsey and Keri are both very active at both ends of the court. Although we lose the next two games, we come back to win the two after that. Rachel and Karmen lead the way in game four, Karyn and Katie in game five. Betsey and Keri play strong defense and do not let those good Xavier guards kill us, as they have often done before.

It is quite a pleasure to see us playing so well against Xavier tonight (especially with several key players unable to be with us). The players are handling the ball well, working hard, and looking for one another. Steals and assists and blocks are all impressive. Playing a top-tier Division I team *is* helping us grow. There was one nice moment as Nancy was leaving the gym before the play began. Seeing that her freshman Rachel was wearing earrings, she told her to "take them off so you don't get hurt."

Sunday, July 30, 7:00 P.M. The last open gym of the summer. Before play begins I meet our new assistant coach, Katie Vieth, who has replaced Travece Turner. This time Xavier brings their best. Their All-American graduate Tara Boothe plays in most of the games tonight, and so does their new recruit Amber Harris from Indianapolis, ranked by the Blue Star Index as the number-one freshman prospect in the nation. She is easy to recognize as a 6-foot-5 wing player. Having printed out a Xavier roster from the Web, I can now identify Alesia Barringer as the 5-foot-6 guard who had been shooting so well all summer, Dar-ryka Martin as the slashing 6-foot-3 forward, and Deana Mason as the 6-foot-2 center who has been such a force inside.

We have a hard night between Boothe and Harris. Boothe hits about 11 of 13 threes. Harris can shoot the three or drive, whichever she wants, seemingly whenever she wants. Those two, with Mason on the inside as a rebounder and team leader, give Xavier the edge most of the time. The only game we win is one in which Boothe does not play. Karyn and Katie shoot well from the outside but cannot match Boothe's long-range bombs. We cannot score much at all inside. The most interesting part of the evening is watching our defensive matchups. Brittany takes on Amber Harris and has some good moments against this quick and imposing player. Karyn guards Boothe most of the evening and at least has a hand in her face on most of those long threes. Angela and Karmen work hard in the block against Deana Mason, who is impossible to move if she gets position. Keri and Betsey do an excellent job on Alesia Barringer, keeping her in check for most of the evening.

Losing every game but one tonight is a tough way to end the open gym for the summer. There is, of course, no shame in getting beat by players like these. Especially without Nicole, Cassie, or Karen on the floor. Even so, the show that Boothe and Harris put on has to be a little hard on the ego. By mid-December entering freshman Amber Harris will have already broken Xavier's all-time record for blocks in a season; Tara Boothe will be averaging 23 points and 13 rebounds as a professional in Neuchâtel, Switzerland.

Our conditioning, our concentration, and our defensive intensity have all improved over the summer. But our players are ready for some vacation time, and they deserve it. Creager, Graham, and Butler have been here since the end of May; they will each be getting home to Ohio before the new semester begins.

Wednesday, August 9. Championship of the Greater Cincinnati Women's Basketball League. Our team made the four-team playoffs, but the players chose not to compete because it is more important to have a decent break before the first week of class. In the title game, Levandusky and the Noll team beat Boothe and the Legends team, 57–52.

During July and early August, while our players were completing their summer classes, workouts, games, camps, and open gyms, I was learning more about Winstel and her program from her colleagues and associates.

Jane Meier has been NKU's athletic director since 1988. In 2003–04 she was named Athletic Director of the Year by the National Association of Collegiate Directors of Athletics. She and Winstel have worked together since 1981, when Winstel became Meier's assistant in coaching both women's basketball and volleyball. Among all the coaches Meier has hired, male or female, she finds Winstel unusual for her intensity, her high expectations of her players, and the trust her players have in her. That trust has deepened over the years as Winstel has become more and more concerned with motivation and team dynamics. Meier pointed to the trip to Australia and the leadership seminars as recent examples of Winstel's evolution as a coach. Because they know she cares, her players play hard for her. "Nancy goes after them to be better, but she doesn't berate them to the point where they're afraid to play. It's just the opposite. She instills confidence in them. And she makes them work to gain that confidence. There's no halfway." Above everything else, Winstel "has shown women how to compete. The ones who can accept it and survive will be successful."

Senior associate athletic director Scott Eaton came to NKU in 1997 from Brown University, where he had been assistant men's basketball coach. He loves Division II women's basketball because of the "purity" of the game. "You're still seeing kids being coached and playing the fundamentals of the game. That's the beauty of it." For him, Winstel exemplifies the "true, caring, knowledgeable coach who runs her program with integrity, nothing but family-oriented style. She makes the kids better people than when they came in. You can't have anything more than that." Her players "love her because they know that she loves them and that if she pushes them hard it is for a reason. I'm not going to say that it takes a special kid to play for Coach, but I think that they have to be mentally strong and they have to be willing to work as hard as they can." Although she pushes them hard, she would never do anything to hurt a player "physically, mentally, or emotionally. The player's welfare is always first and foremost with her."

Rick Meyers, like Nancy Winstel, was a student at NKSC in the early 1970s. He wrote stories about our women's teams for the *Northerner* and the *Cincinnati Enquirer* and eventually became sports information director at NKU, a position he later held with the Great Lakes Valley Conference until 2006. As we spoke, he brought out old scrapbooks he has kept from the 1970s, one of which has a photo from the *Northerner* in which Nancy Winstel is wearing cutoff jeans while playing defense in a scrimmage as a member of the school's first team in November 1974. During two decades as sports information director of the GLVC, Meyers got a unique sense of how Winstel is viewed throughout the league. "When you talk to other coaches, they will say that Nancy's the hardest person to coach against because she's so intelligent; she can figure out what you're doing and counteract it. She can find the weakness and she can go right after it because she's so good. I would hate to be a rookie coach going against her." Meyers compares her coaching style to that of a chess champion. He considers one of her greatest moves ever to be withholding Chiodi from the point guard position in the first half against Drury in the 2006 conference championship game. "The whole Drury team was ready to go after Nicole Chiodi and here was Brittany Winner bringing the ball up the floor. For a time, they weren't sure what to do, and Brittany broke down the press like it was nothing."

During his years as the league's sports information director, Meyers always got to sit near the coaches in the press row; he could see firsthand Winstel's care and passion as she put players in a game and took them out. She could be emphatic when telling them exactly what they had done wrong, but she always had her arm around them as she told them so. "She is a master at turning a negative play into a teachable moment. She can be tough in a practice or a game, but when the game is over she is always there for them. I think, if you asked, every player that she ever coached would feel that way. They just feel incredible loyalty. Years and years down the road they always come back; they're almost like her kids. This is her family."

Ken Shields was the men's basketball coach at NKU from 1988 through 2004. He first got to know Nancy Winstel when she was a student in his biology class at St. Thomas High School in Fort Thomas. That was the school that had no basketball team for women. Shields was extremely impressed that Nancy was able to go on and become a "self-made basketball player" in college. He sees her decision to go to Indiana University for graduate school as a key to her subsequent success as a coach. Bobby Knight was "the hottest coach in America" at the time. When Nancy studied with his assistant Jim Crews, "she had an opportunity to learn from some of the real trailblazers in the coaching profession." From then on she has been a "voracious" reader and student of the game. After each practice as a walk-on in college, Winstel remembers, "I would write down everything Coach Moore had said and try to understand." When she began coaching at Midway, she would read anything she could get her hands on about the game.

Like others, Shields sees Winstel as having become more personable over the years, without losing her intensity on the court. She has become "less like Bobby Knight, more like Mike Krzyzewski." Shields has always been impressed with Winstel's skill in preparing for every opponent. "She puts heart and soul into learning the game and the adjustments that go on in the game." He has also seen her adjust to new technology: "When cell phones came into vogue, she would collect every player's cell phone every night on the road." During his 16 seasons as head coach of the men's team, his and Winstel's players would travel together on nearly every road trip. He would see every minute of every game the women played, "from the tip-off to the end," and he and Nancy would compare notes from their front-row seats on the left and right sides of the bus. What Shields remembers most about all those road trips is how hard Winstel took losses. "When she lost, she couldn't talk to anyone for hours."

Dealing with losses has been Winstel's biggest challenge ever since her first coaching job at Midway. "When I began coaching, losing was the end of the world. I took defeat really, really, really hard." Her mother, though not in good health, had come down to see several of the games. She always worried about how badly Nancy wanted to win. "She would say to me, 'Okay. If you win, good for you. But if you lose, Nancy, don't get so upset about it.'" Nancy would still get upset about it. She will never forget the day her mother finally told her, "In life you're going to win some and you're going to lose some, and you'd better be able to handle it when you lose, because you're going to be pretty miserable, you're going to be pretty miserable, Nance." She always tries to remember this in both good times and bad. But any loss is still hard to take. Fortunately, the first year at Midway has been her only losing season as a coach.

Winstel admits in the afterword to this book, "I am not fond of losing." She goes on to declare that "winning does not make me feel superior; it makes me feel worthy." This sense of self-worth is what the game is ultimately about for her and her players. Doing well at sports helped her feel worthy as the youngest of her parents' five children—and as the only girl among the older boys she and her brothers played with in the streets and alleys of Newport. The young women who play for her today sometimes come from more privileged or protective situations than she had known, but they still need to discover that deeper sense of self-worth that comes from digging deep in the face of adversity, delivering one's best no matter what the outcome.

Matt Schmidt learned how Nancy Winstel responds to losing when he arrived as her assistant during the season that began with five losses in a row. Since then he had seen Karmen, Karyn, and Betsey, and their younger and subsequent teammates, evolve to the status they had achieved by summer 2006. After the loss to Grand Valley in March, he saw their need to become "bigger, stronger, faster." By "bigger" he did not mean "in bulk, but just stronger, tougher." As for "faster," he was thinking of how Grand Valley "just beat us off the dribble. We struggled defending them laterally and side to side. We need to work much harder on our nose-on-ball defense." Strength and conditioning can make a "huge" difference in addressing such deficiencies. But it is also a matter of "intelligence" in playing "the game within the game." You have to force your opponent to go in the direction that "takes away her strengths, not allowing her to catch the ball in a position where she will have the advantage, making life just a little more difficult for her." As his players were working to improve their skills and conditioning over the summer, Coach Schmidt showed his devotion to them by turning down an attractive head coaching position for the upcoming season.

Coach Winstel had a one-week vacation in early August. When she returned she gave me some helpful comments on the chapter I had written about the 2005–06 season. That was the day I asked whether she could remember when she first knew she hated to lose—and she had told me about being a five-year-old girl who wanted a machine gun more than a doll for Christmas and loved playing sports with the other kids who "ruled the neighborhood" because there "were no adults to be found." Now, as she was looking forward to her 24th year as head coach at NKU, the young women on her team were completing an entire summer in which they had taken increasing responsibilities upon themselves. Individually and as a sisterhood, they were still following the passion for the sport they had developed as young girls. They were trying to preserve the fun of the game while trying to master it more than ever. They had voluntarily given up the usual summertime pleasures of college girls so they could lift weights together, run conditioning drills, play in a summer league whose teams were laughably uneven in quality, and play every Sunday night against one of the best D-I recruiting classes in the country, courting absolute embarrassment if they let down their guard only a little.

Why did they do this for the entire summer? Because of their passion for the game, their love of competition in any form. For the solidarity and joy of being together, no matter how hard the work or how tough the competition. And for the dream of making themselves good enough to be the national champions. Whether they reached that goal or not, they had spent the entire summer striving to reach it. "We had a little taste of what it is to succeed," Brittany Winner told me in May, looking back at the victory over Drury two months earlier, "and we want so much more."

I had enjoyed my own work during the summer—interviewing players, coaches, and other followers of the team; watching the players work out with Livey, play in the summer league, and test themselves against Xavier; writing the early chapters of this book as I then envisioned them. But I had not yet seen the players and coaches working together on the practice court. That is when I would really begin to learn how a women's college basketball team is made.

5

PRESEASON PREPARATION

In everything imposingly beautiful, strength has much to do
with the magic.
—*Herman Melville,* Moby-Dick

I be up in the gym just working on my fitness.
—*Fergie, "Fergalicious"*

Labor Day was yesterday. We are beginning the third week of the
fall semester and four players are on the court for "individual"
drills of the kind that are allowed before October 15. The time clock
is set at 50:00. The players have been stretching and then jogging
lightly up and down the court before the work begins.

Winstel stands out beyond the free-throw line, four players under the basket. Three cones are placed along the three-point line—
one to the left of the players, one straight ahead, and one to the
right. These are known as 1, 2, 3. The first player is in the "ready"
position right under the basket, feet going up and down in place like
pistons. Winstel shouts, "Shot 1!" Player 1 rushes out at cone 1,
arms thrusting up to block a shot, body twisting around to block
out for a rebound. "Drive 3!" Player 2 rushes out at cone 3, going
down low to slide quickly to the right to guard against a baseline
drive. "Shot 2!" Player 3 rushes out to block cone 2 and block out for
the rebound. "Charge 1!" Player 4 rushes out to take a charge from
cone 1, falling backward onto the court and yelling out from the
pain of an imagined hit. The pace quickens slightly during the next

round as Winstel calls out, "Drive 2! . . . Charge 3! . . . Shot 1! . . . Drive 3!"

This drill is quick, intense, and confusing—like playing defense in a game. Players must listen hard, run hard, move hard, every move as instantaneous as the command, almost unconsciously knowing where to go and what to do as soon as one teammate has gone, with another to follow right at her heels. This drill is a pleasure to watch because Winstel loves to bark out those commands— and because I can see so much about the players as they carry them out. The pace is so quick and intense that even some of the most experienced players take a false step toward the wrong cone or go down on the drive when she should be going up on the shot. Some players have each of these movements down pat: arms fully extended, butt already swiveling to block the shooter cone; feet seemingly skating on air as she beats the driver cone to the baseline; back straight out to hit the floor after the foul from the charging cone. Others are not quite there yet: one's arms wave like noodles as she swipes at the shot; another stands too upright as she slides against the drive; another is a bit cautious about taking the fall.

You see a lot about conditioning, positioning, and concentration in these drills. You also see incremental learning, for as soon as one set of moves is mastered on a particular day, Winstel adds something new. Maybe during "Drive 2" she will yell "Shot!" and the player defending the drive will have to go up immediately to block a shot. Or she might announce "Combinations." This time each player goes at two successive cones before Winstel barks to her teammate. Player 1 might begin with "Shot 1 . . . Drive 3" before player 2, at the ready, hears "Shot 2 . . . Charge 1." This Shot, Drive, Charge drill might occupy only 5 to 7 minutes of the 50-minute session. It might then be followed by something more relaxing, like shooting free throws. This, too, mimics the game itself—flat-out intensity followed by a relative pause.

These preseason drills alternate offense and defense as well as fast and calm. Early in the semester the offensive moves are pretty basic, working on the fundamentals of shooting, passing, and dribbling. The individual drills may occur on the same day players have lifted weights in the morning or conducted a workout for a recruit in the afternoon. They require the kind of intensity and stamina that each player will need throughout the 13-week preseason that runs, this year, from August 21 to November 21.

On Wednesday, August 23, Winstel calls the first team meeting of the new semester. The meeting is in the locker room, each player sitting on the stool in front of her locker. The first day of class was on Monday, and each player is still adjusting to her new teachers and course schedule, so this meeting is mostly informational, passing out the workout schedule for the next two weeks and reviewing team policies and expectations.

Regents Hall has been reserved for the team from 12:30 to 3:00 P.M. every Monday through Friday for the whole semester. During the week before Labor Day, however, the players will meet in the Albright Health Center. Monday, Wednesday, and Friday will be weights and conditioning. Tuesday will be the annual diagnostic mile-and-a-half run. On Thursday they will do agility tests and timed wind sprints. After Labor Day the team will continue with weights and conditioning every Monday, Wednesday, and Friday; open gym or individual drills on Tuesday and Thursday, usually with additional individual drills on Friday; and an early-morning workout on Saturday. This basic rhythm of workouts, conditioning, open gym, and drills will continue until October 15, when actual team practices can begin.

Winstel is very clear in reiterating the academic policies of the team. "Attend every class." "Tell me if you are having trouble in any class." "Do your own work." "Don't be tempted to cheat in any way." She and the players discuss when study table should be. Last year it was twice a week two hours at a time. This year the 12 schedules are not meshing well. A three-hour stretch from 6 to 9 on Sunday evening seems to be the only time when everyone can get together. Winstel decides this three-hour period will be sufficient this year, since each player was so responsible in her studies last year. She does point out, however, that "your three hours begin when the last person arrives." If someone arrives at 6:30, the whole team stays until 9:30.

With regard to their recent physical exams, Winstel announces that "everybody is in pretty good shape." She asks each player to thank Noriko and the other trainer, Molly, for arranging the physicals, and the doctors for doing them, since they are volunteering their services. With respect to injuries and rehabilitation, she stresses the importance of icing, mentioning several players for whom it did "a lot of good" last year. She reminds the whole team that "if you have ankle issues, tape your ankles or wear an ankle brace. Neither you nor the team will be happy if anything happens." She emphasizes the importance of bringing their student IDs any time the team works out in the Albright Health Center. "Don't put the people who check the IDs in a difficult situation" by just saying you are on the basketball team. "Don't ask for special treatment."

Quite a bit of the meeting has to do with special events the team has to participate in. After the meeting today they have a "Party in the Park" event to help raise money for their winter trip to Florida. Next week they are required to attend the university's welcome party for freshmen. Winstel acknowledges that this time of year, with all these mandatory events, is "crazy." But it is important to attend them all and to present a positive image. "We need to let those freshmen know we want them to come out and watch us play." Winstel says she has not heard of any problems concerning the players who are living in the dorms or the seniors who are sharing a house. She encourages her players to "mingle with other people. Don't just stay to yourselves. Support the other teams in our program." She gets a laugh when she adds, "Not just men's soccer" (someone must have a special interest).

After going over other mandatory events scheduled for the next week and asking whether anyone has any issues she would like to discuss, Winstel devotes some time to the team's alcohol policy. She is not expecting any problems with this team, but over the years she has learned that if there are going to be problems they are "likely to occur prior to the start of the season." "Make good decisions." "If you are underage, you should not be drinking." "Drinking and driving is the dumbest thing—two dumb things!" "There are some times when I cannot help you. I know these district courthouses in Campbell and Kenton counties all too well." "If there is bad news, it will be in the paper." "They write good things about us, but if there is something bad about us they will make that a headline. That has happened with the team and with myself, and it is not pleasant."

After going over a few more details about the preseason workouts, Winstel speaks briefly about the season itself. This is "a very exciting year for us. . . . We have built up our exhibition season this year. Last year we had good workouts with Butler and Indiana State, but this year we will have exhibitions with the University of Kentucky [UK] and Indiana. UK, that's an SEC [Southeastern Conference] school. That's pretty cool. Indiana University, the Big Ten. That's going to be fun. There's no use playing exhibitions with the Little Sisters of the Poor and beating them by 80 points. We are going to see very soon WHERE WE ARE."

Winstel then reminds her team that "our program is not about Ws. It is about a level of excellence that we adhere to. As I said last year, you have probably gotten tired of hearing it, 'There's a certain way that we play and we are going to play that way every freaking time we step on the floor.'" She speaks of the importance of setting goals both individually and as a team. Winstel's goal for the team is "playing the game the way it is supposed to be played every time." She admits that such high goals are "not attainable." As an example she tells the team, "I want to hold a team scoreless." After pausing a minute to let that sink in, she says, "I want to coach a perfect game. It may be crazy to want that, but I do." Lifting one hand high in the air, she says, "If your level of excellence is that high, everything will take care of itself."

Back in May Winstel had told me that in the fall she always works out a detailed plan of what she wants the team to achieve in the preseason workouts and practices. A few days after the first team meeting I stop by the office and ask if she can show me what she does. First she opens an informal notebook containinng a written sequence of activities for each day's workout. Then she pulls out a three-ring binder with all the workout sheets from last year's preseason, so she can measure this year's progress. Then she pulls out another binder, the team's playbook from last year, printed on gold paper. She updates this playbook each year and passes out the new one to each player when practice begins on October 15. She will then collect these books at the end of the season, not wanting her trade secrets to get into the wrong hands.

Before I leave she gives me the schedule for the first week of individual drills, beginning immediately after Labor Day. She says that "all of the individual drills are adapted to game conditions; all of the moves the players are working on are moves they will be making when they play." She tells me, "There won't be too much shouting" in these sessions; she really enjoys the opportunity to work with each player in "a true teaching situation." She schedules these "individual" workouts for three or four players at a time, each player having two per week. Often the guards work with the guards and the post players with the post players. That is how it is on the first two days after Labor Day. On Tuesday, September 5, Winstel schedules four guards at 12:30. On Wednesday the other four guards will begin at 11:15, the four post players at 12:05. Having never seen our players do individual drills, I make it a point to attend this first full set of workouts.

When I arrive on Tuesday the workout is already under way. Brittany, Betsey, and Rachel are on the floor; Winstel, Schmidt, and Vieth are coaching. (Keri has to miss this workout because of a pulled muscle in her back; we do not yet know how serious the injury might be.) The three players are in the middle of the Shot, Drive, Charge drill. At first this is as much of a challenge for me on the sidelines as it is for Rachel Lantry on the court. Winstel is barking her orders like a drill sergeant, and the players are moving very quickly and shouting loudly as they do so. All this is much easier for Brittany and Betsey, who have done individual drills for several preseasons now, than it is for Rachel as a freshman. Winstel has to break the drill a couple of times to show her how to hold her hands all the way up when going out to block a cone, while also remembering to shout, "Ball, ball, ball." When it threatens to be too much to take in all at once, Winstel tells her, "It doesn't have to be perfect. Do it as well as you can."

As soon as the three of them have the Shot and Drive defenses pretty much under control, Winstel throws the Charge command into the mix. Even Brittany and Betsey take a while to adjust to this one.

On this day the Shot, Drive, Charge sequence is followed by a series of dribbling exercises led by Schmidt. The first sequence involves dribbling in place; imagine the control it takes to dribble the ball between your legs with only one hand. Next they dribble while running half court and full court. I like the Start and Stop drill in which each player continuously dribbles two balls full court, stopping in place when Schmidt raises his hand, moving forward again when he lowers it. This takes a lot of concentration and coordination because you have to hold your head up as you dribble both balls. This is hard for Rachel, physically and mentally, after all that has come before, but she continues working on it until she has completed the set.

The dribbling drills are followed by a long set of shooting drills. In the first one each player shoots immediately off a pass from a coach, starting in the right-hand corner. After they make 25 as a group they move to the top of the key and then around to the other corner. After this first group makes 10 shots from the top of the key, someone makes a mistake and dribbles before she shoots, so they have to start counting again. After they finish this sequence they have another round of shooting off the coaches' passes, this time dribbling once to the left or right before taking the shot. By the time they have made their 25 shots from each of the three areas, 15:30 remains on the time clock. Winstel gives them until 14:30 for a water break. This has been an intense 35 minutes, and they all walk slowly to the cooler.

After the one-minute break they resume the Catch and Shoot drills, this time from behind the three-point line. Two players are shooting, another rebounding the shot and passing it to the coaches. You have to make three threes before you can move in to rebound, and no one is making very many. Brittany is the first to make three, but her form is off and Winstel says to her quite often, "Shoot it straight." Rachel makes what appears to be a nice three but Winstel immediately says, "Two doesn't count. You had one foot over the line." Betsey is really struggling with her threes, with quite a few air balls; I imagine her shoulder is still bothering her. Whatever the case, Winstel says at one point to the whole group, "Start over. This is half-ass. We don't do it this way." After this encouragement they

123

start doing better. Brittany and Betsey do a good job of yelling "Ball, ball, ball" as they call for the pass, but Rachel has not yet internalized this part of the drill.

When they are done Winstel says "Good job" to the group. She says to Rachel, "You'll have to talk out there. It helps in conditioning." Rachel says, "Our workouts in high school weren't like this." After Lantry has showered and changed she comes back out and tells Winstel she might need a tutor in math. Winstel asks about her grades in high school. "Bs to Cs." Winstel says that Keri Finnell is a math major and very good. She is glad that Rachel told her about this so early.

Beginning at 11:15 the next morning the same set of drills is performed by Karyn, Nicole, Karen, and Danyelle. They are already doing the Shot and Drive when I arrive, and Karyn Creager is exceptionally good at this. She moves her feet extremely well, holds her hands very high to contest the imagined shot, all the time shouting, "Ball, ball, ball." The others also do quite well, though no one has her concentration and technique.

As Matt supervises the dribbling drills, Nancy comes over to say how relatively simple these early drills are. She says that she likes to have her assistants run some of them, not only to give them experience but also so the players get to "hear another voice; it is good for them to hear the same thing from another voice." Matt is leading many of the drills today, and his T-shirt has a deep sweat stain down the front long before the first "individuals" are over.

This group does very well dribbling up and down the court, Karyn typically saying, "Let's go, girls," for motivation. They also do quite well in the Catch and Shoot drills. Karyn and Karen are both shooting very well off the pass and off the dribble. Winstel is working with Danyelle, however—something about her right foot as she shoots. A bit later she pulls Nicole aside to work on her shooting form, especially on the motion of the hand at the release. Winstel gives this group a one-minute break too, saying, "Enjoy the water."

This group struggles with the threes from behind the cone. Karyn is smooth, accurate, and consistent, looking more confident with her shot than she did for much of last year. The others are very inconsistent. Winstel has to stress the importance of calling for the ball, coming forward as you receive the pass, taking advantage of that forward motion for your shot. "No standing still on the basketball court. No standing around." Today Danyelle is not showing that three-point touch she was known for last year. Nicole cannot find the range either; you can still see that hitch in her shot, which is rather flat, but it is very authoritative when it goes in. Just from watching this drill you can imagine she might be a streaky shooter with her threes. After Karyn swishes three in a row Winstel says to her, "You can't hop and then shoot. You're traveling." She adjusts immediately and continues to hit a very high percentage of her threes. Apart from Karyn, at this point we seem to lack a true three-point shooter—at least among our guards.

As this group is finishing the four post players arrive early. As Karmen, Angela, Cassie, and Katie lightly jog up and down the sideline, their feet sound like four big butterflies flapping their wings.

The next 50 minutes are a pleasure to watch. The first drill involves sprinting to a cone, sliding to the next cone, backpedaling to the next, and then sprinting forward, over, and back again—all the time shouting, "Ball, ball, ball." This is an excellent drill for the way post players have to move in a game. Karmen and Angela are nearly flawless, having had several years of such drills. Katie and Cassie are both beginning their second year in Winstel's program; each does well, but not yet *as* well.

All four do very well at the Shot and Drive drill. So Winstel quickly adds the Charge, saying she had forgotten to do this with the guards who preceded them. There are some funny moments when players are afraid to fall right, and at one point everybody, the coach included, breaks out laughing. "This drill has some potential," Winstel tells them.

The four post players do very well with the whole sequence of dribble drills. They also shoot very well off the pass and off the dribble, making their respective 25 shots faster than either group of guards. On the drill in which you fake a shot and "go somewhere," Winstel asks them to "picture yourself going past the Panthers of Wesleyan or the girls at Drury or Coach Schmidt." In this drill Angela is shooting the bank shot with so much finesse and command that it is a pleasure to watch, even in practice.

After a one-minute water break with 17:00 remaining, Winstel confers with her assistants and announces a drill involving receiving passes in the block. A coach passes the ball to the post player, who catches it and turns immediately with a drop step to the basket, clearing the way with her elbows out. Winstel says, "I don't care if you travel today. The important thing is to lead with your elbows." The new assistant, Katie Vieth, had been a post player for the University of Kentucky. She enters into this drill with great enthusiasm and skill in feeding the passes at various angles and speeds.

After the Drop-Step drill, the post players work on baseline jumpers, then on going up and under with no dribble. This group is very proficient and attentive until the buzzer rings. Winstel says, "Nice job." She huddles with them for some quiet, intimate talk.

As this is Wednesday, a regular conditioning day, all 12 players now gather down in the Albright Health Center to work with Livey Birkenhauer. This time they will do more weights than conditioning, since eight of the players have already had 50-minute individuals today. For a while they all stretch and relax on the intramural court as the post players cool off and take some ribbing from their teammates. Karyn looks at Cassie, fresh from her individual, and praises her "tomato cheeks." Looking at Karmen she says, "tomato cheeks and raccoon eyes." They all seem at ease with one another, just as they were last spring and summer.

In the weight room everyone seems relaxed and highly motivated. The guards tend to work out with guards and posts with posts, but there is some variation. Everyone rotates through the same exercises before they are done. Some are beginning with leg exercises, some arms. The big overhead machine seems to have more weight on it than in the summer. Each player pulls that weight no matter what her strength, the difference being in the number of repetitions. They all put in time on the bench press too, always with a teammate to spot them. When they have finally done their work and recorded it on their charts, they give their books to Matt. Afterward, as I am chatting with Matt and Katie Vieth out in the hallway, five of the players join us for 20 minutes or so, everyone enjoying one another's company in a relaxed way.

The next full set of individual drills is scheduled in four back-to-back 50-minute sessions on Friday morning beginning at 9:15. I decide to watch these too. The 12 players are now in groups of three. When I arrive at 9:15 Angela, Karmen, and Nicole are shooting jumpers over the arms of the coaches. Nancy comes over to say that the players are very tired. They are already 30 minutes into their 50-minute drill; they decided to start early, right after the team finished the weight work that began at 6:30 in the morning. On this Pass and Shoot drill the player cuts inside, calls for the ball, and shoots the layup. When Nicole gets careless and misses the layup, Winstel stops them and says, "Anyone else misses, you all run." No more misses.

After shooting some foul shots for a change of pace, these players get a new drill focused on protecting the ball. You catch the ball, elbows out, and look at the basket. No shot. Just get used to protecting your space. "Get your elbows off your body!" To a player who hesitates: "You're not trying to hurt anybody, but if their head is in your space, you say, 'Get out of my space!' There, that's it."

Throughout these drills Angela stands out, as she had earlier. She shows excellent conditioning and technique in every workout. She looks as much at ease shooting threes from above the key as when releasing those laser bank shots. Her athleticism, originally shaped on the soccer field, is now finding its form on the basketball court.

The next group is Brittany, Cassie, and Katie, and I get to see the whole 50-minute workout. I can certainly see why Karmen, Angela, and Nicole had been tired 30 minutes into it. The first drill is the Sprint, Slide, and Backpedal around the cones, shouting "Ball, ball, ball" as you slide. They are doing this well, so Winstel changes the backpedaling segment by telling them to defend with "your butt to the basket" and "hands up at the close out!" At 45:48 all the players are breathing heavily after just a few minutes of this drill.

Next is the Shot and Drive with the cones. Winstel creates a great tempo as people are going every which way while someone new is in the ready position. When she switches into the Combination there is confusion, because the player at the ready has been conditioned to go herself when she hears that second command.

Now when the first player hears that second command she has to "get there as fast as you can." The players have to "move and listen."

To ease the pace after this, Winstel gives them some stationary dribbling work—around the right leg, between the legs, dribbling low—saying from time to time, "Catch your breath." At one point she holds Cassie's chin up to help her keep her eyes up while dribbling low. Quietly, tenderly, no words.

At 39:17 they begin the dribbling drills up and down the court. Brittany has incredible stamina and speed. I can see that all her summer conditioning has paid off. Coach again says "Catch your breath" in the very short pauses between drills.

At 36:32 they begin the next drill, shooting the shots they will do in warm-ups before the games: layup, bank shot, stop and pop— five each from each side. For a break at 29:36, five push-ups each.

The next set of drills begins with taking the pass, using the elbows to create space, and driving for the layup. Again Nancy mentions to me, "We've done a lot this week, four days, so they're getting tired." For the next 20 minutes they continue shooting off the pass in every variation. "Elbows out." "Exaggerate your fake." "Good sharp cut." "Give me a target for the pass." At the end, "Good job." They are all tired but they all looked good, followed the drills well, got it done.

The next group was supposed to include Karyn, Karen, and Danyelle, but Danyelle has a doctor's appointment and will have to consult Noriko before her next workout. So Karyn and Karen get an extra dose of what the earlier groups of three had done. They both do the Sprint and Slide very well. To announce the variation on the Backpedal Winstel says simply, "Deny outside the cone, butt to bucket." During the Shot and Drive I am amazed by how Karyn moves in one fluid motion from contesting the shot to blocking out.

Karyn and Karen are mostly working on shooting today. The sounds are trancelike—the sweet swish of the net, the hard bounce of the ball. The bodies are in continuous motion. Bracky's arms and shoulders are beginning to glisten with sweat as Angela's had earlier. Working with only two players allows Winstel to concentrate on Karen's shooting form. "Bracky, follow through on that three-shot!" "Way to shoot, Bracky." "Shoulders square. Knock those shots down when you're tired." Karyn is shooting her threes well, 6 of 6 at one point. She moves quickly on the post-and-cut move, in motion the moment she gets the ball, the way Nancy says Cott used to do.

While Karyn and Karen are shooting and moving, a big guy, about 7 feet tall with some real meat on him, is standing in the doorway, mesmerized. Must be one of Dave Bezold's new recruits for the men's team. Would love to read his mind.

As soon as Karen and Karyn are done it is time for Betsey and Rachel and Keri to begin their 50-minute session. Keri is still unable to practice because of the pulled muscle in her back, so it is another two-person drill. This allows Winstel to give Rachel a lot of attention—which she needs. This is only her second day of individual drills at the college level. She is apprehensive after the initiation she got on Tuesday. Before the drill begins she asks, "Will you ask us to do anything we can't do?" Betsey and the coach assure her she will be fine. She will be pushed beyond anything she knew in high school, but it will not be more than she is able to do.

Betsey is a good partner for leading the freshman through this long sequence of drills. Rachel does well on the Sprint and Slide drill, once she gets her feet moving in that "ready" position. On the Shot and Drive drill she does not realize she has to be out at the ready while Betsey is still completing hers. Coach explains with an edge: "You don't want to sit next to me on the bench all year, do you?" When the Combination drill gets tough, Winstel assures Rachel that "everybody gets confused. Do the best you can. You really have to listen." As they transition into the dribbling drills, Nancy has a little joke for Betsey and Rachel, saying, "You are so lucky there are only two of you. Your conditioning will be twice as good. Some days you are just lucky."

There are so many things for a freshman to learn. Rachel works hard at dribbling back and forth between her legs with the left hand only. She has to be reminded to keep her "elbows out" on the Catch and Drive drills. She is tired and she is not hitting her threes, holding Betsey back in completing her drills. Winstel takes a look at her form, making a couple of suggestions. As soon as Rachel finally does make a three, Winstel says, "That's a two. Foot was over the line." Rachel then makes 4 of 5 to finish that part of the drill. She and Betsey get a half-minute rest at 23:00.

The rest is dribble and shoot, free throws, catch and shoot in the patterns the others had followed. "Elbows out." "Both hands up when you call for the ball." "Offensive basketball is all about giving yourself room." Rachel has some cross-body motion on her shot that Winstel spots and corrects. But she also has a lot of bounce at the end of the session, tough as it was. That is one advantage of being a freshman.

It has been a long morning for the coaches and even for me, watching for four straight hours. I like the spirit of the individual drills. Serious but relaxed. Challenging but humane. A joke now and then to relieve the tension. Although quite a few of Nancy's jokes do go over the players' heads. Matt says she would be a great stand-up comic if they only got her humor.

After this intense week of drills the players actually get to scrimmage the next week, in open gym sessions for two recruits. The Monday recruit is a post player, lanky and strong. Like Angela Healy in high school, she is the goalie on her soccer team. NCAA rules allow her to work out with our team, but her soccer coach does not want her to, so she sits and watches our players play, sizing up next year's teammates should she come our way (she is also being heavily recruited by a Division I school). Our players clearly love to be playing together after all the drills, workouts, and conditioning. We are developing some classic matchups—Brittany and Nicole out front, Karmen and Angela inside. Brittany stands out in each one of the 10-point games. She is in exceptional shape, showing speed, strength, concentration, and hustle. You could not ask for anything more. Karyn also looks strong, blocking Rachel a couple of times with those long arms, making several of her threes, and trying out some new power moves to the basket, a direct result of the individual drills the week before. Fortunately, Danyelle and Keri are well enough to play, so all 12 players are on the floor.

The guard who tries out on Wednesday *is* able to work out and not just watch. She shows a great deal of talent and energy (though at one point, exhausted by the pace of college ball, she says, "I need a break"). Again, the matchups are a joy to watch. Great plays are being made at both ends of the court. Our players know one another so much better than last year and can anticipate their teammates' moves. Winstel does interrupt once to call out, "Illegal screen by Karmen Graham." She says to her All-American, as she had to her freshman last week, "You don't want to be sitting here with me, do you?" Reading Karmen's face, she says, "Yes, that might have been a payback for what was done to you, but I can't tell that. We just don't play that way."

The one breathtaking moment this day is when Cassie Brannen makes an incredible move off an awkward pass, whipping it right up like lightning into the bucket. Winstel's immediate sideline comment to Matt is, "That's why I go with them to the hospital." This is too cryptic for me to understand, so Nancy later explains to me that Cassie has a problem with the circulation of the blood that sometimes makes her lightheaded, a condition for which the best medication is still being sought. Winstel has been taking Cassie to the hospital herself to get the diagnosis from the doctor firsthand.

Another sideline comment caught my attention that day. Right after Nicole blocked a shot, Winstel said to Matt, "Sometimes I wish her arms were not so long." The reason: those long arms allow her to make plays without moving her feet the way she needs to (which also happens quite often when Katie Butler blocks shots). I was learning to watch practices like a coach. In both these workouts Brittany was more than holding her own against Nicole at point guard. I had wondered to myself whether the post recruit on Monday could have known, just from watching that workout, what an outstanding point guard she would have if she played on a team whose offense was run by Nicole.

Right after the workout for the post player on Monday I had my first full-length interview with Rachel Lantry, our one incoming freshman. I was impressed, as I had been with her teammates in May, with her poise, expressiveness, and maturity. She had been tested under fire during the individual drills the week before and had come through well, both physically and mentally. She still had a lot to learn but was already showing the potential to get quite a bit of playing time as a freshman. Not yet officially part of the team during the summer, she had shown her seriousness of purpose by playing in the summer league games on Thursdays as well as the open gyms on Sundays. By the time I interviewed her on the afternoon of September 11, it was clear that she had sufficient spunk, talent, and presence to hold her own as part of this year's "delightful dozen."

Rachel's favorite memory from the summer league at Thomas More was a game in which she shot well, moved well, and began to feel like part of the team (the one in which my informal stats had her scoring about 25 of our 77 points). Her worst memory was the time she lined up in our half-court offense and was kindly told by her opponent, "Honey, you're supposed to be on defense." (Because she is a freshman, her teammates revel in any moment when they can call her ditzy.) The biggest challenge this summer was playing Xavier on Sunday nights. Lantry really liked this challenge because Xavier was "so much bigger and stronger. Playing them will only make us better." Even as an incoming freshman, Lantry could see that the only way to improve is to play those who are better than you. She was looking forward to the upcoming exhibition games with the University of Kentucky and Indiana University in exactly that light.

After the workout with the guard recruit on September 15, four full weeks remained until the first official practice on October 15. During this entire period the team continued its six-day-a-week routine of workouts, conditioning, and individual drills, followed by study table on Sunday nights. The coach says this is always the toughest part of the year, and you can see that the team feels it too, itching to play the game.

Wednesday, September 20. Today is set aside for team conditioning rather than individual drills. Many of the items on Winstel's practice sheet are new to me: Line Jumps, Quick Lines (High Knees, Butt Kicks), Ladders (Quick Feet). Instead of improving their skills with a basketball in hand, the players are testing their bodies: their strength, their quickness, their endurance. When I arrive nine players are doing Line Jumps in groups of four and five. Karen Brackman is present but unable to participate; her knee is on ice. Keri and Betsey are not currently in the gym; Noriko is attending to the back of the one and the arm of the other in the trainer's room.

The nine who are doing Line Jumps do them side to side, then up and back, followed by wall touches. With Quick Lines they sprint past the foul line and back in groups of four and five. They do this four times, then three times. Then the groups run the same course the same number of times backward (the Backpedal). In the next set they move forward again, this time with High Knees. Butt Kicks are the opposite, lifting their feet as high as possible behind them as they run.

The next set is not listed on the practice sheet, but it is one of the most interesting to watch. Each group goes into a defensive slide from the end line to beyond the foul line, the oral command for which is "Slide, spread feet, low with the hands." The idea is to achieve the lowest, slowest motion possible—a total contrast to the sprints they had just done over the same portion of the floor. They are again calling "Ball, ball, ball," as they were during the Backpedal sprints, but here the effect is entirely different. Before they sounded like flocks of squawking seagulls. Now they look like sedated penguins, barely moving as Winstel calls out, "Keep arms straight . . . move arms . . . butt down."

After enduring the glacial slowness of this drill the players have to run the same drill in quick, real time, after which Winstel sends them into low, slow gear again. The one player she chides is the one who finishes first, because the goal in this drill is to be the slowest. Angela and Danyelle are easily the best at this frozen motion. Now Winstel tells them to do the same motion "not fast but real fast." They yell as they do it, the penguins becoming seagulls again.

After two more quick-action drills at this end of the court Winstel says, "Go to the ladders." At the other end of the floor are two cloth ladders side by side on the floor. The player "runs" the double ladder in a variety of patterns. Each pattern involves a combination of different steps, all of them quick. Some who have done this before handle each variation with relative ease, but Lantry needs guidance from her teammates, especially when they do the "Ickey Shuffle" (a variation on a former Cincinnati Bengal's touchdown dance).

When Winstel announces "three minutes' water break," her assistants roll up the ladders while her players go for the water on the scorer's table. Some of them lean, exhausted, against the table itself, seemingly barely able to breathe. There is a little bit of chat after the first minute, but some players simply stay to themselves, reserving energy for whatever is coming next. Next on the list are the flat-out sprints, running the court in two sets of eight laps, two sets of six laps, three sets of four laps, and three sets of two laps. Each set has a targeted speed at which it should be achieved, such as 55 seconds for the eight, which Winstel tells her players is "very makeable."

The first group consists of Brittany, Karmen, Karyn, and Nicole. They all run well, but none can touch Brittany, who each time finishes far in advance of the rest of her group, whether it is in the eight, the six, the four, or the two. Rachel similarly outperforms the rest of her group, which includes Danyelle, Angela, and Katie. As the sprints continue I look for Cassie. I see a player being attended to by Livey on the sideline, her legs propped up against the edge of a folding chair, her back flat on the floor. Soon Noriko is out from the trainer's room. She helps Cassie up into the chair, gives her some water, and gently strokes her arm, restoring her from one of those lightheaded moments that Cassie simply has to put up with.

The sprints are a challenge for all our players after the other conditioning they have already done. While one group is waiting for the other to finish, Winstel sometimes has to tell a player, "Stand up, away from the wall." Danyelle is really struggling with the sprints now, so she is allowed to drop out and catch her breath. After one group finishes a set Winstel says, "I bet Grand Valley's kicking ass on these runs. That's the bar, ladies. That's the bar."

After another set she says this: "When we play—whenever is the date of the first game—you're going to be ready. When you step out on the court you know you will win. You don't have to worry about whether you are ready because you *will* be ready. The other team will be afraid because they won't know if they are ready. If you are *not* ready, I need to be fired, and Matt needs to be fired, and Katie needs to be fired, and Livey needs to be fired. No team is doing this."

Group 1 runs the last set. Group 2 runs the last set. Winstel says "Good job" to all. "Take six minutes. Take a drink of water. Cool down. Lots of water. Then we will go down and do weights."

Nancy gives a five to each player. Some keep to themselves, some chat a bit. Cassie is still sitting in that chair. Most are smiling, though not widely. They know they have survived something good. As they cool down, D is completing the laps she missed when catching her breath. Betsey calls out, "Halfway there."

As the players were running their sprints, some workmen had come in to install a new series of banners high above the bleachers in Regents Hall. Each displays the historical achievements of one of our athletic teams. The one for women's basketball is by far the most impressive. Not only because it records the only national championship and the most Elite Eight appearances but also because of the early history of KWIC and AIAW championships, with national appearances in 1975, 1976, and 1977. I realize that Nancy Winstel has been a player or coach on every team celebrated on that banner from 1975 to 2006.

As the rest of the team is heading down to the weight room, Nancy is having a long, intimate talk with Cassie. The only fragment I hear is, "I don't want to put you in a situation. . . ." I will see all the players an hour later when they have a team meeting in the locker room after their work with the weights.

Shortly before the meeting I have a chance to speak with the coach in her office. After discussing Cassie's condition and how badly Cassie feels when she cannot complete a particular workout, Winstel discusses conditioning in general. All the conditioning during the summer was designed to strengthen players "between the shoulders and the knees." She will never give a player more than she is able to do. Today's workout tested some of them, but it was nothing more than they had done at this point last year. She could sense a real feeling of accomplishment at the end of the session (as I did too).

Winstel said that in the days when Katie Kelsey was point guard she had the team run outside a lot, but during practices they would still get tired. That was when she began to rethink conditioning and design drills that came closer to what actually happens in a game. She tries to have all her drills in that category now. This helps the players much more when they get to the actual season. Most of the drills she has invented herself. She knows there are other coaches who are now approaching conditioning in the same way, but she does not have time to study what they are actually doing. She has developed her approach based on her own needs here.

The meeting in the locker room begins shortly after 3:00 and runs for 20 minutes. Though tired, the players are loose before it begins. Rachel is entertaining her elders with some kind of discourse about "power gel." Brittany is asking Angela and Karmen, and also the whole room, "Can you crack your sternum?"

Winstel begins the meeting by saying, "Really quick." After asking if everyone is doing okay in school and announcing that she will be at study table to speak with each of them briefly on Sunday, she addresses the health of the team. "We have some people injured with this or that. We just have to stick together and hopefully people will get back. I can tell you, ladies, it can be a lot worse." Shifting into a slightly different emotional key, she adds, "Hopefully, we'll have everybody healthy. It's not right until I have all my lambs here." Spreading her arms, she says, "It's like Jesus the shepherd and his lambs." Looking slowly at four of her players, she says their names in succession: "Bracky, Cass, Keri, Bets. Let's hope we all get well and do not lose any lambs while we're at it."

As Winstel reviews the next round of mandatory activities, she acknowledges how busy everyone is. She then brings up the subject of team captains again, reminding her players that the choice is up to them. "It's your team. Don't wait for me to tell you. I want you to think about it and decide what you all want to do." Looking at Rachel she adds, "Lantry, you probably won't be a captain this year. But you should be the best darn follower you can be."

After going over the alcohol policy again she tells them to get enough sleep so they do not get "crabby" like she does when sleep deprived. She tells them she is developing the new playbook, "but we probably won't do too much that is new. We are going to do what we do better. There is more to what we do than we've been doing."

Near the end of the meeting she comes back to conditioning, asking, "How do you feel condition-wise right now?" After addressing some individual situations she says to the group, "It's important for me to know how you feel. The next few weeks, you know, are the toughest. Team pictures tomorrow at 1:30."

Individual drills continued for the next three weeks, in preparation for the first official practice on October 15. One exciting bit of news was that Diondra Holliday, the guard from Clark Montessori in Cincinnati who had tried out recently, committed to NKU. We lost the post player to a Division I school, however.

Two players suffered personal losses. In late September Karmen Graham lost her grandfather after a stroke. The same week Karyn Creager's grandfather died in Leipsic. Karyn and Karmen had come to NKU together as freshmen, and now their grandfathers, both octogenarians, were going out together—deep, unpredictable rhythms, deeply shared.

At the October 6 workout I got to be a participant rather than merely an observer when Winstel invited me to do some passing. I was wearing tennis shoes, so I put down my pen for the next 37 minutes. I dropped the ball once, and one of my passes glanced off the defender's head into the right hands. Otherwise, I did okay.

At one break between feeding the shooters Winstel said to me, "They all want to play. When I was a player I wanted to play. But you have to have the fundamentals. When the practices start, if they show weak on the fundamentals, we will be back to drills until they are doing it right."

October 15 is a Sunday this year. Winstel has scheduled the practice from 10 in the morning until 1 in the afternoon. Three hours, with a few water breaks, is a long time, even for someone watching from the sidelines. Winstel tells her players before they begin that they are ahead of where they started last year. Three hours later she and her two assistants seem to feel that things have gone quite well.

The first great thing about this practice is that all 12 players are able to play. Staying healthy will be one of the keys to our success this year; having everyone on the floor is an auspicious start. Although a full practice session with all 12 players allows the coaches to run 5-on-5 scrimmages, much of today's work is done with smaller groups, such as 3-on-2, 4-on-4, or 5-on-0. Like the individual drills with three or four players at a time, these drills are designed to mirror game situations for versatile and often interchangeable players.

One of the first drills today is 3-on-2, working on the transition to a fast break after a missed shot by the other team. The first two times down the floor the team on the break throws the ball away before getting a shot. "Ladies, let's get a shot." "Ladies, that was as poor of a 45 seconds of basketball as I've seen from you in a long time." "Be intense, but relax." "You can't pass four times on a 3-and-2 fast break."

At 10:25 the players are separated into black and white teams, last year's starters wearing the white jerseys. Groups of three defend against perimeter passes and cuts until the ball is finally shot; the defense takes its rebound to half court in a fast-break formation. Offense and defense are both intense. Everyone is making that squawking seagull sound. "Come on, seniors." "The only one doing it right is Katie."

In the next variation the team making the transition goes full court against the defenders at the other end. "Too slow. The pass from the middle to the wing has to be faster. That's why they call it a fast break. You have to think, 'I'm no longer on defense, I'm on offense.'"

After more full-court work the action moves into close quarters at one end of the court. They work at taking the charge, 2-on-2. One after another a player is knocked flat on her back under the basket (the made shot occasionally dropping through the net into her arms). They have all learned to shout as if wounded when taking the fall. But Winstel wants more. Especially from the player who is supposed to rebound. "Put your butt in her belly and shove her out."

At 10:48 they get a one-minute water break during which they jabber quite continuously.

This kind of rhythm goes on for the remaining two-plus hours. I love watching the defensive drill, 4-on-4, that Winstel announces by saying, "Defend for 30 seconds; you are not going to shoot." With no one shooting, the defenders are in the spotlight. If a player steals the ball she gives it back and defends some more. Defenders have to "help" and "rotate" and otherwise adjust to what the offense does. When one of her guards gives too much space to the player with the ball, Winstel stops the drill to give a personal demonstration. She rushes with her own large body right up on the player with the ball, almost suffocating her, shouting all the while. Stepping back, she then says to the slack defender, "I may be slower than dirt, but that's pretty intense, isn't it?"

After more defensive drills Winstel finally announces, "We're going to play." But in this game the points go only to the team on defense for making a steal or a stop. Three teams of four alternate, and the one that fails to "score" on defense does push-ups during the next 90-second water break. During this break Coach Schmidt whispers to Zach Cook, the team manager who runs the clock for all the drills, "Man, I'm beat."

The next 18 minutes are 4-on-4 transitions, with the defense picking up the offense at various spots on the floor and defending against screens and cuts. Winstel explains that she would like to run our four-spread offense higher this year (out closer to midcourt) because this makes "the cut harder to defend." She tells our defenders, "We need to do a better job picking up the ball early" (out toward midcourt). Taken together, these commands suggest we are going to be utilizing much more of the court on both offense and defense. This drill is an equal challenge to the four on either side of the ball. "Don't throw the ball away to begin our offense! There's going to be a substitution!" "You guys are seniors. You can't play five feet off your man and have two captains who aren't even denying the ball." (A week earlier the team had elected Graham, Creager, and Winner as cocaptains again.)

After a drink they work on down screens and flare screens, 2-on-2, the coaches passing the ball. The cutting and moving motion is quick and strong, again equally intense for offense and defense. The coaches are under scrutiny too. "GIVE THEM PASSES THEY CAN CATCH AND SHOOT!" When Matt throws a pass that hits Danyelle on the head and Winstel rides him, Grammy brings up a moment from a previous season in which Winstel had done something similar herself, though with a shoe, not a ball.

At 11:55 they finally get to open up and play some 4-on-4 the full length of the court. For about 40 minutes they do variations on their "four" and "four-spread" offenses, running different kinds of cuts and screens. The players enjoy this chance to play freely (though punctuated by Winstel's censure or praise). This back-and-forth action puts a lot of pressure on the point guards to start each offensive set, and Nicole is making too many bad passes, some that Winstel cannot let go by. "You're too old to make that crappy pass." Yet, right after that, "Great drive and pitch, Nicole." And "Betsey's busting her butt." But then, "Don't let her have the layup. Kelsey has three kids now, but I could put her out here to show you all how to play defense."

Near the end of the practice they move to a variation on the "spread" offense they call the "open," with everyone widely spread out and moving constantly. Winstel tells them, "I would like to use this offense more this year. If we get better at this, what are they going to be able to stop?" It takes a while to get used to moving in this openly improvised way, but they are doing it quite well. Winstel says, "Last year, this was the second week of practice, so we are doing a lot."

The practice ends with foul shots. Each player, one after the other, has to make a single shot. But anyone who misses has to run a lap before shooting again. B-Dubs goes first and makes hers. Danyelle is next and misses. After running her lap she misses her next three, each miss followed by another lap, as her teammates wait and watch. After she makes her fifth shot her 10 remaining teammates each make their first. Impressive.

This practice has been all about ensemble, pattern, effort. Individual players stand out now and then with a spectacular move or a conspicuous lapse, but it is all about the energy and intensity of the whole, on a team whose parts are increasingly interchangeable. I was beginning to understand why Winstel says she "never pays much attention to statistics." This is not about statistics at all but about moving, adjusting, listening, communicating, being in the right position. I am now understanding more of the reasons for which Winstel will take a player out of a game—all the little things, invisible to most fans, that cumulatively determine the outcome of a game, especially the close ones.

As the players are dealing with the moment-by-moment demands of the first official practice of the year, they are also dealing with some longer-term personal feelings. Such as those Brittany expressed in her journal when she wrote of the "unspoken sense" for her and the other seniors "that this day marked the beginning of the end. There's no getting around the fact that this is our last year of basketball. Ever."

"Meet the Norse Night" is October 18. Our team gets to play in front of its home fans for the first time since late February. They put on quite a show. The 20-minute scrimmage ends on a last-second, 35-foot bank shot by Nicole Chiodi, giving the white team a 27–24 victory over the black team. Hopes and expectations are high. Coach Winstel declares to Marc Hardin of the *Cincinnati Post*, "I don't think there's anything wrong in trying to win every game you play." Karyn Creager gives Jami Patton of the *Northerner* this list of the team's goals: "Win our conference, go undefeated at home, beat Grand Valley State, win the conference tournament, make it to the Final Four, and win a national title." However the season plays out, the players have already had seven months since March to dream of a national championship—and to do everything possible to prepare for winning it.

I had to miss "Meet the Norse Night" because I was lecturing in my home state of Washington (where I enjoyed watching part of a practice by the women's team at Peninsula College). Two faculty fans sent me their impressions of how this year's team appeared from the stands. John and Cheryl admired the energy, conditioning, and talent of this year's team. John took particular note of "Brittany's added quickness and confidence, the agility and athleticism of all our post players, and Nicole's now unquestioned floor leadership." But his main impression was "how evenly talented the team was. It was hard for any player to stand out." Cheryl agreed, although "I have to say that Brittany and Angela were the hustlers of the evening. Brittany was everywhere on the court and she outhustled everyone." They were both delighted to see Keri on the floor "without braces or bandages!"

When I arrive at my next practice on Monday, October 23, the fun of the public scrimmage is over; the challenge and excitement of playing the University of Kentucky are nine days away. After some relatively light shooting drills, the team works on five different ways of breaking a press. The whole practice becomes a two-and-a-half-hour workshop on the "press break." This is one of those transitional drills in which there is equal pressure on the offensive and defensive teams. Winstel encourages the offensive effort by saying, "We have four options on every one of our fast breaks. How can anyone stop four options? They can't." She challenges her defenders to have good footwork when she instructs them to "keep your hands behind your backs," defending with feet only.

After a short water break the offense runs the press break against a man-to-man defense, five players against six. Winstel is unhappy with the defense, saying, "You are a 4 on a scale of 10. On a good day you may be a 6." Later she tells the offense, "If a team is going to press you, shove it down their throat. Very few teams are good enough that five players can press very well." The team has been making progress today, but there are too many stretches when neither the offense nor the defense is doing well enough. At one point, truly furious, Winstel stops the practice to say, "We're not putting pressure on the ball [to the defense] and still we're throwing the ball away [to the offense]." A Winstel team does not want to hear that too often from her.

In addition to trying to motivate the entire team, Winstel has been trying to motivate individual players. When the players are sluggish early on, she shouts to Katie Vieth, "I want *you* to get on them. Don't make *me* do it!" She tells one of her players to "trap the crap out of her. You are all too easy on each other." Today the seniors are getting in as much trouble as anyone else. When Winstel stops practice after Karyn throws a "crappy pass," she elaborates with true exasperation in her voice: "You have Butler open for a three and you throw a pass that bounces a couple of times!" When Karmen misses an easy shot she initiates a brief dialogue: "Did you get fouled?" "No." "Then make the shot!" Each of these is a teaching moment, a way of demonstrating a point to the entire team.

The issue becomes more deeply personal when Katie Butler is too loose on defense. "Remember the first two months of last season? You and I spent at lot of time on the bench. Our relationship could USE SOME WORK!" Working hard on defense is the best way to repair one's relationship with this coach.

Although Winstel is more likely to stop a scrimmage to point out errors or lapses, she will also do so when she sees unusual effort or a great play. She stopped today's drill to say, "Danyelle, that was a great pass to Cassie! Great cut Cassie! Our sophomores are much better than you were last year. Way to play!"

Friday, October 27. We play UK next Wednesday. We begin today by working on our motion offense. One small component is a defensive drill in which players go one-on-one on each side of the floor. A coach holds the ball while the offensive player moves for the ball and the defensive player denies. Always great to watch. Next are a series of shooting exercises with every kind of cut and motion but with one continuing refrain: "Passes you can catch and shoot." This is followed by more work on passing and cutting plus "skipping," passing the ball across court for a quick shot.

Now Winstel elaborates on "the way we attack a zone." In order to have "good ball movement to overload a zone," the ball has to "move faster than the defense is moving." When you drive into a zone, you have to find where the "gap" is. "So you drive the seam into the double team, but you pass the ball before they trap you." At the next water break everyone is talking about the gaps and the seams.

At about 100 minutes into the practice the players finally get to play full court, possession plus one, putting all this into practice. They are moving the ball quickly against the zone, but twice Karyn fails to shoot the ball after it is "reversed" to her for a three. Winstel stops the practice to explain, "If you don't shoot that shot, we are playing them four against five. We are losing an offensive player." Karyn shoots the next couple of times the ball is reversed to her, but she misses. She is clearly down, but Winstel says, "Shoot it till you get hot."

Winstel's anger flares up just once during this full-court scrim-mage. Grammy shoots a long jumper that misses, but she hustles in to get her own rebound and scores. Winstel is angry at Nicole, who stood watching Karmen when she should have been crashing the boards herself. Winstel stops the practice to say, "That's an auto-matic sub if that shot goes up and you don't crash the boards." The term "automatic sub" helps me understand, in retrospect, some of Winstel's seemingly arbitrary substitution patterns last year.

At the end of the workout Winstel says to the whole team, "Good job." She seems quite satisfied with how it has gone. "Usually we aren't too hot against the zone," she tells me. The bus leaves for Lexington at 2:45 on Wednesday afternoon.

6

RISING TO THE CHALLENGE

'Twas not as much as David had
But I was twice as bold.
—*Emily Dickinson*

Kentucky is a blue state in basketball. Walking into Memorial Coliseum you see the blue banners celebrating the dynasty Adolph Rupp built in the men's game, the kind that Coach Mickie DeMoss would like to build in the women's game. Last year's UK women were 20–9. Their 9–5 record in the SEC included a win over Tennessee. This year they are number 16 in the national preseason Division I poll, compared with NKU's number 15 in Division II. This matchup will provide an interesting comparison between the two divisions.

Memorial Coliseum holds about 8,000 fans and about 2,500 are present, a very large crowd for our players. Before the game begins the lights go out, the sound goes up, the wide-angle Jumbotron goes wild, and we visitors from Highland Heights get a taste of D-I atmospherics. Once the game begins we hold our own and play very well against a much taller team. We are tall for a D-II team, with four players at 6-foot-1 and another at 6-foot, but we are dwarfed at the tip-off by Sarah Elliott, the 6-foot-6 center, and Jennifer Humphrey, the 6-foot-3 forward. One measure of how well we play this night is that we outrebound UK, 30–28. Another measure is the score, five minutes into the second half, when NKU trailed UK by only three points, 48–45. UK then went on a 10–4 run and eventually pulled away, winning 77–60.

Throughout the game we played with a poise and confidence that showed we belonged on the floor with this team. We had great difficulty getting the ball inside on offense, but our motion offense had UK off balance until they slowed it by going into a 3–2 zone. In the first half Brittany Winner played with great intensity at both ends of the court, scoring 8 points with 6 rebounds and several assists. Katie Butler came off the bench with the same kind of flair she had shown last season, scoring 11 points in only 15 minutes, giving us a huge offensive lift each time she entered the game. Karyn Creager was our next leading scorer with 10 points, hitting one three-pointer but also showing she was not afraid to drive against this much taller team. Keri Finnell was very strong off the bench, scoring 7 points in 16 minutes and looking good on defense. One of the most enjoyable moments came when Rachel Lantry entered the game with 8 minutes remaining and immediately drained her first college shot—a three-pointer from the corner. This cut the lead back down to six, keeping us in the game and forcing UK to call a time-out, quite an impressive debut for a freshman.

In the first half, when a number of our inside passes and shots were being blocked, we stayed in the game, in part, by hitting all six free throws. Our biggest difficulty the entire night was our inability to stop UK's All-America candidate Samantha Mahoney, a 5-foot-10 guard who scored 28 points. Her quickness and versatility were too much for our perimeter defenders, who were also challenged by 5-foot-8 guards Carly Omerod and Jenny Pfeiffer, the only other UK players in double figures.

In the press conference after the game Coach DeMoss praised NKU's motion offense and wished she had had a chance to scout us. Coach Winstel was pleased with her team's effort for the entire 40 minutes and especially the first 25. I had been impressed by how we responded to UK's press, but Winstel on the bus ride home was wishing we had done more; if we had been quicker with some of our passes we might have not only endured the press but broken it. Another thing she mentioned on the bus ride home is that we had been invited to play an exhibition game this year against the University of Maryland, the reigning Division I national championship team (which had defeated Duke for the title in an exciting overtime game back in March). She would have loved to accept, but we had already scheduled Kentucky and Indiana, and she felt that two exhibition games would be enough for our team.

Because this was an exhibition game, our players were not interviewed on the radio after the game. But a few of them gave me their brief impressions of how they felt after playing a nationally ranked Division I team. For Karyn Creager, "it was a great experience and it was really neat to compete with one of the top teams in the SEC." For Angela Healy, "we learned that we are not where we want to be. We can hang with a D-I team but we have to work on our offenses and our team defense." Brittany Winner wrote in her journal:

> Walking into Memorial Coliseum reminded me almost instantly of my freshman year at Elon University, when I walked into a packed house at Cameron Indoor Stadium to play the No. 2 Duke University Blue Devils in our season opener. . . . The atmosphere in Lexington was surprisingly similar. When we arrived at the gym, more than an hour before tip-off, there was already a large crowd of UK fans filling the seats. . . . Once the game started, though, it was the same old basketball game that we've all been playing for the better part of our lives.
>
> It took us a couple minutes to settle into the atmosphere, I think, but after a turnover and a few early bad decisions, we realized that we could play with this team. We battled tough with them for probably the first 30 minutes of the game—there were spurts here and there where we really played exceptionally and had them back on their heels. I don't think that they were as prepared for us as we were for them. Later in the second half though, we hit a funk and couldn't get much accomplished on offense, and this proved to be the difference maker in the game. . . . We learned from this game that we were capable of playing with the best teams in the nation, but that we also had a lot of room to improve.

Friday, November 3. The bus got back late at night from the Wednesday game with UK, so Winstel gave her players Thursday off. This put extra pressure on Friday's practice in preparation for the Monday game with Indiana. The team could be proud of how they had played in Lexington, but that did not lessen the challenge awaiting them in Bloomington.

When I arrive at 1 P.M. they are doing what they call the 5-4-3-2-1 drill. As soon as a shot is missed, the team that was on defense begins a fast break. Their five opponents cannot run to defend until Coach Schmidt calls out their respective numbers. Players 1 and 2 get called right away but 3, 4, and 5 have to wait, giving the breaking team a 5-on-2 advantage if they move and pass quickly enough. In spite of this advantage, the team running the break, our usual starting five, is not doing well. Winstel stops them to say, "Passing and catching are the two worst things we do right now."

Next time down they again fail to convert the break. When this happens the point guard is supposed to set up the offense. But Nicole fails to call a play. Winstel asks her, rhetorically, "What is the position you play?" "Point guard." Coach announces to all: "Everyone is thinking she is going to call the offense except the one who has to do it."

Soon after this the tension increases when someone throws the ball away on the 5-4-3-2-1 break. Coach says, "I'm tired of messing with this crap! You throw the ball like you have your head up your butt!" She throws her whistle into the stands—always a bad sign.

Next time down the second team makes a great play. Rachel reverses the ball across to D, who makes the three. The coach praises both the pass and the shot. "But we've got a junior and a senior who aren't playing like that. You guys had better get your heads out of your butts!"

The drill resumes after a time-out for substitutions. Cassie passes to Katie for a shot that goes in, but the guard who should have been in a position to rebound was standing far from the basket. "If I have to tell you not to be standing out there for a rebound—" the coach shouts loudly. "Seniors, captains, whoever you leaders are, you take care of this, because otherwise we are going to RUN." To run means to run laps, up and down the court, for a long time.

Soon after play resumes Brackman makes a careless mistake. "We are all going to get better at this. We are close to running, serious running." When Bracky makes another mistake Winstel says, "Karen Brackman, the difference between you and D is that she knows what she's supposed to do. You've got to get your act together. You're getting passed by, sweetie." She tells the team, "We didn't win by 17 on Wednesday. We lost by 17. We got our butt kicked."

Now the offense begins working upcourt against a nontrapping zone. Once they do quite well and score on a jumper. That is not good enough for the coach in her current mood. "I'm looking for a layup. I'm not looking for jump shots."

Next they work against a trapping zone. Winstel adds a sixth player to the trapping team to make it harder, but the offense does very well. So she tells them, "Best yet." But now she turns her scrutiny on the defense for making it too easy. "This practice stinks. You have six people on defense and you're giving up layups. THAT'S WHAT I GET FOR GIVING YOU YESTERDAY OFF!" She makes them run 13 laps.

Now they have to work on "telling your teammates where to be." The defense has to be more vocal in switching or otherwise adjusting to the offense. She warns, before the water break, "Nicole, if you get lackadaisical, I get really upset." This is the most animated water break of the day. The players are all talking about who guards whom and the various offensive and defensive sets.

Before they scrimmage again, Winstel puts them at four different baskets shooting free throws. They have to make 15 in a row as a team before they can play again. Schmidt shouts out the running count. They are not doing well. Winstel walks by the table where I am sitting and says, "Practice was like this every day last year." After 10 full minutes they finally make 15 in a row.

Next they do a half-court scrimmage. The rules for this one are: "Make it, take it, 3–2 zone." All seems to be going well until one team "makes it" and someone is slow taking the ball out of bounds. "Let's run 10 laps," she suddenly says. As they do, she pulls out her cell phone and talks to someone as the laps go on and on. She stops them after 19.

Now they try other offenses against the 3–2 zone (the kind that hurt us in the Kentucky game). The offense has to drive the seam. And also crash the boards. Again, one player fails to. This does it. She reminds them, "Everybody's in the paint except the safety on every shot. LINE UP."

To Katie Vieth, "Go take a shower." To the team, "As of now, you don't have next Tuesday off" (the day after the Monday night game in Bloomington). This time she lets them run 52 laps.

This was by far the most upset I have seen her during a practice. Winner had written about a similar practice before the UK game:

> Today was one of those days where I just feel like our practice is predetermined by the mood Coach is in when she walks in the gym. If she's not happy, it's not going to be a good day. Period. Yesterday I had not practiced as well as I should have/could have, and I know this. But today I thought I was doing considerably better and thought that practice as a whole was going pretty well. Au contraire. It ended up lasting an extra 25 minutes. . . . Just one of those days, I guess. . . . Many more to come, I'm sure.

After the tense Friday afternoon practice ends with the 52 laps, Winstel reminds her players that tomorrow is NKU Fan Day, when they and the men's team will be entertaining several hundred children in Regents Hall from 10 A.M. to noon. This means that their Saturday morning practice begins early, at 5:45 rather than 6:30. The players are done for the day after they run their last set of laps, but the coaches are not. Winstel, Schmidt, and Vieth drive two and a half hours to get to Bloomington in time to see Indiana, our Monday night opponent, beat Indianapolis, our GLVC rival, by 31 points, 66–35.

Indiana is a red state in basketball. Assembly Hall is a cathedral of the college game. Bright red banners at both ends of the court celebrate the achievements of Bobby Knight's men's teams. There are many fewer banners for the women's program that has recently become more of a presence on campus and in the Big Ten. This year the women have a new head coach, Felicia Legette-Jack (who last year took Hofstra to the National Invitational Tournament). One of the national championship banners for Knight's men's teams dates from 1976. In November of that year Nancy Winstel played in Assembly Hall as a senior with her NKU teammates, losing to Indiana 65–58. One year later Winstel ran the 30-second clock for all the women's games at Assembly Hall when she was a graduate student in Bloomington. Now, 30 years after playing for NKU on this court, she is bringing her own team to do the same. Our entire group is in awe as we walk out on the floor, seeing 18,000 seats rising high into the rafters, yet in such a way as to give this enormous space an intimate feel.

Indiana's team is not as overwhelming in size as Kentucky's (except for 6-foot-7 Sarah McKay, who is not a starter but does get considerable playing time). But they are still Big Ten, and they are well coached, and they had beaten Indianapolis badly in their first exhibition game three nights earlier. The game starts poorly for NKU. On our first possession Karmen Graham is blocked by Whitney Thomas. On our second, Nicole Chiodi is stripped by Kim Roberson. On our third, Karmen Graham is blocked by Carrie Smith. Fortunately, we get a shot off on our fourth possession, and it is a good one—a three-pointer by Karyn Creager gives us a 3–2 lead. The lead changes hands seven times in the first half, and NKU goes into the locker room with a 26–24 lead—on a half-court three-point shot by Nicole Chiodi at the buzzer.

The second half is quite a bit like the UK game. The score is tied with 14 minutes to go, but we hit a dry spell in the next few minutes as Indiana builds up a 14-point lead with 11 minutes to play. We continue to play hard and reduce the lead to 9 with 3:37 remaining, but we eventually lose by 13, 74–61. We played excellent defense in the first half, allowing only 24 points, but Indiana scored 50 in the second half.

This was a tough game to lose because it had seemed for a long time that we might actually win. Indiana's zone was tough on us throughout the game. Neither Winner nor Graham made a field goal, and Chiodi's only goal was the half-courter at halftime. Cassie Brannen and Katie Butler kept us in the game with their scoring off the bench, finishing with 12 and 11 points. Our free-throw shooting kept us in the game too; we made 13 of 16 for our first-half lead and another 14 of 18 in the second half. The fact that we were fouled so often showed how hard we were playing against Indiana's rock-solid team. In her postgame interview Winstel compared Kentucky's team to a Corvette, with "more finesse"—whereas Indiana was "more like a diesel, or maybe a tank. Indiana has a ton of power, which is exactly what you think of when you think of Big Ten basketball."

The biggest measure of Indiana's power is that they rejected eight of our shots. Still, we did block four of theirs (the most dramatic being when 6-foot Chiodi blocked 6-foot-7 McKay on an attempted layup). The biggest measure of *our* power is that we outrebounded Indiana, 42–41. Healy played a stellar game on defense, pulling down 12 rebounds and fronting their post players so they had a very difficult time getting the ball. One of her best rebounds came on offense, when Karmen was blocked by McKay; Angela got the ball and immediately laid it in for an 11–7 lead. Butler and Brannen showed *their* strength and resourcefulness when Indiana was ahead by one and had the ball with 0:07 remaining in the first half; Katie blocked a shot by Jamie Braun, their leading scorer for the evening, making possible Cassie's swift pass to Chiodi for the half-court three-pointer.

Although it always hurts to lose, we had much to be proud of in both our exhibition games. We held our own against both UK and Indiana, playing hard for 40 minutes against both teams and outrebounding both. We were not fearful of either team, and we gave as good as we got. We were already showing more depth than last year, especially deeper down on the bench, with Finnell and Lantry playing especially well against Kentucky and Echoles getting in good minutes against Indiana. Some of the difficulty we had scoring underneath in the two exhibition games should even out when we begin playing Division II competition. We need to improve our offense against a zone and our perimeter defense, but our interior defense was very impressive.

"After our respectable showing against #16 UK only 5 days before," Winner wrote in her journal,

I thought we had a very good chance of sticking close enough to this team to be able to pull out a win. . . . In the first half, it almost appeared that way. We were playing them evenly, keeping the game close, and not letting them go on any big runs. If we could keep this up, we might just slip out of Assembly Hall with a victory. . . . But IU came out to start the second half with a new level of intensity. The difference in body type between DI and DII really became apparent in the final twenty minutes. . . . Our posts seemed to be getting mugged, and any time a guard tried to attack the gaps of their 3–2 zone, we were met with the same lack of hospitality.

So while we were not able to sneak away with a victory, we did learn a lot from this game, just as we had from UK. We need to take care of the ball at all times. We can't fall into spurts where we go three or four possessions without getting a good shot. . . . But like Coach said after the game, the most important thing after these two exhibition games is the fact that everyone is still healthy, and that we have two weeks to prepare for our season opener.

Kentucky and Indiana each opened their regular seasons the next weekend at Memorial Coliseum in Lexington. In the first round of the Women's Sports Foundation Tournament, Kentucky beat Washington State 80–51, and Indiana beat Wake Forest 75–53. Indiana then beat Kentucky, 54–51, in the final. The fact that NKU did much better than either Washington State or Wake Forest against these two teams was another reason for pride. When I asked Winstel what she took away from our games with Kentucky and Indiana, she said, "I was happy to see the competitive nature of our team. I thought that our team was not intimidated by players that were bigger, stronger, and faster—more athletic. . . . I was impressed by the fact that they never at any point in time seemed like they were in awe. Not just the players, or the game, but just the atmosphere, the aura. I think it's just them and their confidence. It's the confidence they have in each other. And the confidence they have in each other helps them have confidence in themselves."

The two weeks remaining before the season opener on November 21 were not easy. After taking two hard losses, a team wants to get on the floor and put up some wins. After seven months of hard work since the last season ended in March, the players want the new season to begin right away. But Winstel's practices can be harder than the games themselves, and two more weeks of them remained. The practices I saw between the Indiana game and the opener against Midway College showed a fast-improving team that was working hard to prepare itself for the regular season.

Practice is going well when I arrive for the last half hour on the Wednesday after the Indiana game. The black and white teams are scrimmaging, working on the need for the point guards to attack the zone. Everyone is making plays: Rachel, Karmen, and Karyn all hit quick threes; Nicole steals for a score. Winstel gives a big smile when opposing post players topple together as they go for a rebound; she loves to see equality of strong, hard contact. My notes are full of more great plays: "Power move, Healy. Healy out to Keri for a 3. Katie hits a 3 with one second on the shot clock. Bracky, great feed. B-Dubs, great pass. Pleasure in playing. All of them. A two-pass fast-break: Brittany to Cassie to Grammy, split-second-quick."

They finish practice with a continuous full-court fast-break drill in which the ball is not allowed to touch the floor. Twelve times the ball speeds from out of the net at one end of the court, into the net at the other end, and then back again, 12 rotating players running each pass-pass-layup sequence without a single dribble. It is an exhilarating exhibition of body, mind, and timing.

On Friday, November 10, there is more of the same. It is another practice of great energy at the same time we are working through a whole series of offensive and defensive sets. From the beginning, the noise level is high. The press breaks are going very well. Grammy makes two great passes. "Assists are so much better to watch than turnovers. Your energy is great. Keep it up." Three more great assists, Karen to D, Betsey to Katie, Karen to Rachel.

The players are relaxed and feeling good about themselves at the next water break. They tease Grammy about how often she got blocked by UK and Indiana. She says she liked that one they swatted all the way into the stands.

As we go five against five, working against our various man-to-man defenses, Winstel is praising plays as often as she was critiquing them the other day. At the end she reminds them that tomorrow is Saturday and practice will be at 7 A.M. "I know sometimes it's hard to come in that early to practice. A lot of teams do not practice like we do. We are getting better. Today your energy was 500 times better." Afterward Winstel was unusually pleased, saying to me, "We didn't run or anything."

On Wednesday, November 15, practice begins the same way. They move to two ends of the court, Matt working with the guards, Katie with the posts. Katie has a pad and is pushing them hard as they shoot, each player unfazed, keeping her balance and making her shots. Even when pushed with pads from both sides, Healy shows impressive force in breaking through to score.

Today the 5-4-3-2-1 drill goes very well, players making excellent plays on both offense and defense. Winstel stops it once to praise two consecutive passes by Lantry. "Rachel just made two good decisions and two good passes. That gets you playing time."

When they break from scrimmage and have to make 15 consecutive free throws, everyone begins to get frustrated when someone different misses at 14, 14, 12, 14, and 14 in a row. Winstel's body language gets increasingly tense after a full nine minutes of this, but Brittany finally makes number 15 and the scrimmage can continue. We fine-tune various offensive sets with screens, without them, against both man-to-man and zone. Everyone is working hard, talking well, competing well with one another. This level is what Winstel has been aiming for during the whole preseason, and the praise comes out strong and direct. "Now we are working harder. Now I don't have to coach effort. Now I can start coaching. You're a whole lot better offensively than you were last week. Our defense is making our offense better and our offense is making our defense better."

At 2:02, 92 minutes into this practice, Winstel calls a 2-minute water break. Soon after play resumes Cassie blocks a shot by Angela. Soon after doing so she comes to the sideline and sits down, holding her head. Noriko sits down beside her. Nicole passes to D for a three. B-Dubs makes a great drive. Nancy looks over to Noriko to see if Cassie can come back in.

Cassie is sitting in a folding chair close to the scorer's table where I am sitting. I see her right leg begin to tremble. As this starts, her teammates sneak a glance at her whenever they can. Katie Vieth goes in to take her place on the court. I've never seen one of these lightheaded episodes so closely, or from the beginning. Now the left leg is trembling too.

155

On the court Karmen makes a two. Angela blocks Butler. Keri fakes Bracky, passes to Butler for a three. Noriko is putting Cassie on the floor, getting ready to raise her legs against the edge of the chair. Winstel, watching closely, says, "You can take her into the training room."

For me it has been scary to see, close up, the physical disability this strong, active, resilient young woman has to deal with intermittently as an athlete. Everyone else is concerned too, even though they have seen it before and have every reason to believe Cassie will be fine when it passes. This condition, called syncope, is caused by reduced circulation of blood to the brain. Watching Cassie experience its effects right next to me deepens my appreciation for her quiet courage in playing a game that makes her susceptible to such unpredictable attacks. I am glad to hear from Matt, at the next day's Basketball Tip-Off Luncheon, that these occasional episodes do not pose any threat to Cassie, her career, or any part of her life beyond the court. I am also happy to see Cassie arrive at the luncheon with her teammates, entirely herself, as if nothing had happened the day before.

The event is hosted by Cincinnati television personality George Vogel; he will introduce our women's and men's coaches to give a preview of the season. It is a pleasure to see Nancy's team dressed for the banquet hall rather than the basketball court. Today Karmen Graham is the player whose appearance differs most strikingly from her usual on-court look. No longer bunched in a ponytail, her beautiful soft hair falls on either side of that lovely, open, smiling face, which for once is not flushed tomato red from the heat of the game. Wearing a scooped black jacket over a flesh-brown tank top, this young woman would warm the heart of many a young man having nothing to do with basketball. Freshman Rachel Lantry is said to be the most fashion-conscious of all our players, but her taste differs from Karmen's classic look today. Winstel will introduce *her* by saying that Rachel's wardrobe contains very little without holes in its knees.

Winstel's players show impressive poise in a roomful of middle-aged males prone to the kind of roasting and joshing more appropriate to the culture of the men's game. Angela Healy sets the tone by delivering the prayer that opens the program. Winstel introduces all her players to the Tip-Off crowd by their academic aspirations rather than their athletic exploits. She announces that Brittany Winner, in addition to being a Spanish education major, has just been approved to do her practice teaching in Argentina next year. Her remarks about the new season include a couple of references to the film *Hoosiers*, which she happened to see on cable the night before. Winstel calls that film "a love story about a group of guys, a coach, and a ball." The film is "all about the team, and hard work." But what she really noticed this time was the moment when one player says, "Give me the ball, Coach. I'll make the shot." Her comment: "You have to play as a team but there comes a time when a player steps up and is ready to shoot." Her players are occasionally unselfish to a fault, and this was a way to send that message to them as well as to the roomful of friends and fans.

"Since last season," she says, "we have done a lot to get better." Over the summer her players worked a lot on their own "to prepare for this season." Referring to *Hoosiers* again, she says there are David games and there are Goliath games. "To UK and IU we were the David. But we will be the Goliath for a lot of the teams that play us. We are very ready to play."

I was eager to have one more interview with Coach Winstel before the preseason was officially over. We had scheduled it for immediately after practice on November 20, the day before our opener with Midway. When I get to practice Karmen is not on the court. She is sitting at the scorer's table in street clothes, awaiting a trip to the doctor with the coach as soon as practice is over. She had twisted her knee in practice the day before the Tip-Off Luncheon. She did not think much about it at the time, but it did bother her when she wore her dress shoes to the banquet the next day. She had wanted to practice on Friday, but Winstel would not let her. Winstel wanted Karmen to get an MRI to be sure there was no damage to the meniscus, no condition that needed surgery or could be aggravated by practice or play. Karmen, our queen for a day, our cocaptain, our honorable mention All-American, would now miss the first game of her senior year, and most certainly the second one too. We could only hope she would not miss more.

Katie Vieth was now completing her first preseason as Coach Winstel's assistant. She knows about knees. After her career as a post player at UK, she was enjoying a season of professional ball in Switzerland. When she reaggravated a leg injury that had required surgery during her junior year of college, she was faced with this life decision: "Do I want to be able to walk when I have kids?"

Katie has played for many coaches and coached in several programs, so I wondered what, if anything, distinguished Nancy Winstel's approach to the game. "She knows the game very, very well. She knows how she wants to run her stuff. The kids work hard every day because that is what she demands. She is also very good at adjusting to what the other team is doing. I am amazed at her ability to see the floor and to see everything that's going on."

What is the biggest challenge facing our team this year? "I think for any successful team coming back the year after, it's having the hunger to come in day in and day out and give it your all at practice. We have a good core of leadership with the five seniors. But we have to take care of the little things. Rebounding. Turnovers. Some people don't realize it but the little things will come back and haunt you."

As a former D-I player, what do you see as the main difference between the two divisions? "D-I athletics have gone so much more to the money side of it, whereas D-II is still focused on the student-athlete. D-II is good to coach at because the kids are in it for the right reasons, developing them into responsible adults. That is kind of what your goal is. To win games, for them to graduate, and for them to become people that are successful in society."

Matt Schmidt was now in his third preseason as a Winstel assistant. This was the ninth season of his coaching career. What distinguishes Winstel's approach to running preseason drills and practices? "Her consistency from day to day. In all of our drills we are working on every phase of the game as opposed to one or two phases. And she believes that practice should be more difficult than the game, that if you can handle practice, the game should be relatively easy. She is also able to tell her players what they need to hear. The great coaches are able to do this. Our players might get ticked off at her but they know that Nancy really cares about them. The thing about Nancy is that she knows who she is. She doesn't change her personality to make somebody else happy. She'll listen, but she believes strongly in what she believes."

How would you evaluate our team's preseason work? "Pretty darn good. Some people have had deaths in their families. We have some seniors that are now thinking about their future and what is going to happen—life after basketball and school. That can be a bit of a distraction at times and I think they have all kept it in perspective. I think they have done a good job of keeping focused and having balance in their life and having fun, but also wanting to accomplish certain things in their athletic career before they are done. So I think we have been real good. Can't complain."

What do you see as our biggest challenge as the season begins? "Understanding the situation we are in, whether it is offensively or defensively, and taking care of the basketball. Right now, turnovers are killing us. When you are playing great teams, you have to get a shot on every possession."

This had been Nancy Winstel's 24th preseason as head coach at NKU. What were her most important goals for this preseason, and how well had her players met them?

"Last year we learned a lot, we came a long way. Right now we are at a better place than we were at this time last year. Our conditioning level is better. Our players have a better understanding of what it takes to be successful. Now we have to try to get our leaders to take that next step. Our seniors, last year they were excited that they weren't seniors. They really liked each other and they really thought not having any seniors was kind of neat because they really didn't have pressure and there wasn't any finality to what was going on that year.

"But this year my seniors see that finality; they talk about it. Sometimes they stress over it. They love their team, their teammates, and they want to take it all in, cherish each minute of it. They do have more confidence in themselves as leaders. The juniors are a little older and the sophomores are a little older. But also one of my big things is to just get out of the preseason and be healthy. We're not 100 percent healthy, but you just hope you don't lose anybody in preseason."

After watching the UK and Indiana games in the context of our preseason practices, I wondered how Winstel handles a player who does better in the game situation than in practice. "Well, here's my philosophy. Practice gets you notice to play. But I do tell my players that at some point it does become about performance. If you are a 'game player' but you stink in practice, you're going to have a hard time getting on the floor. But on the other hand there are kids who aren't good practice players but are great game players and vice versa. You don't want to be accused as a coach of playing kids who don't work hard. So if you've got a great game player who is not great in practice, you try to make her work harder and get better."

Regents Hall, Northern Kentucky University, completed 1972. (Schlachter Archives, Northern Kentucky University)

Nancy Winstel (in cut-off jeans) guarding Teresa Rump in a scrimmage of NKU's first women's basketball team. (Photo by Joe Munson, *Northerner*, November 22, 1974)

Players from NKU women's basketball team in Sydney, Australia, May 2005. (Photo courtesy Keri Finnell)

Proud members of the Great Lakes Valley Conference, NCAA Division II, 2005–07. (Photo courtesy GLVC Headquarters)

Nicole Chiodi driving against Molly Carter of Drury University, Regents Hall, December 3, 2005. (Photo by Tim Downer)

Betsey Clark splitting two Drury defenders, Regents Hall, December 3, 2005. (Photo by Tim Downer)

Coach Winstel with sophomore point guard Nicole Chiodi,
Regents Hall, December 22, 2005. (Photo by Tim Downer)

Katie Butler driving against Drury in the GLVC championship game, Roberts Stadium, Evansville, Indiana, March 5, 2006. (Photo by Joe Ruh)

NKU fans during the GLVC championship game with Drury University, Roberts Stadium, Evansville, Indiana, March 5, 2006. (Photo by Joe Ruh)

NKU team with the GLVC championship trophy, Roberts Stadium, Evansville, Indiana, March 5, 2006. (Photo by Elizabeth Randolph Courtney/GLVC)

NKU players at the NCAA banquet, Great Lakes Regional Tournament, Springfield, Missouri, March 9, 2006. Front row: Betsey Clark, Nicole Chiodi, Katie Butler, Karen Brackman, Danyelle Echoles, Keri Finnell; back row: Karyn Creager, Karmen Graham, Angela Healy, Cassie Brannen, Angela Estes, Brittany Winner. (Photo courtesy Angela Healy)

Karyn Creager scoring the game-winning basket against Michigan Tech in the NCAA Great Lakes Regional Tournament, Springfield, Missouri, March 10, 2006 (with Nancy Winstel and Scott Eaton looking on). (Photo by Tim Downer)

Brittany Winner going up for a shot against the University of
Kentucky, Memorial Coliseum, December 1, 2006. (Photo courtesy NKU Sports Information Office)

Cassie Brannen shooting against the University of Kentucky, Memorial Coliseum, December 1, 2006. (Photo courtesy NKU Sports Information Office)

Freshman Rachel Lantry taking her first college shot, a three-pointer against the University of Kentucky, Memorial Coliseum, December 1, 2006. (Photo courtesy NKU Sports Information Office)

A serious moment on the sideline during the season opener
against Midway College, Regents Hall, November 21, 2006
(standing behind Coach Winstel are Betsey Clark, Angela Healy,
Karmen Graham, and Matt Schmidt). (Photo by Tim Downer)

Team photo immediately after Coach Winstel's 500th career victory at NKU, Regents Hall, November 21, 2006. Players in the first row: Finnell, Clark, Lantry, Brackman, Echoles, Butler; second row: Healy, Brannen, Winner, Chiodi, Graham, Creager. (Photo by Tim Downer)

Karen Brackman shooting against Wayne State, Regents Hall, November 25, 2006. (Photo by Tim Downer)

Keri Finnell driving against Wayne State, Regents Hall, November 25, 2006. (Photo by Tim Downer)

Karmen Graham shooting against Bellarmine University,
Knights Hall, Louisville, Kentucky, December 9, 2006. (Photo
by Tim Downer)

Danyelle Echoles driving against Northern Michigan, Regents Hall, December 18, 2006. (Photo by Tim Downer)

Brittany Winner shooting the last-second game winner against the University of Wisconsin–Parkside, Regents Hall, February 10, 2007. (Photo by Tim Downer)

The team mobbing Brittany Winner after her game-winning shot against the University of Wisconsin–Parkside, Regents Hall, February 10, 2007. (Photo by Tim Downer)

Angela Healy scoring what would have been the game-winning basket against Ferris State, NCAA Great Lakes Regional Tournament, Romeoville, Illinois, March 9, 2007. (Photo by Tim Downer)

The five seniors on Senior Night after NKU's victory over Bellarmine, Regents Hall, February 19, 2007. Left to right: Karmen Graham, Karyn Creager, Betsey Clark, Brittany Winner, Katie Butler. (Photo by Tim Downer)

Three future cocaptains as young girls: Karmen Graham, Brittany Winner, and Karyn Creager. (Photos courtesy of Matt Schmidt and the players' parents)

NKU celebrates its 2008 national championship victory over South Dakota at Kearney, Nebraska, March 29. From left: Nicole Chiodi, Angela Healy, Jessica Wendeln, Jessie Slack, Karen Brackman, Cassie Brannen. (Photo by Tim Downer)

7

LOSING WHAT WE HAD

Experience is the angled road.
—*Emily Dickinson*

The regular season begins with a home game against Midway, the small college near Lexington, Kentucky, at which Nancy Winstel began her coaching career in 1978. After the three-month off-season and the three-month preseason, it is finally time to play. The first good news upon entering Regents Hall on November 21 is that Karmen Graham is going to be okay. The MRI revealed no serious damage to the knee, so she should be playing again soon, hopefully in time for our GLVC opener against Quincy on November 30.

The next good news is that NKU wins against Midway, 98–42, and looks good doing it in spite of the mismatch. This is Nancy Winstel's 500th victory at NKU, and it is fitting that she achieved it against the only other school at which she ever coached (she won 39 games at Midway during the 1978–81 seasons). She and her players are interviewed for a long time after the game. Karmen Graham hated to miss this milestone in her coach's career. "Obviously, I wanted to be out there for this. Coach has worked so hard, and she can still relate to young women. She has a lot in common with us."

When I asked Coach Winstel to reflect on the importance of the 500 wins, she began by saying, "I hate to lose. When you look at my career—so many wins, so many losses—I look at the 160-some times that I lost. That is half a year in a life. I look at losing. I want to win. My team, I would hope they would say, of all the things that

161

Coach Winstel did, she's one of the most competitive people I've ever met." When I asked her to respond to Karmen's comment that she and her players have a lot in common, she said, "I enjoy being with my players. I enjoy riding the bus, sitting in a restaurant. But I don't pry into their personal lives. I don't try to be 20. I let them know I have a life of my own. But it's nice to feel that you can relate to them.

"Day after day I get to be around these young women and see them grow and mature. I get to see them strive academically, professionally, personally. I get to see them go through the ups and downs of life like we all do. We're probably more similar than we are different."

November 21 and 25: Midway College and Wayne State

Midway College is midway between Lexington and Frankfort in the middle of the state. Its team had already played nine games and lost six. Going over the scouting report at practice, Winstel had told her team, "They will have trouble with our size and athleticism if we come to play." This was evident when the two teams lined up for the opening tip. We were the Goliath tonight, dwarfing them the way UK had dwarfed us.

Brannen started in place of Graham. For the first three minutes Winstel got a little taste of that perfect game she dreams of coaching. After Cassie controlled the opening tip, Healy passed to Creager, who swished a three from the corner. After Healy rebounded a Midway miss, Healy passed to Creager for another perfect three. Next time down for Midway, Chiodi stole the ball and drove to score. Midway scored next to make the score 8–2, but now Chiodi answered with a three on a feed from Healy. Midway's next attempt was blocked by Brannen and rebounded by Healy. She made two free throws after being fouled. Before Midway could shoot on its next possession, Brannen stole the ball and was fouled doing so. Cassie made two free throws. We were already ahead 14–2 when we made our first substitution, Clark for Chiodi, with 16:55 remaining. When Butler came in for Healy 20 seconds later, Katie was aware that we had made all three three-point shots and all four free throws. She worried that she might break the streak. She did not. She made her first three-pointer on an assist from Winner after a steal by Brannen. That made the score 20–4 with 14:48 remaining in the half, setting the tone for the rest of the game.

Even against a team unable to apply much defensive pressure, it is impressive to make 70 percent of your field goals (19 of 27), two-thirds of your threes (6 of 9), and all your free throws (11 of 11) in building a 55–14 halftime lead. By the end of the game Creager, Butler, and Chiodi led in scoring with 18, 14, and 13 points. But the biggest story of this game was our depth and quality off the bench. Not only Clark and Butler but also Brackman, Finnell, and Echoles got to play almost as much as the starters did. This was a breakout game for Danyelle Echoles, who had 11 points, 5 rebounds, and 3 steals while also playing excellent defense. She was a force in this game in a way we had never seen before, giving us—with Finnell now healthy and Lantry on the squad—much more depth at guard. Brackman, who had been hampered in the preseason by her knee in-jury, also showed a lot in this game, with 8 points, 6 rebounds, and 3 assists in only 14 minutes. Although Lantry played least, she did score 4 points in 9 minutes, two of them on her first official shot as a college player (continuing the streak she had begun with her first exhibition shot at UK).

The most satisfying element of the entire game was the energy and concentration with which the whole team played. We had only one slow stretch, at the beginning of the second half, when Winstel started a five-guard offense of Clark, Lantry, Echoles, Finnell, and Winner. Midway came out strong against the smaller lineup, play-ing for pride and holding its own until Winstel began slipping her starters back in. From then on we continued to play extremely well no matter who was on the floor. Winstel, in her postgame com-ments, was happy that so many of her players were able to play so many minutes and that all of them played with success. Her most significant overall comment may have been that "our energy was really good." High energy from the five on the floor, at both ends of the court, following our game plan but improvising too, seems to be all she really wants or expects for any given game, all 40 minutes of it. She came about as close to that as she could hope to get in an opener. In every subsequent game she will judge and encourage her players by this standard, no matter who the opponent.

Over in the parents' section after the game I was able to reacquaint myself with some of the mothers and fathers I had already met at the exhibition games in Lexington and Bloomington. The Creagers were here from Leipsic, and so were the Butlers from Findlay, the Winners from Minster, and the Grahams from Kettering. The Brannens were here from across the river in Cincinnati, and so were the Finnell, Clark, and Echoles families. Among the northern Kentucky contingent, Rachel's parents had now joined those of Angela and Nicole.

Everyone seemed happy and relaxed after this game. Karmen's parents were extremely grateful to Coach Winstel for "pushing along" the medical evaluation of Karmen's knee, including the MRI. They remembered with affection the first time they had worried about their daughter's legs, immediately after Karmen had a growth spurt in the middle grades: "She was like Bambi out there, and her legs would get all tangled up." Karyn's parents tonight were showing off their infant grandson Lincoln, whom Karyn carefully cradled after the game. I was glad to meet Keri's parents and to congratulate them for bringing two such talented athletes to our basketball program (Keri's brother Billy was now a sophomore on the men's team).

The most interesting bit of news from chatting with various parents came from Nicole's mother, who mentioned that Angela had been hit so hard in the mouth in the Indiana game that she had since had root canal surgery. I had seen that smash-mouth moment near the end of that game, and I had also seen the plastic mouthpiece Angela had been wearing to practice since then (I could hardly miss it the day I was chatting with Karmen on the sideline and the mouthpiece whizzed past us, Angela evidently expecting Karmen to catch it). But I had not expected a root canal, nor would I have been likely to hear about it from Angela or any of the players themselves.

Last year we had gone up to Detroit to play Wayne State two days after Thanksgiving. This year they came down to play us. Last year's game was the one in which Karmen had suffered a concussion while scoring 17 points in a 28-point victory. This year she had to sit out the rematch as we won by 41 points. In the locker room before the game Winstel emphasized its importance in the regional rankings at the end of the season, since Wayne State is a member of the GLIAC, our sister conference in the Great Lakes Region. Our 97–56 victory got us off to a good start.

The three other post players played extremely well in Karmen's absence. Cassie Brannen again joined Angela Healy in the starting lineup. She scored a career-high 20 points on 7 of 8 from the field and a perfect 6 of 6 from the line. Cassie also pulled down 9 rebounds, as did Angela, who scored 14 points. Katie Butler, our only true post player off the bench, added 11 points and 7 rebounds. All-purpose 5-foot-9 Betsey Clark also played the post during part of the game. "Spark" scored 10 points while rotating through all five offensive positions. She helped our inside players hold their Wayne State counterparts to a total of 3 points while scoring 55 among themselves.

The game started out quite a bit like the one with Midway, with NKU running out to leads of 9–0 and 20–5 on the way to a 41–16 halftime score. Our bench began getting significant play midway through the first half. By the end of the game Brackman, Finnell, and Clark had as much playing time as Winner, Creager, and Chiodi. The three starting guards were all outscored by the trio off the bench, who finished with 12, 11, and 10 points. These three subs also outrebounded the starters and had more steals. Something similar had happened the previous day in practice when the second team, running Wayne State's plays, had beaten the first team in a long scrimmage. Winstel had not been pleased with the first team's effort. She ended the practice with these words: "You just got beat by 'Wayne State' today. You'd better show up tomorrow. Because if you get beat in your own gym by Wayne State, your dreams of hosting the regionals are dead."

Wayne State offered a much greater challenge than Midway in terms of height, rebounding, and Division II skills, but we did meet the challenge in impressive fashion. To have six players in double figures with our leading scorer from last year unable to play is an impressive measure of depth. Some memorable moments: Cassie making those twisting, jigsaw shots; Angela setting those unforgiving picks and delivering passes just where and when they needed to be; Keri sticking with Joy Nash, Wayne State's speedy 5-foot-1 point guard, not giving her an inch of daylight.

The parents' section was quite relaxed and happy after this game too. One regular was missing; Brittany's father, Earl, had to stay home to harvest his corn and soybean crops. Karyn's father, Dale, had been plowing his own fields through the previous night until seven in the morning. He made it to the game just in time and would be returning to the harvest immediately after his three-hour drive back home. Brittany and Karyn bring a similar work ethic and stamina to Winstel's day-after-day practices. Brittany's parents were not surprised she had been reelected cocaptain this year: "She's always been a pusher and a leader. Back in high school she pushed the entire team." I was surprised to hear from Karyn's parents that she had torn her ACL during her junior year in high school; they had been extremely impressed by her dedication to getting back in shape for her senior year and college career.

In the locker room after the victory over Wayne State, Coach Winstel praised her players and briefly looked ahead to the home game with Quincy on Thursday night. She stressed that "every game in the GLVC is a freaking war. A freaking war. We have to win every home game and do the best we can on the road. Being picked as favorites of the conference means *nothing*. Being the favorite can be a medal or an anchor. It can help you or it can drag you down. Last year Drury was the favorite and they ended getting beat by some podunk team picked to finish third or fourth in the East [NKU]. This year in the region Grand Valley has a huge target on its back. The other night they only beat Drury by three at home. I can't wait till they come to play us here. They are a target and I have a gun. I hope you will be my bullets." Winstel assured Keri immediately after saying this that she was not planning to hurt anybody.

The day after our victory over Wayne State we got some help from our friends at Bellarmine up in Michigan. They upset Grand Valley, 62–60. Now Grand Valley would not necessarily be the overwhelming favorite to host the Great Lakes NCAA Regional in March. But now we had to worry as much about Bellarmine as Grand Valley. And our first Bellarmine game was still four games away.

November 30 and December 2: Quincy and SIU–Edwardsville

The cumulative stats looked great after our first two wins. We were averaging 97.5 points a game, eight of our players were averaging 8 or more points a game, and our opponents had scored only 14 and 16 points against us in the first half. But none of this mattered from 12:30 until 3:00 on Monday afternoon. Arriving shortly after 1:00, I had never seen the coach so riled up so early in a practice. When I come in, she is shouting at her two assistants, "COME ON COACHES, EXPLAIN THE DRILL RIGHT!" Zach, the manager, whispers, "It's been bad."

One reason Winstel is so volatile today may be that *two* of her seniors are unable to practice: Karmen's knee is not ready yet, and one of Betsey's knees is swollen. One thing Winstel wants from her players on the floor is more communication. Looking at Angela and Nicole she says, "We have two seniors out today; work on your leadership." Looking at Karyn she says, "If you don't do better, I'll find a new captain." This is one of those days when she and Nicole have their wires crossed, and the voltage is higher than usual.

The drills are designed to prepare the team for Quincy's screens and traps, and still the players are not talking to one another. "We are going to talk during this drill. Four or 40 minutes, it is up to you." The words today are not so different from what I have heard before, but the vehemence is more extreme.

The players probably feel a jolt of relief when the fire alarm goes off in Regents Hall. But that only makes it harder to hear Winstel's voice above the alarm as she continues the drills for the next 10 minutes. Regents Hall is built in such a way everyone could escape if this should be anything but a false alarm. But it is still highly disconcerting to try to see and hear the practice with the alarm ringing. Finally we do go outside, on a beautiful late November afternoon. After 15 minutes of outdoor calm, practice resumes. The starters are now working quite well against Quincy's offensive scheme, but Nicole has another lapse and is abruptly demoted to the second team.

On Wednesday things are better. Betsey is still out but Karmen is back. Cassie was out yesterday with flu-like symptoms but is back on the court today. The workout is intense today, but more cooperatively so. The players are working hard and communicating well, and Winstel is delivering her advice in private tutorials on the sideline rather than in public harangues. After several of her starters tip the ball with good effort on defense, Winstel stops to praise them and encourages them to do more. "If you can tip it, you can steal it." She wants them to give that extra effort and get the ball. Today's scrimmage "won't be too long." Everyone plays quite well, and she sees as much to praise as to censure. The practice ends early at 2:30.

At 5:30 on Thursday we come out ready to play. So does Quincy. This is another classic matchup between two well-matched teams. Quincy plays excellent defense and has a motion offense that is difficult to stop. One of our defining moments last season was to beat them 73–70 on their court. Our subsequent victory over them in the conference tournament was one of our finest games of the year. Their center Deana McCormick has graduated, but guards Crawford, Wisser, and Weiser are back, and freshman Janette Burgin is making a big impact at forward. The GLVC preseason poll had ranked Quincy second to Drury in the Western Division. NKU had jumped up to 10th in this week's national poll. But Quincy came very close to beating us on our own court.

After an exciting first half in which the lead changed hands many times, Quincy led 33–30. Quincy remained ahead for most of the second half—until the last 23 seconds. NKU was behind by six points with two minutes to play. Butler cut the margin in half by driving for a layup and making a foul shot for a three-point play. On Quincy's next possession Chiodi stole the ball from Crawford and passed to Winner for a layup. After Quincy got those points back on two free throws, Butler immediately answered with a long three-pointer (our only one of the night) to tie the score. With 33 seconds remaining, Quincy regained the lead on two more free throws by Burgin. But Graham powered in for an acrobatic layup while being fouled, making a three-point play for a one-point lead. When Quincy missed at the other end of the court, Chiodi got the rebound and was fouled. She made the first of two shots to put us ahead 63–61 with 8 seconds remaining. Quincy had one more chance to score, but Chiodi forced Crawford into a turnover without a shot being taken.

Butler's ability to come up big in game after game has been remarkable. She did not feel comfortable with her three-point shot tonight (she had missed two), but Karmen had told her that if she was open she was going to get the ball. When the shot went in Katie made huge windmill motions with her arms we had never seen before. Nicole had struggled with turnovers, especially in the first half, but she led us in rebounds with seven, in assists with five, and in steals with three. Her defensive pressure against Crawford at the end of the game made Butler's offensive heroics at the other end of the court possible. As Katie said in her postgame interview, "Nicole stepped up for us when the coach got on her about her defense. She knows what's going on out there and she's a great point guard. She has like a sixth sense and she knows where people are on the floor. Not once did we think we were out of this game. We kept saying that if they were in front of us, we were going to come back and that we were fine."

How did we come so close to losing to Quincy at home? We committed 22 turnovers. We allowed 21 offensive rebounds. And we played 31 minutes without Angela Healy, who committed two quick fouls in the first half and then suddenly fouled out midway through the second half—when she was charged with a technical foul immediately upon receiving her fourth foul. Angela's absence for all but nine minutes of the game put a lot of pressure on the other post players—especially as Karmen was still recovering from her bad knee, Cassie was still a little under the weather, and Katie was not in the habit of playing so many minutes.

How did we win under these conditions, apart from the great plays in the closing minutes? We made 50 percent of our field goals while holding Quincy to 33 percent. We blocked 10 shots (4 by Brannen, 3 by Winner) compared with their 1. And we had balanced scoring (six players between 8 and 12 points). Winner's 12 points came on 5 of 7 field goals. She had 3 assists, 3 blocks, and a steal. Her all-out play was one reason we were still in the game for all the heroics at the end. Her jumper with 2:51 remaining ended a three-minute drought during which we turned the ball over three times.

As Winstel had predicted, it was a freaking war, and it took last-minute heroics by several players to pull it out. Quincy played extremely well on both offense and defense, but we dug deep and did what we needed to win. In a team meeting the next day Winstel gave special credit to Chiodi and Butler, saying, "I've been on Nicole and Katie for defense lately, but last night, Nicole and Katie, your defense made a difference in the ball game. Nicole, at the end of the game, you could see it in her eyes, number 40 didn't want to have anything more to do with you."

The Edwardsville game was the reverse of the Quincy game. We played a strong second half that put us in a position to win, and we let it get away at the very end. We had taken a three-point lead with 1:29 remaining on a layup by Healy. Amber Shelton made two free throws with 1:08 remaining, but we had the ball and we still had the lead. When Chiodi missed a layup, Winner got the rebound, so we still controlled the ball. With 28 seconds remaining, however, Chiodi threw a pass out near the center line that was intercepted by Shelton. As Shelton streaked up the floor for the layup, Winner streaked after her and knocked the ball out of bounds as she was going up for the shot. It was an extraordinary burst of speed and concentration, but it left Edwardsville 24 seconds in which to win the game. They got the ball to Shelton, their high scorer for the game with 24, who made her last 2 points on a jumper with 4 seconds left, giving them a 65–64 victory.

These two games together, losing 65–64 after winning 65–63, show how tough the GLVC will be this season. Quincy has been a perennial power, but Edwardsville is turning its program around this year. They are doing so with the help of three D-I transfers, including Amber Shelton from Illinois State (who entered our game averaging 19 points a game on .633 shooting from the floor). We knew Edwardsville would be tough—not only because of their transfers and their 4–0 record but also because of the way they had beat Bellarmine at Bellarmine two days before, 71–61. That victory had been all the more impressive since Bellarmine was coming off its upset of top-ranked Grand Valley at Grand Valley. I had been impressed with Edwardsville as they warmed up. They were big, strong, and confident. They had some blue-collar heft and seemed ready to use it.

Edwardsville outplayed us on our own court during nearly the entire first half. They challenged us to shoot from the outside and we were painfully cold, missing our first four three-point shots and making only 2 of 14 for the game. With three minutes remaining in the first half, Edwardsville led by nine. NKU then responded with seven unanswered points. Healy scored five of those points and Winner the last two on a brilliant play that ended the half. Winstel had called a time-out with 12 seconds remaining. The play she called put the ball in Brittany's hands at the top of the key. She dribbled one way, cut back the other, and sliced through the zone to close the deficit to 31–29.

This good momentum continued through nearly all of the second half. We immediately tied the score on a layup by Healy, and we took a six-point lead with 11:19 remaining when Chiodi converted a three-point play on a pass from Winner. Edwardsville then scored eight unanswered points to take a two-point lead with 7:39 remaining. By the 4:30 mark we had fought back to a six-point lead of our own. We were still leading by five points with 2:31 remaining, setting up the slow erosion that ended with Shelton's game-winner with four seconds left.

Had we won, rather than lost, by a point, there would have been much to celebrate. Healy played a powerful, commanding game both offensively and defensively, with 21 points and 9 rebounds while committing only 2 fouls. Winner was equally inspiring, with 16 points and 9 rebounds. Many of her best plays came at crucial points in the game—the drive to score at the end of the first half, the hustle to stop Shelton's shot at the end of the second half, the steals when we were building our lead in the closing moments. Chiodi had scored 10 of our points, but that last bad pass allowed

Edwardsville to win—just as her defensive heroics had allowed *us* to win in the last seconds against Quincy. The one bad pass was exactly the kind that drives Winstel wild wherever it occurs—at practice, in a summer league, or with a GLVC game on the line.

Of course, every minute of a 40-minute game counts as much as the last minute toward the final score. Perhaps the toughest aspect of this loss is that Edwardsville held Graham and Creager to three and two points. One of the great strengths of NKU this season is that we have nearly everyone back. One of the great strengths of Edwardsville is that they have added outstanding D-I transfers. It will be very interesting to see how these contrasting strengths play out in the course of the season, not only with Edwardsville but also with other GLVC teams that "stocked up" over the offseason. Rebounding from this painful loss will be a challenge for Coach Winstel as well as her players. Last year's home-court loss to Drury, also in early December, brought our team closer together and made us better. Our games with Georgetown and with Bellarmine next week will begin to show whether the Edwardsville loss has the same result.

On the Tuesday after the Edwardsville game, Brittany wrote in her journal:

> Of all the ways to lose, losing on a last-second shot is the worst. When you lose to a team by 15, it's more of a general feeling of a lack of performance, whereas a close loss makes you rethink every play and every possession that could've made a difference. I was up late on Sunday night working on projects that were due this week and finally went to bed at 2:30 A.M., exhausted. But I didn't fall asleep until after 3:00 because I was replaying the last 20 seconds of the SIUE game in my head. . . . But it doesn't really get you anywhere. A loss is still a loss and you can only hope to learn from it so that when the situation presents itself again, you will know what to do.
>
> We had hoped for an undefeated season, or at least to be perfect at home. That goal will have to be amended.

Brittany was not the only member of the team to replay the end of the Edwardsville game in her head. At practice on Monday something quite dramatic took place: the team asked Winstel if they could hold a meeting among themselves without the coaches being present. Angela Healy recalls that "the captains asked the coach if we could have the time alone." This was after the coach had signaled to the captains that "she was looking for ideas." Betsey Clark recalls that the meeting itself "took 45 minutes to an hour. We just sat down and we went through everything. It was beneficial to talk among ourselves. We would then relay back to the coach what we thought was necessary and what she needed to know."

The captains negotiated two changes before the game with Georgetown on Wednesday. The players as a group felt that the coach was asking them to arrive too early on game day, causing them to shoot too much or to lose focus before game time. She agreed to give them a later arrival time. The players also felt they would play better if they had a few minutes to themselves, without the coaches, in the locker room immediately before a game. Winstel granted this request too. For just a few minutes the players could do whatever they wanted, among themselves, in the locker room. As Betsey recalled, "This gave us time to be college kids. Even if it was right before the game, and it was only a two-minute period, we got to be us. We were feeling, if you don't have fun on the floor, what's the point of being there?"

The journal entry that Brittany wrote on Tuesday about the Edwardsville game does not directly address the team meeting or the negotiations with the coach, but it does show some indirect results of the initiatives the players had taken the day before: "I think we're stronger now and have a new energy in us that we didn't have before. We'll see if I'm right or not when we play Georgetown tomorrow."

December 6 and 9:
Georgetown and Bellarmine

Georgetown, like Midway, is about 10 miles from Lexington in the center of the state. It is home to a large Toyota manufacturing plant as well as a small Baptist college. The college's basketball team is coming to Regents Hall with a 9–2 record. Georgetown is currently ranked number 18 nationally in the NAIA Division I poll, compared with NKU's number 12 in this week's NCAA Division II poll. So this game will test two teams and two divisions, quite like our recent exhibition game with UK. In this matchup, we are the Goliath and Georgetown the David, but both teams remember the way Georgetown brought us down in the opening game of Karmen's and Karyn's sophomore year (which was also Brittany's first game as a transfer from Elon). Georgetown's coach, Sue Johnson, is one of the few coaches in the country who can compete with Winstel for both longevity and wins. Now in her 28th year at Georgetown, she began this season with 495 wins and 312 losses. The 9 new wins brought her to Regents Hall with 504 wins, the same number Winstel would have had at NKU had we not lost to Edwardsville.

Georgetown played hard and shot well, especially in the first half, but they were no match for an energized and rededicated Winstel team. NKU won 92–69, and the senior cocaptains led the way. Karyn Creager led the scoring with 21 points, hitting all five of her three-point shots, four of them in the first half. Karmen Graham scored 13 points on a perfect 5 of 5 from the field and 3 of 3 from the line. Brittany Winner had 5 assists to go with her 14 points and played with great intensity at both ends of the court. The inside-outside game was working to perfection. Creager's third three-pointer with 11:58 remaining in the first half gave us a 6-point lead. That grew to 13 when Butler hit her first three-pointer with 7:23 remaining, making the score 32–19.

NKU's shooting remained torrid throughout the game. We made 63 percent of our field goals, 67 percent of our three-pointers, and 87 percent of our free throws. Brannen and Butler scored 14 and 10 points off the bench, and Chiodi and Healy each scored 8. But this game was as much about all-court intensity as it was about scoring. Chiodi had 8 rebounds and 7 assists with her 8 points. Brannen had 8 rebounds and 4 blocks with her 14 points. As a team we made 25 assists, after only 12 against Edwardsville. Georgetown played hard and well, but whenever they would threaten to pull closer we would hit a couple of threes (we were 10 of 15 for the game), block a few shots (Brannen had 4 of our 8), or make a pass to a cutting player for an easy basket. Chiodi played an inspired game at point guard, with 7 assists against only a single turnover, but we had some excellent interior passing too, including a single minute in the second half when we scored 6 unanswered points on interior passes between Brannen and Healy. When Karmen scored on an assist from Karyn near the end of the first half, the two friends gave each other a quick chest bump as they headed back upcourt. For the moment, they had both put the Edwardsville game well behind them.

I had missed Monday's practice to have skin cancer surgery. Zach told me the next day about the meeting the players had asked to have among themselves. This sounded like an important development, so I was hoping to learn more about it during whatever brief interviews I could get immediately after the Georgetown game on Wednesday night. There is no press room at Regents Hall. After each game I would camp out under the stands with Marc Hardin of the *Kentucky Post* and the interviewer for NKU's sports information office, deferring to them as the three of us did our best to catch our targets as they came out of the locker room.

Coach Winstel, when I got to her, was not particularly interested in talking about that team meeting her players had requested. After telling me that I looked like I had been in a car accident (because of the huge bandage over my nose), she said that whatever happened with the players was "between them." Although she did not seem thrilled about the meeting itself, she was willing to support "anything that helps us get our spunk back and play better. Anything short of something absolutely, ridiculously, crazy and stupid, I'm all for it." With regard to the impressive victory over Georgetown, she singled out our "senior leadership. I just think our seniors took control of our team, and that's what they need to do. When you have a tough loss, you either fall apart or you regroup. Our seniors stepped up and did some really good things and the others followed. Leadership is tough. It's easy to lead when things are going well. When things are going tough, that's when you have to take a look at yourself. We're not a finished product. We have to get better. We have to continue to get back to the level we want to be at, but today was a good step in the right direction."

When I asked Brittany whether the new energy in the game tonight had anything to do with the special meeting the players had called on Monday, she said, "Yeah. But it's not a big deal. It's just something that we went in and talked about, and we kind of sorted things out. We just talked about our goals and what we need to do to get them done, and we talked about coming out with intensity. So we just got everyone on the same page, and we changed some things around today in our pregame, and really got our energy up today."

When I asked Karyn about her splendid shooting in the game tonight (21 points, 5 of 5 three-pointers, 4 of those in the first half), she said she had decided "just not to put pressure on myself by thinking about it too much." She said she had also been energized by her teammates in the locker room before the game. "We were pumped up, we were jumping around, and we just wanted to go out there and have fun."

At the time I had no idea that Brittany's pregame energy and Karyn's jumping around referred to something new that was happening in the locker room as a result of the team meeting on Monday. This pregame self-expression continued for the rest of the season. These student-athletes played loud music. They jumped up and down. They danced together. They got in a crazy huddle that Winner proposed, in which they laughed like hyenas. Anything to get relaxed, have some fun, be ready to play.

The victory over Georgetown was very satisfying because of the intensity and skill with which we played. But Bellarmine at Bellarmine would be a test of a different order. Not only had they beat Grand Valley in Michigan on November 28. Last Saturday, while we were losing to Edwardsville in the closing seconds, Bellarmine was beating Quincy by 66–44. Our in-state rivalry with Bellarmine goes back to when Winstel was playing for NKU in the 1970s. Winstel's rivalry with Bellarmine's coach, David Smith, goes back to when he was coaching for St. Joseph's in the 1980s. Neither will ever forget the game in Rensselaer in 1988 when his St. Joseph's team beat her NKU team in five overtimes, 131–130, the best game either had ever seen. After moving from St. Joseph's to Shippensburg in Pennsylvania, Smith was now in his ninth year at Bellarmine. He was on track to become another 500-game winner this season; the 485 career victories with which he entered the season placed him number 10 among current Division II coaches.

Coach Smith granted me a telephone interview in advance of our visit to his court. When I asked what, if anything, distinguishes Nancy Winstel from other coaches he has known, he spoke of her ability "to get her teams able to play their best every night. We all start in late November and play until mid-March. With 4½ months, 27 games, and all the practices, it is pretty difficult to be able to play your best every night. But somehow she is able to get her teams to do that. The rest of us, it seems that we have two or three times a year when we give away a game we just shouldn't have lost, but they don't ever have a bad night" (he had not seen last Saturday's game against Edwardsville). Preparing to play a Winstel team is always a special challenge, but "as a coach it has just made me better to have to play against her all these years." When I asked what the NKU rivalry means to Bellarmine, he immediately said, "A lot. Two games a year when we don't have to say to the kids, you have to get up for this game."

This year's Bellarmine players are undoubtedly still smarting from the surprisingly large 12-point victory we scored on their court last February. Our players are quite chatty in the back of the bus as we leave campus for the ride to Louisville. My faculty friends are unable to make this trip, so this is an opportunity for me to sit with the players' parents immediately above the visitor's bench. Our players look fit and ready to play as they come out in their black razorback uniforms. And they do play quite well. But Bellarmine plays extremely well, scoring 85 points to our 78. They play an up-tempo game, getting the ball upcourt and running their sets quickly. Tonight they get exceptional play from Dana Beaven, Angela Smith, and Taylor Kopple, who score 18, 20, and 24 points. We know Beaven and Smith from last year, but Kopple is a Division I transfer from Western Kentucky.

Taylor Kopple was as difficult for us to stop as Amber Shelton had been in the Edwardsville game. She drove at will, whoever was guarding her, making 6 of 10 field goals and 12 of 15 free throws. Her ability to take it to the basket made it difficult for us to force them into a deliberate half-court game. When we did do so, Bellarmine ran its complicated screens to perfection, getting three-pointers from Angela Smith or Dana Beaven whenever we made a run. NKU only led for one four-minute stretch early in the second half. Even so, we did play hard, on a court where it is always extremely difficult to win, forcing Bellarmine to make one great play after another to beat us, setting up what should be an exciting rematch when they visit Regents Hall in February.

NKU played a good offensive game in many ways. We outshot Bellarmine 51 to 46 percent from the floor. We had balanced scoring from Healy, Creager, Butler, and Winner (16, 14, 13, and 11), followed by Chiodi and Graham (8, 8). But the flow of the game was such that we were battling uphill all the way. Winner blocked a shot by Kopple to begin the game, but then Bellarmine took the lead until we tied the score with 13:41 remaining in the half. When Healy then blocked Ashley Lewallen, it appeared as if the momentum would swing to NKU. But turnovers by Graham and Echoles helped Bellarmine take a five-point lead—at which point Brittany's second foul sent her to the bench for the rest of the half. Creager reduced the lead to two with a three-pointer, but Beaven answered immediately with a three of her own. Beaven's next three-pointer, with 4:40 remaining in the half, gave Bellarmine its largest lead of the game, 28–16. NKU then rallied hard to reduce the lead to one on a jumper by Cassie Brannen with 0:17 remaining, but Beaven again answered with a killer three for a 33–29 halftime lead.

NKU started the second half with a crisp pass from Winner to a cutting Chiodi for a layup. We took the lead for a few minutes early in the half. That is when Angela Smith began to heat up, scoring 18 of her 20 points in the second half. When Winner tied the game at 42 with 13:51 remaining, Smith immediately answered with a three. When Winner made another three-pointer three minutes later, Smith again responded with one of her own. Creager scored five straight points to cut the lead to four with 3:29 remaining, but Smith immediately answered with a three-point play, keeping the game out of reach. Bellarmine made nine free throws, mostly by Smith and Kopple, to seal the victory.

The one bright spot of the game, apart from our continuing effort after Bellarmine made play after play, was Healy's game on the inside. Bellarmine's tag-team post players Ashley Elmore and Ashley Lewallen had given fits to most of Bellarmine's opponents, including Grand Valley. Healy held Elmore to 5 points and Lewallen to 4 while scoring 16 herself—while also getting 9 rebounds and making 4 assists. The scariest moment for NKU came late in the second half, when Nicole went down hard, holding her neck and shoulder, after running into a pick. Noriko attended to her for quite a while before she was able to get up and leave the floor. I was surprised that she was able to reenter the game and make two free throws in the last minute.

Coach Smith was gracious after the game, saying it was a typical NKU-Bellarmine game—if it had gone another five minutes, either team could have won. He thought that many of our top GLVC teams would match up well with Grand Valley this year. We will see how true that is for ourselves in a week and a half. In the meantime, our players will take a week off from basketball, and from their daily practice, for final exams.

Winner wrote in her journal about the Bellarmine game:

There isn't really much to say. As a team we need to make changes, especially defensively, and until that happens, our season could continue to go this way. We executed and did good things on offense, but we couldn't stop them defensively. Yes, they shot a ridiculous 72% from behind the arc, but when you consider that figure you have to take into account our defensive intensity. Sometimes, yes, they just flat out knocked them down and they were "in the zone" or whatever you want to say. But other times we didn't have a hand in their face and they had wide open looks. Not to mention how many trips to the free throw line they had. Way too many.

I, for one, know that I need to do a better job on defense. But it's also something we need to work on as a team. Last year, it took us until about halfway through the season before another team scored more than 60 on us. Where did that defensive tenacity go? That's the difference between last year's team and this year's. We have improved tremendously on offense, but we're letting our D slide. . . . How can we get it back?

December 18 and 19: Travel America Classic Tournament—Northern Michigan and Grand Valley State

Our holiday home-court tournament would provide the toughest test of our early readiness. The four teams include three of the top 20 in the nation; number 3 Grand Valley State would be playing number 2 Emporia State in the first-night opener, followed by number 17 NKU against unranked Northern Michigan. The schedule for the second day matched Emporia State against Northern Michigan and Grand Valley against NKU. The two successive nights would give us a clear idea of whether we are currently good enough to be considered true contenders for the national championship. At this point, the answer has to be no.

Grand Valley and Emporia State played what felt like a preview of a national championship game. Grand Valley prevailed, 73–71, in overtime. The game was extremely exciting and very well played. NKU played well in its 68–46 victory over Northern Michigan. There was no reason, while watching this game, to think we could not compete on an equal basis with Grand Valley. Our comparatively easy victory over Northern Michigan, plus the home-court advantage, positioned us perfectly to establish our national credentials—and avenge last year's loss in the NCAA Regional—by beating Grand Valley. We did not. Their 74–58 victory over us was even worse than the score reflects. But first, the victory over Northern Michigan.

Northern Michigan came in with a 3–6 record. Three days earlier, however, they had scored an impressive 92–70 victory over Ashland, one of their GLIAC rivals. Our game with them, like those with Wayne State and Grand Valley, would affect our regional ranking at the end of the season. Winstel had stressed the importance of defense at the end of the 7 A.M. practice on Saturday the 16th. "We have a reputation as a defensive team. We have to get our reputation back. These teams are coming into our house and we have to send a message about the Great Lakes Valley Conference. We are going to give it our freaking best shot." This we did well against Northern Michigan, holding them to 46 points, half of what they had scored in their previous game. We held them to 32 percent of their field goals and 11 percent of their three-point shots, showing the kind of defensive tenacity that Winner had called for in her journal entry and Winstel in her last practice.

The offensive intensity was there too, in large part because Karmen Graham was back. The time off during finals week had obviously helped her injured knee, and for the first time this year she was playing like her old self, with 17 points on 5 of 7 from the field and 6 of 6 from the line. Brittany Winner was again exceptional in this game—14 points, 6 rebounds, 4 steals, 3 assists, and only 1 turnover. NKU came out strong, running to a 13–0 lead in the first five minutes. We then had a terrible dry spell for the next nine minutes, during which Northern Michigan cut the lead to 15–13 with 6:28 remaining. Katie Butler answered by scoring 8 points in the last six minutes to build a 30–18 halftime lead.

Winstel was quite happy with the defensive intensity in her postgame comments. She was happy that we held them in "the 40s," and she felt like we were getting back some of the defensive strength we had shown in the two preseason exhibition games. She was very happy to have Grammy back playing like herself. Karmen attributed our offensive success to our defensive intensity. "When we get stops on defense we're excited, we're ready to go, and then when we get to the offensive end of the court things will open up more for us."

Much of what worked against Northern Michigan did not work against Grand Valley. They beat us nearly as badly as they had in March. We simply could not stop them from scoring. Crystal Zick and Erika Ryskamp were nearly unstoppable at guard, much as they had been against Emporia State the night before. Zick had 27 points on 11 of 14 shooting, making 4 of 6 three-pointers. Ryskamp had 15 points on 5 of 7 from three-point range. Grand Valley as a team shot 62.5 percent from the field in building a 38–22 halftime lead. We shot much better in the second half, matching their 36 points in that period, but we never got closer than the 16-point deficit with which we began and ended the second half. Grand Valley was leading by 26 points with 10:43 remaining. Soon after that Karyn Creager scored 8 points in a row to keep the final score from being much worse than it was.

Any chance we had of mounting a challenge in the second half was dimmed when Grammy's head hit the floor hard, seeming to disorient her. She sat out much of the half and was taken to a hospital immediately after the game, where it was determined she had suffered a concussion, continuing the extreme bad luck of her senior year so far. Her cocaptains Winner and Creager led us in making the most of the rest of the game. Winner led NKU in scoring with 13, in rebounds with 6, and in assists with 4. Healy and Creager each scored 10. This was one of the few games in which neither Butler nor Brannen was able to provide much punch off the bench, with 4 and 1 points, respectively.

This game showed again our vulnerability to guards who can both drive and shoot. Zick and Ryskamp were Kopple, Smith, and Shelton all over again. At a practice after the Bellarmine game Winstel had tried to strengthen our perimeter defense with a new strategy. Instead of fighting through a screen at the top and getting beat for the drive if we could not get through, she had our defenders work on a high-and-low strategy in which the second defender would hedge high, above the screen, hoping to slow the player with the ball, while the primary defender dropped quickly under the screen to deny the drive on the other side. When introducing this possible adjustment, Winstel pointed out that it would also be "giving something away." It necessarily gives the player with the ball the space to shoot a quick three if she wants to take it. That was our problem with Zick and Ryskamp—each is equally adept at the drive and the three. In spite of NKU's best defensive effort, Grand Valley made 11 of its first 13 shots, with both Zick and Ryskamp making 3 of 3 three-pointers in the first half.

Before the season began, one question about Grand Valley was whether they could maintain their national-champion quality after losing All-American Niki Reams to graduation. Their back-to-back play against both Emporia State and NKU suggested that they could. One question about NKU before the season began was whether we could improve enough over the offseason and the preseason to be truly competitive with Grand Valley when they arrived here in December. This game showed that despite all our efforts we were not at their level. This emphatic 16-point home-court loss—

coming so soon after the losses to Edwardsville and Bellarmine—suggested we were moving farther from, rather than closer to, our goals. Things will not get any easier during the first week of January, when our first GLVC road trip takes us up to Parkside and Lewis. But before that, we have a holiday trip to Florida, with two basketball games followed by a day in the sun.

In an interview before the Emporia State game, Grand Valley coach Dawn Plitzuweit told me how she, upon arriving at Grand Valley five years ago, had studied the success of Winstel's program at NKU when deciding how she would like to build her own program. Now Grand Valley was raising the bar for others. In addition to the uniquely aggressive, assured, and often inspired level of play, Grand Valley exuded an energetic spirit that was absolutely palpable. Their warm-up drills included a team huddle in which they chanted at length as if they were warriors pumping up for the hunt. During the pregame introductions, their starters gave one another running chest bumps that put me in mind of Brittany Winner's earlier locker-room question: can you crack a sternum? During the game itself their bench was highly engaged and vociferous, generating a noise level that helped counter the home-court advantage of our fans, soon half-silenced by Grand Valley's sterling play. But Winstel always adjusts well, so if we should happen to meet Grand Valley again in March, the game will be well worth watching.

A few days after the loss to Grand Valley, Coach Winstel made an adjustment in my relation to her team. She asked me to "take a step back" and stop taking notes when I was watching a practice. She said it was beginning to bother her that "you have that pen out all the time"; this was inhibiting some of what she said to her players. I asked if she thought my note-taking had become a problem for the players too. She did not know. She did not yet see it as a "problem," but it was a "concern."

I had come to her office hoping to get permission to meet with the captains to learn how they were working through this devastating loss to Grand Valley so soon after the ones to Bellarmine and Edwardsville. She asked that I not seek a meeting with the captains at this time. She did not think it would help them to have someone asking them questions about what they were feeling while they were still struggling through the middle of it. "You can't imagine how emotional it is," she said, "either for me or for them." I was disappointed, but I understood her position. I knew she had her reasons for saying what she did, even if it was not something I wanted to hear. I was beginning to experience some of the ups and downs that Winstel and her players were themselves feeling.

This conversation made me reconsider my plans to travel to Florida with the team. I had been looking forward to that trip as a chance to spend a little more time with the players themselves—whom I had enjoyed getting to know during our interviews in May, but with whom it was quite difficult to have any extended conversations during the pressures of the regular season itself. And now, what I was most interested to learn—how they were adjusting to this extremely difficult time in the season—was off-limits for me. Since Winstel had already asked me to "take a step back," I decided not to go to Florida, inviting her to use the plane ticket I had purchased in September for whomever she would like to take in my place. She surprised me by saying, in response, "We need you to go." I was not sure why she said that, or exactly what she meant by it, but I decided to take her word for it and make the best of it.

December 28 and 29: Florida Southern Holiday Classic—College of St. Rose and Mercyhurst

Florida was not the best state for the skin cancer that had prompted the recent surgery on my nose. But Frank Lloyd Wright had designed much of the campus of Florida Southern University, and he had connected all his buildings with shady esplanades. A few steps in either direction and you could be in sun or shade as you pleased. This warm, sunny campus was the perfect place to ease a variety of hurts from the Grand Valley game by playing two days of quality basketball before having a day at the beach.

Our first opponent was the College of St. Rose from Albany, New York. They came into the game ranked number 22 in the nation with a 9–2 record—compared with our number 17 ranking now that we were 5–3. St. Rose's players were probably more aware than ours that NKU had given St. Rose one of its toughest losses in school history when we upset them in the Elite Eight on the way to the national championship in 2000. They had come into that game undefeated and ranked number 1 in the nation. They had two players from the Nigerian Olympic team, one of whom was a strong contender for National Player of the Year. Winstel recalls that the turning point of that game came when one of the Nigerian all-stars "drove nearly from midcourt to the basket and Michelle Cottrell stood up to her and took the charge. In addition to giving us the ball, Michelle's play gave their player her third foul. I wasn't sure Cott would get up, but when she did, the momentum had begun to change." The star of the second half of that game had been freshman Bridget Flanagan, who came off the bench to score all 13 of her points to seal the 60–50 victory. "Bridget had not done much in the first half," Winstel recalls, "and at halftime I told her, 'we need you.'"

The St. Rose program had no doubt looked forward to any chance to avenge this upset in the intervening six years. Nancy Winstel's current players were more concerned with showing that they could beat a nationally ranked team after losing so badly to Grand Valley. St. Rose was a well-balanced team averaging 72 points per game. Their three starting guards, Linsey Onishek, Mary Lewis, and Courtney Ludwig, gave them quickness, power, and points; they were averaging 15, 14, and 9 points a game. Lauren Revesz, a 6-foot-1 transfer from Ohio University, gave them plenty of punch on the inside; she was averaging 17 points a game. To win, we would have to play very well outside and inside at both ends of the court for 40 minutes. We did.

NKU led nearly all the way, taking a 31–26 halftime lead on to a 74–63 victory. These were the most aggressive 40 minutes we had played this season. But our play was still uneven. Early in the game we were pushing the ball hard upcourt and taking it with real force in toward the basket, but our timing was off and we missed far too many high-speed layups. St. Rose was ahead 13–9 after the first five minutes, but we then went on a 12–2 run on points from seven different players (including a three-pointer by freshman Lantry soon after she came off the bench). In the second half we maintained our lead as both teams played very well. Our defensive aggressiveness was very impressive, especially during the four-minute period in which we had four steals—two by Winner, one each by Creager and Chiodi. St. Rose answered this with a suffocating press. They reduced our seven-point lead to three with two consecutive steals and layups. This must have momentarily reminded our players of the way we had buckled under Drury's press a year earlier. But we then adjusted to the press, got a three-point play by Winner on a pass from Creager, and went on to clinch the game with 7 of 8 free throws, 5 of them by Healy.

Healy anchored this victory with perhaps the biggest game of her career, scoring 24 points on 6 of 9 shooting from the floor and 11 of 14 free throws. Equally impressive were her 16 rebounds, 13 of them off the defensive boards. No less remarkable was her defense against Revesz, who was held to 3 points in the first half and finished with 11. Our other double-figure scorer was Brittany Winner, who had 5 steals, 4 rebounds, and 3 assists in addition to 11 points. Her high-pressure floor game energized our offense in a way that is giving us an entirely different look this year. Her 5 steals were part of a team total of 9, something we could not have achieved against such a quality opponent last year. Our perimeter defense also pressured St. Rose's high-scoring guards into missing 16 of their 18 three-point shots. Our offensive pressure fouled four St. Rose players out of the game and resulted in our hitting 31 of 44 free throws. If we can play this hard for the rest of the season, strong and aggressive inside and out, we might indeed be national contenders before it is all over.

What Winstel liked most about the St. Rose game is that "our will was very strong, and in the end that goes a long way. We were focused. We worked hard. We played hard together. We didn't do everything great but we did a lot of good things. Late in the game we got a little sloppy with the ball, so we called a time-out. We kind of organized ourselves and told our players exactly what we wanted them to do, and they were able to do it."

Mercyhurst College in Erie, Pennsylvania, is another member of the GLIAC. They entered our game with a 4–8 record after losing a hard-fought game to tournament host Florida Southern, 72–67. They are a young team with some strong senior talent, which includes 6-foot forward Julie Anderson, who is completing a sterling four-year career that began with her winning GLIAC Freshman of the Year honors. Anderson hurt us with 23 points, 15 of them in the second half, but the game was never in doubt as we led by 34–18 at halftime and cruised to a 76–50 victory.

The star of the game was Karmen Graham, scoring 17 points on 5 of 8 from the field and 6 of 6 from the line. After having injured her knee on the day before the Tip-Off Luncheon and suffering a concussion in the second half of the Grand Valley game, she was now battling flu symptoms that had her going to the sideline during the pregame warm-up. Even so, she played with her customary reckless courage, diving to the floor for loose balls and once running almost full speed into the padded wall beyond the end line trying to make an impossible save. After that one, we all thought again, "I hope she gets up."

This was a game in which our motion offense continued to improve. One measure of this was four other players in double figures with 10: Winner, Chiodi, Creager, and Butler. Our 23 assists were also widely distributed; Chiodi had 6, Healy 5, Creager 4, and Winner 3. Many of these assists were pinpoint exquisite—such as the dart that Chiodi threw to Creager under the basket from well beyond the three-point line. We made more of our driving layups in this game, and we had three or four that were totally uncontested due to exceptional ball movement. If we can do this against top-notch teams at the end of the season, we will be a formidable offensive unit.

One reason that Anderson did so well against us is that Healy missed 11 minutes of the first half and much of the second half with foul trouble. Brannen, Butler, and Graham all filled in for her with some strong defense. Brannen intimidated Mercyhurst with four blocks. The one major disappointment in this game is that we let Mercyhurst make a 12–0 run early in the second half, keeping the game much closer than it should have been and reducing the playing time that otherwise could have been given to a number of our nonstarting players. Winstel was upset with her starters for not putting Mercyhurst away more convincingly so that their teammates, who contribute so much day after day in practice, could have had the playing time they deserved.

Two moments involving Karyn Creager sum up the impressive athleticism of the two games in Florida. When St. Rose put on the press near the end of the game, Karyn tried to break it once by throwing a long pass down the right sideline. That pass was absolutely gobbled up in an instantaneous leap by the defender right in front of her. Karyn matched that move when her opponent was launching a three in the Mercyhurst game, cleanly wrapping the ball in her long arms before it was even released. Karyn made all 6 of the free throws she shot in Florida, giving her 26 in a row, one shy of the school record she had set as a sophomore.

Our players had a large contingent of family and friends to witness the two victories in Florida. After saying good-bye to the Creagers, Grahams, Butlers, Clarks, Chiodis, and Brannens, who had cheered them on, the team piled into three vans driven by the coaches and streaked for the beach at Clearwater. A midnight curfew on the first night was followed by a full day in the sun on the beach. (One could only hope this would not result in too many burns on the bodies that would be playing up north at Parkside in Wisconsin on Thursday night.) All sun and no shade was a fine way to end a Florida trip whose two victories brought our record to a much more respectable 7–3.

Rather than dissect another game, Winner could write in her journal about a "spectacular" day that was "sunny, in the 80s, with a slight breeze. We used our time wisely—relaxing on the sand, wading in the chilly-but-bearable water, 'people watching,' browsing the shops, and even making new friends on the sand volleyball courts. A few of us stayed to watch the sunset over the Gulf from Pier 60 before finally heading back to the hotel after a full day in the sun." This day was Karen Brackman's birthday, so Brittany, Danyelle, and Keri went out with Bracky for dinner and then "spent the night celebrating and sharing stories . . . before turning to bed to get some sleep before an early morning departure for the Tampa Airport."

It was a delight to see our team in an entirely different atmosphere in Florida. The funniest moment came when we were all sitting in the lobby of the hotel in Clearwater and Katie Butler launched a hilarious burst of recollections by asking her teammates, "Do you all remember when Coach examined Angela's _____?" She was referring to a road trip during the previous season when some of the players had seen water seeping from the bathroom directly upstairs and had called on the coach to investigate whatever was plugging its toilet. Katie's way of phrasing the question provoked immediate laughter and commentary from all her teammates. Her mother is proud of her daughter's "way of saying just the right thing to loosen things up." I had now seen that firsthand.

My roommate in Florida was Mike Tussey, who announced the live radio broadcasts from Lakeland (his broadcast partner, Denny Wright, was currently with the men's team in Alabama). His biggest frustration as an announcer was trying to get a read on the players' exact medical conditions, especially that of Karmen. All he could get Coach Winstel to say is, "We're as healthy as we are going to be." This was not very specific, but it turned out to be quite accurate, especially in relation to Karmen. She had a few games, like Mercyhurst, when she played like her old self, but she never fully recovered from the injury to her knee. Nor was she able to lead us, day after day and week after week, in the way she had throughout the previous season.

I had not been able to learn much more than Tussey had about Karmen's injury, in spite of having attended so many practices. Noriko, as a medical professional, is not authorized to comment on a player's physical health to anyone beyond the coaching and medical staff. The coaches and players do not like to speak of injuries because they do not want to be seen as making excuses. I would not actually know the specifics of Karmen's knee injury until my exit interview with her when the season was over. Then she explained that it was a fracture of the femur behind the kneecap. At first she thought she had only "tweaked" the knee when she took an "awkward" fall in practice, since it was several days before the serious swelling began. The doctors had wanted her to sit out longer than she was willing to wait during the early weeks of the season, and she was still hoping surgery would not be required to repair the way it had healed as she had continued to play on it over the course of the season.

On the last day of the year Winstel's team flew from Tampa to Atlanta and then on to Dayton, Ohio, where the university bus met us for the two-hour ride back to campus. On January 3 the bus took the team on its first GLVC road trip of the season: to Wisconsin–Parkside and Lewis. After that trip was over, the final spring semester for Creager, Graham, Winner, Clark, and Butler would begin.

January 4 and 6:
Wisconsin–Parkside and Lewis

DeSimone Gymnasium in Kenosha has been one of our most difficult places to play, even in the best of seasons. Last year Wisconsin–Parkside ended our 16-game win streak with that 70–62 victory, in spite of having a 6–19 record at the time. Joking with our team in advance of the trip to Kenosha, Winstel had said, "They may as well take me straight to the bar when we get up there." This year Parkside was a much improved team, especially with the addition of two D-I transfers, twin sisters Kari and Carly Score. The Parkside team entered the game with a 9–3 record and a four-game win streak, one of those wins being over Quincy at Quincy. Coming off our two victories in Florida, we were hoping we could win this one before the even bigger challenge at Lewis two days later.

NKU played quite well in the first half against Parkside. We took a 29–27 lead into the locker room. We had played extremely well the first five minutes, building up a 14–8 lead. Then we hit a dry spell that allowed Parkside to pull to within one point with nine minutes remaining. At this point Katie Butler provided her customary lift off the bench, scoring seven points in the next five minutes to help us keep the lead at halftime.

The second half was a different story. Parkside outplayed us the entire half, scoring 39 points to our 28. Kari Score and Mackenzie Heise, who finished with 20 and 18 points, respectively, were driving for layups on pick-and-rolls that we were powerless to stop. Parkside shot 67 percent in the second half while we were shooting only 35 percent. We were getting very few shots from outside and were missing a high percentage of the layups we had in the paint.

The two bright spots in this game were Karyn Creager and Angela Healy. Creager was our only player who played extremely well in both halves, scoring 16 points and making all 7 of her free throws to set a new school record of 33 in a row. Healy scored 11 of her 15 points in the second half and led us with 8 rebounds, but she and Creager had very little offensive help in the second half. Butler had no points in the second half after 7 in the first. Chiodi had no points in the second half after 2 points in the first. Graham had 2 points in the second half after 2 points in the first. And Brannen had no points at all.

The second half of this game was extremely disappointing. If our poor shooting was in part owing to good defense by Parkside, their torrid shooting was even more owing to poor defense by us. After turning the ball over only four times in the first half, we made eight turnovers in the second half, often at crucial moments. Chiodi was struggling on both ends of the court during the 31 minutes she played. This was one of the rare games in which she had no assists. Nor did our team have a single block. It was an uncharacteristically weak team performance, even in a season that was itself uneven.

The toughest thing for Winstel to admit in the postgame interview was that our opponents "are competing at a higher level than we are. Last year our competitive level on defense was very high. This year we are not playing as hard as we consistently need to do for 40 minutes. I hate to say that but it's the truth of the matter. Our fire is not there and I don't know why." Last year we had "no pressure" and we played better than people expected. This year we have "higher expectations and we are not handling it very well. Everyone wants to beat us because we have that target on our back. But that target is starting to come off."

NKU and Lewis were reversing positions from last year. Then they were favored to win the GLVC East and we were ranked third. Yet we won the division and beat them both times we played. This year we were favored to win the division and they were ranked third. But we were now arriving at their Neil Carey Arena with a 1–3 conference record compared with their record of 3–1. Their most recent victory was a 76–57 drubbing of Bellarmine on the night we were losing to Parkside. While we were in Florida they had beat Grand Valley State 63–52. We were still ranked number 18 in the nation, and Lewis was unranked. They knocked us off the charts with a 75–64 victory, elevating their own team to number 16.

There was no disgrace in losing to a Lewis team playing as well as they had been playing. They entered our game with a five-game win streak during which they had defeated three of the best teams in the region (Grand Valley, Bellarmine, and Edwardsville). Their one-two punch of Darcee Schmidt and Mary Moskal had been impossible for anyone to stop. Schmidt came into the game having scored 30 against Grand Valley and 33 against Bellarmine; she scored 32 against us. Moskal, after scoring 11 against Grand Valley and 14 against Bellarmine, had 23 against us. Against NKU, Schmidt made 13 of 22 field goals and 4 of 6 three-pointers. Moskal made 6 of 11 field goals and 11 of 15 free throws. Together, their 55 points were within 9 of our entire team's.

We would have needed an exceptional offensive game to win against this team. We did have four players in double figures (Creager and Healy had 13, followed by Graham and Butler with 12). But as a team we shot poorly, making only 37 percent of our field goals, 33 percent of our three-pointers, and 69 percent of our free throws. NKU started the game very well, leading 10–8 after the first four minutes on three-pointers by Graham and Creager and baskets by Creager and Winner. After Lewis went on a run to lead by eight with 10 minutes remaining, NKU battled back to take a one-point lead on a three-pointer by Katie Butler with 4 minutes remaining. But Lewis then went on a 14–2 run to lead 44–33 at the half.

The best thing about this game was the way we bounced back in the second half. After allowing two layups by Darcee Schmidt in the first minute, we reduced a 14-point deficit to 2, at 59–57, when Brannen made a layup on an assist by Winner with 8:53 remaining. Lewis finally missed some shots (four players combined to miss five three-pointers in a row), but NKU could not take advantage. We committed two turnovers and four fouls as Lewis built their lead back up to seven with our hardly taking a shot. We were unable to threaten after that. We walked off the Lewis court with a different kind of record than we had been expecting to set. We had now lost four straight GLVC games, something no NKU team had done since beginning league play in 1985. The most disappointing element of those four losses was that only the first one—to Edwardsville—was even close in the final score.

Winstel did find a few bright spots in her postgame radio interview with Mike Tussey. Schmidt and Moskal were "tough to stop." Even so, "we had them where we wanted them" in the middle of the second half. But then "they made some plays and we didn't." Brittany was called for a key turnover when we had a chance to tie the game in the second half, but otherwise she had another strong game, especially "since she is playing point for us right now." Winner was on the point for most of the game because Winstel had started Rachel Lantry in place of Chiodi. This was the first time Nicole had not started since early in her sophomore year. Winstel was clearly ready to do anything necessary to help her team get its rhythm back, but Lantry and Chiodi were both scoreless in their combined 21 minutes of play. So that put even more pressure on the other perimeter players. Another particular frustration of this game was that "we worked hard to get the ball inside but we didn't finish. We missed too many easy shots inside."

Clearly the team had reached a turning point in the season. To start out 1–4 in the GLVC, with the league being even tougher than last year, makes any kind of postseason success an uphill battle. To drop from number 12 in the nation to an unranked team in a four-week period was a shocking development for a Winstel team. With nearly everyone back from a 27–5 season, these players had expected to make a run at being the best in the nation. At the moment, they were in sixth place out of seven in the GLVC East. Last year these players did not lose their 5th game of the season until the 32nd game they played, in the second round of the NCAA Tournament. This year they lost their 5th game in the 12th game they played, on a GLVC road trip in the first week of January.

Had expectations not been so high, there would have been many things to celebrate. This team, in spite of its many problems, was

shooting exceedingly well. Going into the Parkside game Katie Butler and Angela Healy were leading the GLVC in field goal percentage
at 57.1 and 55.3. Butler was leading the league in three-point shooting (54.5 percent), and NKU was leading the league in team field
goal percentage, making 50.5 percent of its shots (this was the highest in NCAA Division II basketball; only a few Division I teams had
a higher percentage at this point in the season). NKU was second in
the GLVC with a team free-throw average of 78.3 percent. Karyn
Creager made her 34th in a row before missing one at Lewis, giving
her 89.4 percent for the season. She was closely followed by Angela
Healy and Karmen Graham at 88.1 and 86.1 percent. NKU led the
GLVC in blocked shots, having blocked 57 in its first 10 games, far
ahead of the next best team. But our perimeter defense was still
killing us, especially against guards who could both drive and
shoot. It would have to improve dramatically for us to be a factor in
the conference, much less the nation, after returning home for the
new semester.

Last year's season was now, in retrospect, an absolute dream.
Then, the team had played exceptionally well throughout January
and February and into March, putting the December loss to Drury
behind them and becoming one of the most exciting, disciplined,
and captivating teams in the history of the program. Now, 11 of the
same players, who should have been so much better this year, were,
as a team, doing worse—in spite of the devotion they had shown to
the game, and to one another, in the offseason as well as the preseason. In the first 12 games of this season, the team had lost its
national ranking and some of its confidence.

The most obvious reason for the team's situation would have to
be the injuries suffered by Karmen Graham. To lose your best
player, leading scorer, and All-American candidate would be a severe challenge to any team. Karmen had been our heart and soul
last year; this year she was giving her all on a wounded leg. Even so,
something more was missing. Whether the missing ingredient was
best defined as fire, intensity, chemistry, or desire, this year's team
had not yet found the rhythm and confidence these same players
had generated and sustained for two-thirds of the previous season.

As Winstel began saying in December, this year's team had not yet found the chemistry *on* the court that they had *off* the court.

Rediscovering that on-court chemistry will be the most important challenge for the 12 players—and the three coaches—for the rest of the season. If they are able to re-create it, the wins and losses should take care of themselves—at least to the extent of returning to the conference tournament. If they are not able to regain that chemistry, this team might have a real chance of exceeding Winstel's worst-ever record at NKU, the 16–12 record during the sophomore year of Graham, Creager, Clark, and Winner.

The mood of the five-hour bus ride home from Lewis was not at all what the players had hoped for or expected. As they rolled past the cold, empty Indiana farmland in the dark, this team was deep in "the bleak mid-winter" of its season (in the words of a Christmas hymn). They needed the "blade of green grass" (in the answering Easter hymn). And they needed it soon.

8

FINDING WHAT WE NEED

Success is counted sweetest
By those who ne'er succeed.
To comprehend a nectar
Requires sorest need.
—*Emily Dickinson*

Fourteen games remain in the regular season. Eight of the fourteen teams in the GLVC will qualify for the conference tournament. If the selection were made after the loss to Lewis, we would not be among them. Yet if we are able to play at our best for the next two months, we will again be in Roberts Stadium in Evansville for the first weekend in March. And if we are there when the tournament begins, those old dreams might well be rekindled.

Soon after returning home from the Lewis game, Angela Healy poured her hopes for the rest of the season into a poem she posted on the locker of each of her teammates. Its opening section begins by describing everything she loves about their team as a whole:

Each of us has a number behind our name.
Put ten in a gym and you have a game.

The numbers seem to run the show.
But there's way more to it, and this we know.

FINDING WHAT WE NEED

Behind the digits are sweat and tears.
And some of our most precious years.

Do you remember when you were small?
And a basketball jersey is what you wanted, that's all?

Sometimes we forget our childish love for our sport.
And winning becomes our only focus on the court.

Yea, when you win, everything's great.
But working towards our goals, we can't start to hate.

Do you realize what an amazing team we are?
And by team I mean best friends from near and far.

Angela then provides rhymed snapshots of each of her teammates:

Let's start by looking at each individual lady.
The craziest of all would have to be Katie.

And then there's Keri who takes it all in.
And D who gets mad if the socks are not in the bin.

Don't forget about Rachel who gets lost out there.
And Unit who wears too large of underwear.

Creags can brighten your day with her smile.
And Bdubs can run a 4-minute mile.

Brackman looks confused when she makes "the face."
And Gwammy can thrill you with all her grace.

Betsey makes the most delicious Christmas candy.
And Cassie's gramma dancing is really a dandy.

Ed sometimes acts like a funny child.
All twelve are what makes us so fun and wild!

She calls on her teammates to believe in themselves and one another:

No matter which number is the hero that day,
What makes us special is you can't take any away.

The names in front of the numbers are what make up our team.
Put us all together and we start to beam.

God gave each of us talent to make our dreams come true.
He knows your biggest fears, but is still so confident in you.

So dig deep within yourself and find your passion.
Let's play the rest of the season in badass fashion.

That last rhyme provided inspiration for the rest of the season.

Betsey Clark, like many of her teammates, loved the poem because it was "funny." But it also "just kind of calmed all of us. We were so uptight and upset about how the season was going. And then you come in here and have the poem from Angela about the whole team. In kind of a weird way, it put in perspective all the time and work you spend your entire life to get to this point. And then not to enjoy it is ridiculous. It kind of put a different twist on it."

I did not learn about Angela's poem, or the influence it had on her teammates, until she mentioned it casually after the season was over. Reading it gave me a better understanding of something Angela's parents had said when I interviewed them on the night of the Georgetown game. "Angela is one of those persons who initially, until she gets a real feel for a situation, is observant. And then once she's comfortable, and once she kind of has permission and affirmation, she does become a natural leader."

January 11 and 13: Missouri–Rolla and Missouri–St. Louis

The GLVC schedule is finally being a little kinder to us, at least for one week. Missouri–Rolla and Missouri–St. Louis are doing as badly in the Western Division as we are in the East. They currently occupy the fifth and sixth spots in the seven-team division, with league records of 2–4 and 1–4, respectively. If we play well we have a chance for two strong victories that will ripen our record and boost our confidence.

Monday is the first day of the new semester and the first practice after the loss to Lewis. We have now reversed practice times with the men's team, so daily practice will begin at 3:00 and end at 5:30. I arrive a little after 4:00 and we are working at making good passes into the post. All year we have had so many passes just miss—or just miss being converted. All 12 players are out on the floor, and no one seems inhibited in any major way by injuries. Until Karmen goes suddenly down. It must have been a fluke accident. I did not see how it happened. But there she is, crying out in great pain, pounding her fist on the floor in frustration.

For a long time she is on her stomach and I am not sure what is wrong. After Winstel talks to her, and they take more time to see the extent of the injury, Winstel moves the practice to the other end of the court while Noriko attends to Karmen. For at least five more minutes Karmen is not allowed to move. When Noriko finally helps her up, she seems to have severely sprained the ankle on the leg opposite the one with the bad knee and the brace.

For the rest of the practice Karmen sits with Noriko in the front row of the stands beyond the end line, her newly injured leg stretched straight out with a huge ice pack over the ankle. By the time Winstel calls for each player to make 100 free throws at the end of the practice, Grammy has her foot back in the shoe and is rebounding for her teammates. She even shoots a couple of free throws herself. I am guessing she will want to be out there tomorrow, practicing for Thursday's game.

Before this happened, during a water break, her teammates had again been kidding her about how she falls, saying that when she goes down she just dives way out, instead of protecting herself. My stomach dropped when I saw her fall and heard her cry out. Losing even more of her game is the last thing that she, or the team, needs.

The players seem to be playing hard and concentrating well in practice. Had I not known it, I would not have been able to recognize the two-game losing streak in their demeanor. Cassie looks especially strong today. Once she went up for a pass with her back to the basket and, without landing or putting the ball on the ground, spun in the air for a beautiful two. If she can do moves like that consistently, we are going to be hard to stop.

Winstel's biggest frustration during the part of the practice I saw came when the white team (essentially, the starting team) was passing the ball in an offensive formation. Stopping practice, she pointed to the three spot at the upper left and said, "That spot is open for whoever wants it. Doesn't anybody want it? DOESN'T ANYBODY WANT IT? I don't understand."

Nicole was one of the guards who was reluctant to shoot the three that day. She was also reluctant to go to the coach's office to ask about something that bothered her, but she did go. She had been hurt by Winstel's decision to start Lantry at point guard in the Lewis game. She did not understand it, and she did not believe she should be penalized for the failings of the whole team. She had been giving everything she had—in spite of the pain she was still feeling from that shoulder injury at Bellarmine.

"I was not happy at all, and I wanted to get to the bottom of it and figure it out right away, because you don't want things to kind of draw out like that. So I went in and I talked to Coach Winstel. I asked for her opinion and she listened to me and what I had to say. After that we had some good days in practice and things got better again. You want to make sure you get things figured out, not only for you but also the team, because you don't want to be upset and down when you're around your teammates."

After Nicole said what was on her mind, Winstel told her exactly why she had not started her in that game and exactly what she needed to do to return to the starting lineup. Winstel asked Nicole if she was hurt, and Nicole said, "No." They both remember exactly what Winstel said next: "If you're not hurt, then quit playing like you're hurt, because you sure do look like you're hurt."

Winstel was glad that Nicole had come in to speak with her. "I had the utmost respect that she did that. It took a lot of guts, and we talked it out. I know she was upset with me, but I also think her shoulder was bothering her more than she wanted to admit."

Nicole was back in the starting lineup for the Missouri–Rolla game. She remained there for the rest of the season, performing at an increasingly high level as her shoulder continued to heal. She still could not shoot the three-pointer as often as she would like, but she made up for that, in part, by intensifying her rebounding and floor game.

I also made a short visit to the coach's office after the team returned from Lewis. I told Winstel that I had a new chapter of the book for her to read. Until now, she has been reading each chapter and making very helpful comments. Now, she tells me, she can no longer do that. Not until the season is over. She has to focus all her attention on helping her team. She says she is torn between two roles—trying to nurture her players as they all work hard to be better, but also having to take the parental role by showing them where they need to be. "It's just like being a parent," she says. It is clearly not easy for her, or them, to be where they are right now. It probably does not help that this is the one season in her career that I have chosen to write about. She says again, for the second time, how essential it is to win both games this week. "I don't have to tell them that."

After the losses to Parkside and Lewis, I am feeling an even greater need to find out how the players are processing these tough developments in their season. When I explain to Winstel how frustrating it is to write about these losses without any direct access to how the players are responding to them, she gives me permission to seek out a conversation with the captains. But now the players themselves are too absorbed with working things through—and the first week of the new semester—to want to talk about it. They, too, prefer to wait until the season is over.

On Tuesday I again come to practice shortly after 4:00. Everyone but Karmen is on the floor. She is sitting out this practice in the hope of practicing on Wednesday and playing on Thursday. She says the ankle is only a bad sprain, but when she went down it had hurt so bad she feared it was broken.

Today the drama is head high, not flat on the floor. I do not see exactly what provokes it, but suddenly Winstel is on Butler in a way

201

I had not seen before. This is a sequel to the "We have to work on our relationship" speech I had witnessed earlier, when Katie's defensive play had not pleased the coach. But this encounter is entirely different. It is as blunt and forceful as one could possibly imagine. Stopping practice so that everyone has to see, hear, and feel every word, Winstel calls her senior down. I am no longer taking notes at practice, but the gist of it was something like this: "KATIE, I'M TIRED OF YOU NOT PLAYING DEFENSE. I DON'T CARE HOW MANY THREE-POINTERS YOU MAKE, IF YOU ARE NOT GUARDING ANYONE AND THEY MAKE MORE POINTS THAN YOU DO, YOU ARE NOT HELPING THE TEAM. YOU HAVE BEEN WITH US MORE THAN A YEAR NOW AND YOU ARE STILL NOT PLAYING DEFENSE. YOU HAVE 14 GAMES LEFT AND IT IS TIME TO SHOW YOU CAN DO SOMETHING. IF YOU DON'T PLAY DEFENSE, YOU WILL NOT BE IN THE GAME."

Everyone is standing stock still. Katie stands straight and looks at the coach as each word is said. The challenge is clear as can be. It will be interesting to see how Katie reacts. With Karmen's playing time and mobility compromised even more by the severe ankle sprain, we need Katie on the floor in the post. But if she cannot, or will not, play defense, Winstel will continue to use her only as a role player when we need points on the board.

For the rest of the practice everyone seems to be working hard. When someone other than Butler has a defensive lapse, Winstel stops the practice and says, "A while ago I got after Katie for her defense. So I have to get after you too. It is not just Katie or any other single player. It has to be all of us." The rest of the practice goes quite well. But we are still looking to find that rhythm we had for much of last year.

Cassie again started in place of Karmen against Missouri–Rolla. She would start every game for the rest of the season. But Karmen was able to suit up and get in the game. In fact, she played 20 minutes and scored 5 points, giving her 1,003 for her career. She is the twenty-second NKU player to make that 1,000-point milestone, with 13 games left to play in the regular season.

Our team played well against Rolla. Nicole Dierking is one of the outstanding players in the conference, averaging 14 points a game. Brittany Winner, playing 34 minutes, held her to 8 points. (Winner set the tone on the first play of the game, stealing the ball from Dierking and passing it to Chiodi, who got it to Healy for a layup with 19:35 remaining.) Rolla's point guard Tamara McCaskill, averaging 15 points a game, was also held to 8 points by a team of perimeter defenders. In fact, no one for Rolla scored in double figures. We held them to a field goal percentage of 33 for the game, 26 in the first half. We led at halftime 30–17—quite a defensive achievement, since Rolla was averaging 68 points per game.

Our offensive stars were Creager and Butler. Karyn set the tone during the first half in one of the best all-around games of her career. In addition to scoring 17 points she led our team with 5 assists and 3 steals while also grabbing 6 rebounds. The 16 assists by the team were more than we have had for some time; Karyn was cutting for scores as well as she was passing to others. Seven minutes into the first half Healy passed to Creager for a layup and a 12–6 lead. Our next time down the court Creager cut to the basket for another layup, this one on a precision pass from Grammy from out beyond the three-point line. We still held that 8-point lead when Butler came in with 7:55 remaining. Her 5 points, plus three-pointers by Brackman and Creager, helped boost us to the 13-point halftime lead.

Rolla never threatened in the second half. Fifteen more points by Butler helped make sure they never had a chance to. Her 20 points for the game were her season high. Katie played a good floor game too, blocking three shots and pulling down eight rebounds in 22 minutes of play. For this game, to be sure, she had risen to the coach's challenge. Her active play at both ends of the court was essential in a game in which our other three post players were seriously hampered in one way or another. Graham played gamely on her recovering knee and newly sprained ankle, but she was not herself. Healy was having foul trouble throughout this game and eventually fouled out. Cassie also had foul trouble, picking up her second foul six minutes into the game, which sent her to the bench for the rest of the half. She never came back. Before the first half was over she got one of her attacks of lightheadedness that sent her to the locker room with Noriko. She watched the second half from the bench but was unable to play.

As Marc Hardin of the *Kentucky Post* was interviewing Winstel after the game, he noted that Katie Butler had played more minutes and scored more points in this game than in any previous one. He also recalled that Winstel had spoken more than once about Butler's need to play better defense if she wanted to get more playing time. So he asked Winstel whether she had given Butler any special favors in practice this week because her offense was so important to the team. Winstel assured him that she did not (as anyone who saw the Tuesday practice could certainly confirm!). Although this was a good victory, and a much needed one, Winstel was not about to let her guard down. Her team was still "struggling." And "the worst thing that could happen to us is not losing. It's falling apart as a team. And I'll be darned if we are going to let that happen."

Later, when I found out about the poem Angela had written, I asked Winstel if she thought it had helped the team play well that week. "Obviously, it helped them tremendously. We were struggling and trying to find our way, we were trying to do things to help us believe in ourselves, and she went and put that together and put it on her kids' lockers. At the time she did it, I thought, 'If this doesn't help, they're not paying much attention, because this kid is putting her soul out there.' I think she put into words what a lot of them wanted to say."

Last year Missouri–St. Louis had been one of our tougher opponents—especially during the January game on their court, which we had won only because Karmen was fouled while Katie's three-point shot was bouncing high in the air, giving us the five-point play and three-point lead. UMSL still had 6-foot-1 Jennifer Martin, now a senior, one of the best post players in the league. This year she was averaging 12 points and 7 rebounds a game, but their only other double-figure scorer was guard Taylor Gagliano. Again, the NKU defense did a sterling job in the first half, holding Martin to 1 point, Gagliano to 2, and the entire UMSL team to 19. Their 44 points for the game was the lowest total for any opponent since the 42 scored by Midway in the season opener. Healy led the way in our defense against Martin in the post, but she was helped out enormously by Cassie Brannen, who blocked five shots, many of them in the first half, as we entirely shut Martin down. NKU recorded 10 blocks for the game, matching the number against Quincy in the conference tournament back in March. Two of the other blocks were by Butler, but the other three were by guards: Winner, Clark, and Lantry.

Apart from the defense against Martin, the most striking element of this game was the all-around team effort at both ends of the court. In addition to the 10 blocks, the team had 18 assists and 13 steals. Chiodi led the scoring with 12 points, followed by Winner and Butler with 11, Brannen with 10, and Healy with 8. Butler and Brannen led in rebounds with 7, followed by Healy with 6. Chiodi led in assists with 5, one on a pass to Healy on the first play of the game. On our next possession Nicole passed to Brannen for another layup—after Cassie had blocked Martin at the other end of the court. Halfway through the second half we scored four consecutive layups on beautifully executed passes, showing the interchangeability of our players and their skills.

We fans had almost forgotten how fluid this team could look when all was going well. We were beginning to see some of that passion and precision we had seen last year. This was another game in which offense and defense were feeding off each other. Chiodi playing 36 minutes of such efficient, energetic, and tenacious ball does wonders for our team. To see Brannen block and shoot and defend so well, two days after having to leave the bench for the locker room before the end of the first half, was a great relief. Karyn Creager was one player who struggled offensively in this game, scoring only one point and missing all six field goals after having had such a superb game against Rolla. In the second half, however, Winstel put her on point guard Courtney Watts, the only player who had done much damage in the first half, and Karyn shut her down for the rest of the game, getting two steals and forcing other turnovers.

Karyn's play early in the game may have been affected by the absence of her parents, who had attended every previous game she had played in Regents Hall. On their three-hour drive down to this night's game, Dale and Kathy Creager had been hit by another car near Lima, Ohio. Their van, in which their son, daughter-in-law, and grandson were also riding, was severely damaged, but none of its passengers suffered serious injury. After this game I met Karen Brackman's parents for the first time. Her father, Jim, is in the farm supply business and sometimes sells equipment to Brittany's father, Earl. It is a small world in Minster, as well as in Highland Heights.

In the two games against Rolla and UMSL this week the team did more good things at both ends of the court than it had done in a long time. The next challenge would be to do the same against two of the best teams in the conference, on the road. Winstel was very happy with these two home-court victories, but "when you go on the road, you have to have an attitude about you, and I'm not sure we have that. *I* have it." Edwardsville had that attitude in Regents Hall. So did Grand Valley. Our team needs to take that kind of attitude on the road to Kentucky Wesleyan and Southern Indiana.

January 18 and 20: Kentucky Wesleyan and Southern Indiana

Kentucky Wesleyan had clearly become one of the toughest teams in the conference. As we were beating UMSL at home on Saturday night, they were beating Edwardsville at Edwardsville by a commanding 95–87 score. This gave them a 5–2 record in the GLVC and a 12–3 record overall; at home in the Owensboro Sportscenter they were 7–1. Against Edwardsville they made 14 three-pointers, with junior Laura McClintic and freshman Latoshia Lawrence making 5 apiece. Lawrence scored 25 points from her guard position, with McClintic adding 17. Closer in, Lauren Stewart and LaTasha Henry scored 19 and 12 points. This would clearly be another game in which our perimeter defense, and our defense in general, would be challenged.

We met that challenge with the best game we had played all year. The key was our defense, especially in the first half, when we held Kentucky Wesleyan to 16 points; they made only 5 of 26 shots from the field. In addition to shutting down their outside game, we beat them badly inside, outrebounding them 28–15 in the first half and 40–30 for the game. The defensive pressure was relentless as we ran out to a 7–0 lead in the first three minutes. In those three minutes, Cassie Brannen blocked two jumpers by LaTasha Henry, Karyn Creager blocked a jumper by Lauren Stewart, and Nicole Chiodi stole the ball from McClintic. Wesleyan never recovered in the first half. NKU led by 30–16 at halftime.

Yet Wesleyan made a game of it in the second half. NKU was still up by 13 with 9:09 remaining. McClintic hit a three-pointer to cut the lead to 10. She then made three more three-pointers, from ever-increasing range, incredibly high-arching shots. Henry heated up inside too, and suddenly Wesleyan had reduced our lead to 3, 48–45, with 2:48 remaining. NKU met this challenge by scoring 6 unanswered points by Creager, Healy, and Chiodi. With 1:20 remaining McClintic answered with a three-pointer, reducing the lead to 6. Chiodi then made two free throws in a row to give us the 8-point cushion we needed. After Wesleyan made four consecutive free throws, Creager made sure McClintic would not hurt us again by stealing the ball from her and driving for a layup. Free throws by Karmen Graham closed out the victory, as we made 7 of 8 during the last two and a half minutes (and 15 of 16 for the game).

Our balance was again enviable. Creager and Graham led the scoring with 11, followed by Healy with 10, Brannen with 9, and Winner and Chiodi with 8. But it was not so much the evenness of the points as the timing of the contributions that made this victory so impressive. When Wesleyan rallied toward the end of the first half, Karmen Graham came off the bench to score 8 points, 6 of them in a three-minute stretch, to keep our lead in double digits. Winner also scored all 8 of her points in the first half, playing her high-intensity floor game at both ends of the court. Creager, Healy, and Chiodi did almost all their scoring in the second half, as we withstood the Wesleyan challenge and held on for one of our most important victories of the season. Creager and Chiodi scored many of their points in the last 2:33 minutes, with the game on the line. Healy held us together in the middle of the second half, before McClintic made her run. Katie Butler scored only 2 points in this game, but she pulled down 10 rebounds to contribute to our huge advantage in that category.

What enabled our players to achieve such a commanding victory in a must-win game on the road? In part, they may have been responding to the main point Winstel had made in the team huddle at the end of practice on Tuesday. She told her players we have too often waited to respond to what the opponent does to us instead of taking the game into our own hands from the very beginning. Against Wesleyan we did exactly that, imposing our defensive will on them. They never entirely recovered. As Brittany Winner wrote in her journal, "This game really showed everyone that we were not ready to let go of our chance to play for the GLVC Championship."

Also, the team's performance in this game may have been a carryover from the way practice had ended on Monday. That day only 11 players were on the floor; Karmen was in the training room trying to get her right knee and left ankle in good enough shape to be able to practice the next day. After devoting quite a bit of time to defending against Wesleyan's offensive sets, Winstel ended the practice with the drill she calls 4:04. In this drill the players have four minutes and four seconds to make 68 layups while running full speed to both ends of the court in both directions, each made layup being passed to a player running full tilt to the other end of the court. Zach was keeping the time clock. After he saw two missed layups he said, "They're not going to make it." Sure enough, when the buzzer went off they had 32 at one end and 32 at the other for 64, not 68. So they had to run it again.

This time they ran even harder, some absolutely sprinting each time, and they shot with more care, too, making every shot I saw. But one player made an errant pass to the downcourt breaker, losing several full seconds in retrieving and returning the ball, and this proved fatal. This time they made 32 and 34 for a total of 66.

Only on the third try did they master the 4:04 drill. Winstel had given them a little time to catch their breath. Then, with everyone running extra hard, passing especially well, and finishing every shot, calling loudly in encouragement to one another all the way, they ran this one almost flawlessly, without an error, a hitch, or a miss, making 69. The concentration this took for every player for the entire drill, and for the team itself as an organism, was a metaphor for the focus and high-speed intensity they would need for the whole game if they were to beat Wesleyan in Owensboro on Thursday.

When I asked Winstel about this drill the next day, she said it is great for conditioning, passing, catching, and shooting on the run—all areas in need of improvement. She also said that earlier in the season she had required them to make only 66 shots in 4:04. She knew she was raising the bar. So did they. And they responded. They each had to dig deep, individually and as a team, to achieve it in their third attempt.

Winstel has had some previous teams that could not come close to making 66, much less 69, in four minutes. She adjusts her expectations every year according to the skills and conditioning of her players, always pressing the current year's group to get better and better. Monday was the perfect day to challenge the team with this drill because Karmen was not on the floor. Subjecting her knee and ankle to this particular drill, three times over, would not have been good for the healing process, though Karmen, of course, would have done it.

How things change! On January 6, when we lost to Lewis to go 1–4 in the GLVC, Southern Indiana upset Drury to go 5–0 in the conference and 11–2 overall. Since then they have lost three conference games in a row while we have won three in a row. If we could beat them in the P. A. C. Arena on January 20 (where their only loss was to Bellarmine on Thursday night), we would suddenly be even with them at 5–4 in the conference. We do beat them, 70–56, in a game very much like the victory over Kentucky Wesleyan two nights earlier.

In this game too we got off to a good start and never lost the lead. Again we held a high-scoring team to a total in the teens in the first half (our halftime lead was 30–19). Again we totally disarmed our opponent's top scorers in the first half. Guard Katie Thiesenhusen entered the game averaging 13.3 per game; Karyn Creager held her scoreless in the first half. Forward Jasmine Baines, their top inside scorer, was also held scoreless in the first half, in large part by the long arms and quick feet of Cassie Brannen. Guard Akia Alexander, who had scored 22 in a recent game against Quincy, scored only 2 points in the first half—a half in which Brittany Winner stole the ball from her three different times. As at Wesleyan, we also won the rebounding battle.

Offensively we had exceptional balance among our top four scorers. Winner led with 17, followed by Brannen with 14, Creager with 13, and Healy with 12. Each of these players did much more than score points. Brittany's 17 points were her highest total for the season, but equally important were her 5 steals and 6 rebounds while giving Alexander fits the whole game. Cassie had 5 rebounds and 2 blocks in addition to her 14 points; she completely flustered Southern Indiana's inside game in the early going. Karyn played an excellent floor game in addition to shutting down Thiesenhusen in the first half; she finished the game with 4 rebounds, 4 assists, and 2 steals. Angela had 12 points on 5 of 7 from the field while also pulling down 9 rebounds and teaming with Brannen to shut down Southern Indiana's inside game.

The exceptional performances by Winner, Brannen, Creager, and Healy helped overcome relatively low scoring by Chiodi, Butler, and Graham, who finished with 4, 4, and 3 points. In spite of our fast start and early lead, we faced a serious challenge when Healy got her second foul with 9:54 remaining in the first half. Our lead was 11–9 at the time, and this put Angela on the bench for the rest of the half alongside Nicole, who had picked up her second foul with 13:43 remaining in the half. This was a point at which we could have lost ground quickly. But instead we went on a 23–10 run for the rest of the half for our 34–19 halftime lead. In Chiodi's absence Winner took over the point guard position; after Healy's second foul Winner took over the game. In the last nine minutes of the first half Brittany had 9 points, 3 rebounds, 3 assists, and a steal while also keeping Alexander almost shotless.

This game still left us with much to work on. We had 23 turnovers, 8 of them by Winner. Our substitute point guard was somewhat flustered by a pressing defense. Nicole had one of her least productive games of the season; fortunately, Brittany compensated for this in many positive ways. Any weaknesses in this game were more than made up for by the intensity of our defensive play, especially in the first half. In her postgame interview Winstel said, "We were so aggressive in the first half, I thought the worst thing that happened was we had to stop for halftime. Sometimes you leave your aggressiveness in the locker room. I told our players [that] with this crowd and in this place, if they made a run, we could be in trouble. We did not let up, and this was a great road trip to beat a couple of very good teams."

While our team was traveling down the Ohio River for the games in Owensboro and Evansville, some of their local basketball acquaintances were playing a historic game back home in Cincinnati. For many decades the Crosstown Shootout between the men's teams of Xavier and the University of Cincinnati has been one of the premier events of the winter basketball season. This year, for the first time, the game between the women's teams of these two universities became a civic event of real importance. With the help of some prominent boosters, Cincinnati's Fifth Third Arena was sold out. The crowd actually in attendance was estimated at 10,500. They saw a game in which Cincinnati led by as much as 14 in the first half, but Xavier came back to win it by a final score of 89–76. Cincinnati got another strong game from Michelle Jones, Cassie Brannen's former teammate at Mount Notre Dame High School, who had 18 points and 10 rebounds. Her effort was topped, however, by Xavier's super freshman Amber Harris. Harris took over in the second half, when she scored 23 of her 32 points and put the game out of reach. The *Cincinnati Post* covered the game as a major event, and Lonnie Wheeler raised some eyebrows when he called Harris "the most highly recruited player ever to grace our humble city, men included" (move over Oscar Robertson and Kenyon Martin).

Harris's display against Cincinnati made it even more evident that Brittany Winner and Karyn Creager had been playing against two of the best players in the nation when they guarded Harris and Tara Boothe in the open gym workouts against Xavier during the summer. In early November our entire team had shown they could step up against first-rate SEC and Big Ten teams in the exhibitions against Kentucky and Indiana. Now we were beginning to bring some of the defensive intensity we had shown in those two games to bear against some of our better GLVC competition. After these two road victories over Kentucky Wesleyan and Southern Indiana, it feels like we will finally be ready to do better against Bellarmine, Parkside, and Lewis when they come to Regents Hall in February—and even against Grand Valley if we meet them in March. Our

11–5 record at the end of this road trip is quite similar to those of our female counterparts at Cincinnati (11–6), Kentucky (13–6), Indiana (13–7), and Xavier (14–6). All five teams are still in the hunt to make their respective NCAA tournaments.

January 25 and 27:
Indianapolis and St. Joseph's

You could not ask for a better midseason matchup than the Thursday night game with Indianapolis. Our two teams are in a four-way tie for third place in the GLVC East with identical records of 5–4, 11–5 overall. Indy is playing well, having stunned Quincy 64–36 on Thursday night and upset Edwardsville by an impressive 69–55 on Saturday. They are coming to Regents Hall as the top defensive team in the league, allowing only 56.4 points per game. We are second at 59.9 points per game. In the huddle at the end of practice on Tuesday, Winstel stressed the identical records and said, "There is nothing Indy would rather do than come in and beat us in our house. Remember, if you want to play in March, you have to win in January."

This game lived up to its billing. Both teams played strong, tough ball for the first 10 minutes. Amanda Norris of Indy tied the score at 18 with 9:56 remaining in the half. The two teams continued to battle evenly until NKU took a 28–23 lead with 5:11 remaining on back-to-back baskets by Healy and Winner. On the next play, however, Healy got her second foul while attempting to stop a drive by Mandy Geryak. Healy went to the bench for the rest of the half, Geryak completed the three-point play, and Indy finished with an 11–0 run to take a 34–28 lead into the locker room. Without Healy on the court, and with Winner getting her first rest during the last three minutes of the half, we lost our oomph and Indy took advantage. Winstel told the team in the locker room, "If we don't play better in the second half, we could get beat by 15 to 20 points."

NKU began the second half strong, with Healy blocking a jumper by Norris and Winner getting the rebound. Next time down, however, Healy was called for her third foul while trying to stop a move by Norris. Norris made two free throws, Graham came in for

Healy, and Norris scored again to give Indy a 38–28 lead with 18:16 remaining. During the next nine minutes Chiodi and Winner led NKU on a 21–2 run. Nicole began the turnaround with two fast-break transitions in which she rebounded the ball at one end of the court and passed for a layup at the other. After Norris made two free throws, NKU scored 14 unanswered points, 10 of them by Winner, and 6 of those on back-to-back three-pointers that suddenly gave us a 49–40 lead with 9:41 remaining. Both three-pointers came from excellent inside-outside passing against the zone, the assists coming from Brannen and Healy, who was now back in the game.

Just as remarkable as our scoring binge was the fact that Indy had scored only two points in nine minutes of play. Our defense tightened as our offense surged, leaving Indy with no shots, poor ones, or blocked ones. When we were still one point down in the middle of the rally, Brannen blocked Norris on an attempted layup, allowing us to take the lead on our next possession. After Winner's first three-pointer gave NKU a 46–40 lead, Brittany blocked a shot by Karla Mast before making her second three. This was the best team defense we had played all year, especially in the second half, when Karyn Creager finally shut down Mandy Geryak. Geryak had scored 13 points in the first half, 6 of them on lightning-quick three-pointers, even through Creager was guarding her closely. Karyn held Geryak scoreless during the first 12 minutes of the second half and kept her from even attempting another three-point shot.

Indy still had plenty of fight for the last 10 minutes of the game. They answered Winner's second three-pointer with a six-point run of their own, reducing our lead to 49–46 while also drawing the third foul on Brannen and the fourth on Healy. Winner answered this challenge with another three-pointer on a pass from Chiodi, and Indy was unable to get any closer. One reason for this was the sterling play of Katie Butler at the end of the game. She scored all six of our points in the last two and a half minutes while also coming up with two huge offensive rebounds, our only two of the game.

Brittany Winner scored 17 of her 21 points in the second half. She made 8 of 11 shots, with 6 rebounds, 2 blocks, and only 1 turnover. She played 36 of the game's 40 minutes, exceeded only by the

38 minutes Karyn Creager played. Karyn scored 10 of her 13 points in the first half before shutting Geryak down for much of the second half. Angela Healy had 7 rebounds in addition to 10 points. Nicole Chiodi also had 7 rebounds, plus 5 assists, with only a single turnover. Our total of 9 turnovers was the lowest of the season, and we achieved it against Indy's very good press. They pressed in both halves until we hurt them by beating it. Their press was tough enough that they had driven Quincy and Edwardsville to commit 24 and 18 turnovers, respectively, the week before. That we had only 9 is a real measure of the quality of our play. So is the fact that we held Indianapolis to 20 points in the second half, when they made only 5 of 28 from the field, as opposed to 14 of 32 in the first half.

Because of what happened in the other games on January 25, this victory lifted us out of a four-way tie for third place in the Eastern Division into a four-way tie for second place. The other teams now with a 6–4 record—Bellarmine, Parkside, and Kentucky Wesleyan—are all coming to Regents Hall in February. So is Lewis, still leading the pack at 9–1 (and 16–2 overall). In the Great Lakes Regional rankings released on January 24, we are now ranked sixth—after Lewis, Edwardsville, Bellarmine, Grand Valley, and Ferris State. We are now back in the race not only for the GLVC Tournament but also for the NCAA Regional. But we have yet to reappear in the national poll. Lewis (number 9) and Grand Valley (number 10) are the only teams from the Great Lakes Region to receive a single vote.

This week's practice had been a lot more enjoyable and animated after the two strong road victories last week. I saw more smiles on the players'—and the coaches'—faces than I had seen in a long time. The new mood had been most evident on Tuesday. The starting team had responded quite well to the various offensive and defensive sets they were asked to work on. The "scout" team, led by point guard Keri Finnell, had done an excellent job of running the Indianapolis plays as scouted by assistant coach Schmidt. So Winstel ended practice a little earlier than she might have, saying, "We'll finish with 4:04, 34."

The players immediately assembled into four groups at each corner of the court. The moment Zach started the clock at 4:04 they began their race against time, having to make 34 layups at each end for a total of 68 before time expired. This time, amazingly, if one remembered last week, they smiled as they did it. And they did it the first time. With ease. Running hard and loose with total concentration and pleasure. Knowing, by the time there was a minute to go, they had it made. Karmen was with them this week, holding her own. They were all yelling to one another as they ran, Karyn calling Karen "cheetah." But no one can match Winner's sprinting ability as she takes this drill to a whole other level.

The next day athletic director Jane Meier dropped by as I was watching the final practice before the Indy game. Glancing out at the floor as we were chatting she said, "It's amazing how much time and effort people spend preparing for a basketball game that does not mean anything at all when compared to what is really important in life." Our world is driven by "such life forces as war and crime," yet here are "twelve athletes and three coaches working every day to win a basketball game."

Basketball does provide an alternative world, and in some ways a better one. The playing field is even, the baskets are all the same height (except maybe at one of the gyms we travel to), and the result on the hardwood floor is immediately evident for all to see.

Our victory over Indianapolis got some excellent coverage in the local press. Marc Hardin's report on the game itself in the *Kentucky Post* ("Winner Carries Norse") stressed Brittany Winner's emergence as a go-to player during a season in which Karmen Graham was still recovering from injuries. He also discussed Brittany's plans to teach in Argentina and her love for the band Red Hot Chili Peppers, whose album *Stadium Arcadium* has provided her recent pregame inspiration.

Lonnie Wheeler's feature column in the *Cincinnati Post* the next day was entitled "Blessed Assurance, with Her on the Line." Its immediate inspiration was Karyn Creager's prowess on the free-throw line. Wheeler mentioned that Karyn already had a new streak of 12 under way after missing the shot that ended her previous streak at 34. He gave a touching account of the inspiration she had absorbed as a little girl from her late grandfather Orvil, who had taught her to love basketball in the abandoned church on the family farm in Leipsic (in which he had also nurtured the talents of her father, Dale, and her brother Lee). Wheeler also revealed the inspiration for Nicole Chiodi's drastic improvement this year at the free-throw line, where she is now making 78 percent of her shots as opposed to 49 percent last year. Winstel had made Karyn Nicole's free-throw partner in practice this year. Watching Karyn's form helped Nicole to find her own.

Superb as Karyn's free throws have been this year, they are a continuation of what she has always done superbly at NKU. The bigger story has probably been her defense, which has improved dramatically each year. Against St. Joseph's on January 27 she was again given the job of guarding our opponent's top-shooting guard—in this case, Allison Hughes, who arrived in Regents Hall averaging 16.4 points per game. Karyn held Hughes to just 3 points in the first half, a half in which NKU held the entire St. Joseph's team to only 12 points, in one of the most devastating defensive displays NKU fans have seen in years. At the same time that St. Joseph's was making only 5 of 24 field goals for 21 percent, NKU was making 17 of 26 for 65 percent, taking a 42–12 halftime lead. Our starters had come out and absolutely buried the Pumas, not only avenging their upset victory over us on their court last season but also getting playing time for everyone on the bench. This was a game in which Karen Brackman played more minutes than Brittany Winner, Betsey Clark played more minutes than Karyn Creager, and Keri Finnell played more minutes than Nicole Chiodi, with all 12 players getting at least 10 minutes of play.

Brackman, Clark, and Finnell all played extremely well. But the big story of this game was up front. Cassie Brannen played a near perfect game in her 17 minutes on the court, scoring 17 points on 7 of 7 from the floor and 3 of 3 from the line. She also led us in rebounds with 7 while also getting 2 blocks and 2 steals. Thirteen of her points came in the first half. Angela Healy scored 12 of her 14 points in the second half. Angela shot 6 of 9 from the floor while also taking down 5 rebounds and giving out 4 assists. Completing our offensive domination in the paint was Katie Butler, who scored 10 points on a perfect 5 of 5 from the field. She also blocked 3 of the

11 shots we blocked as a team. Our four post players also generated 11 of our 21 assists in the game, 5 by Graham and 4 by Healy. In a game filled with beautiful scoring passes by NKU, an impressive number of them were from post to post.

The motion offense that had often been just a little out of sync was, in this game, a clinic in how to run, cut, screen, pass, and finish. Our 21 assists were made by 11 different players. One test of the rest of the season will be whether we can achieve this kind of timing and execution against the best of our league opponents. St. Joseph's had entered the game with a 1–8 conference record. Even so, it was impressive to dominate them so completely in a game in which our three cocaptains scored only 3, 3, and 2 points in limited playing time. Betsey Clark had one of her best floor games of the season. Karen Brackman had 8 points and 3 steals. But Keri Finnell had the most brilliant game off the bench, scoring a career high of 9 points in 16 minutes. Seven of those points came in the last 1:33 of the first half, first with a three-pointer, then with two free throws, and finally with a circus conversion on a fast break as the buzzer sounded. Healy had pulled down a rebound and made an outlet pass to Clark, who somehow saw Finnell all the way at the other end of the court. Betsey launched a pass that Keri pulled down near the end line and then, as the final second ticked, she spun the ball up and in with a move so acrobatic one wondered how she knew where she was on the floor.

Keri made an equally captivating appearance at halftime of the men's game. The team's scholarship queen and writing champion was one of five finalists for this year's homecoming queen. Trading her white home uniform for a black evening dress, Keri was undeniably the most elegant of the finalists, even though another candidate got the crown. Her parents, Bill and Dolly Finnell, had brought their video camera for the homecoming ceremony; I hope they also had it running when their daughter capped her seven-point run against St. Joseph's with that acrobatic shot at the end of the first half.

Because it was homecoming, the stands were nearly filled for the first time this year for one of our women's games. An impressive number of fans came down from Rensselaer, Indiana, to watch

217

their struggling Pumas play. NKU had a special contingent from Minster tonight, as 19 additional fans came down with the Winners and Brackmans to see their former high school stars play. One of our most beautiful passes was from Winner to Brackman for a two.

When Cassie Brannen was interviewed as the star of the game, she was most pleased with the playing time all her teammates got. "These girls really work hard in practice, and it just goes to show how strong this team is." Winstel, not surprisingly, elaborated on the same theme. "Our subs help us every day; they make us better. Today was a chance to let me say thanks to them and give them some quality playing time. They don't get their names in the paper very often. They don't get a whole lot of pats on the back. They work every day and they want to play. I thought they all took advantage of it."

Freshman Rachel Lantry got her 10 minutes too. She scored six points, making all four of her free throws, in spite of some interference from Katie Butler. "When I was out there shooting them," she told me, "Katie was kidding around to make me smile, asking me if I was trying to be the leading scorer."

February 1 and 3: Drury and Rockhurst

The trip to Drury is the longest of the season, nine hours by bus. They will give us one of our biggest challenges of the year. Drury is leading the GLVC West after back-to-back wins at Edwardsville and Quincy. They are 8–3 in the conference, 14–5 overall. They are on a five-game win streak; during their two years in the GLVC they have never lost a conference game at home. Paradoxically, their two victories last week moved them up to number six in the Great Lakes Regional poll, whereas our two victories dropped us down to number nine. An upset over them on their home court would do worlds for our self-confidence as well as our postseason chances. We do upset them, 52–49, for our seventh victory in a row.

Both teams entered the game with keen memories of the previous season—in which they had demolished us on our own court before we retaliated in the GLVC title game at Evansville. Amanda

Newton, their sharp-shooting All-American center, had graduated, but Molly Carter, the point guard who had scored 28 points against us in Evansville, was back as a junior. She was again leading Drury's pressure defense in which she was ably assisted by guard Becky Flippin and forward Lauren Gregory. These three players had already accounted for 157 steals. Drury as a team was averaging 12 steals a game and forcing its opponents into 20 turnovers a game. How we handled their pressure in the pressure-cooker atmosphere of Drury's Weiser Gym would have much to do with the outcome. Drury did outsteal us 10 to 7, and they also won the turnover battle 12 to 17. We outrebounded them 45 to 33 and blocked 6 shots to their 2. It was a classic matchup of their quickness against our height, and we prevailed, barely.

Our strength showed with five offensive rebounds on the first play of the game. This also showed that we missed our first five shots. This was one of our worst shooting nights of the season—19 of 55 field goals, for 34.5 percent. Healy was 1 for 9 and Chiodi 1 for 8. Winner was 3 for 10 and Creager 3 for 11. Fortunately, Karmen Graham came off the bench for 13 points on 4 of 5 from the field and 4 of 4 from the line while also pulling down 5 rebounds. Cassie Brannen scored 11 points while also grabbing 7 rebounds and blocking 4 shots. Some of the players who did not score well played excellent floor games. Nicole Chiodi played 38 minutes against the Drury press without committing a single turnover. She also had 7 rebounds, 3 assists, and a steal. She and Creager, Winner, and Clark applied excellent defensive pressure on the perimeter all night, limiting Drury to 1 of 19 three-point shots (Drury had not made fewer than five three-pointers in a home game all season). Drury's 49 points were by far their lowest total of the season; their field goal percentage was even worse than ours (17 of 55, for 30.9 percent).

At several points we surprised Drury with our own bursts of defensive brilliance. With 6:52 remaining in the first half Chiodi stole the ball and drove for a layup to cut Drury's lead to 16–15. With 1:54 remaining Clark stole the ball and drove the length of the court to give us a 28–23 lead. In between Butler and Graham had hit three-pointers to help us build a 30–25 halftime lead. We finished the half with 13 points off the bench, compared with none for Drury.

In the second half NKU appeared to take the game away. With 12:25 remaining we extended the lead to 43–32. While doing so, Karyn Creager made two consecutive steals from Molly Carter, a defensive feat few in the conference had achieved. NKU was still ahead by 12 with 7:08 remaining, but we had a four-minute drought during which Drury reduced the lead to 49–45. With 0:39 remaining the lead was 51–49. Carter had intentionally fouled both Chiodi and Winner, and each had missed the front end of a one-and-one. Now Carter fouled Chiodi again, and again she missed. With five seconds left, Carter fouled again. Winner missed the first of two free throws, but she made the second to give us a three-point victory as Carter's three-point shot fell short.

Drury's second-half comeback was furious, but we withstood it. In her postgame interview Winstel was unhappy about the layups we had missed in the first half and the free throws in the second, but she also declared that "we are nine hours from home, and I will take a win over a very good Drury team on this court any day." She attributed the victory, above all else, to our defensive intensity, something we had lost early in the season but the entire team was now finding. "We stayed together as a team" when we were struggling and "now when teams throw their stuff against us, we have those tough times to fall back on, and I think it helps." During their "shoot-around" when arriving on Drury's court, Winstel had been frank with her team about the new regional rankings—in which we had slipped from sixth to ninth in spite of winning two games the week before. "You have to hear this. We have our fate in our hands. You have to be able to handle that. It's not a pressure thing. It's a challenge we have to embrace."

I had felt confident about this Drury game ever since witnessing an impromptu burst of emotion at practice on Monday. We were working on how to beat Drury's press. Winstel stopped the workout to address some technical matters. Then she said, "You remember what we did last year when WE BEAT THEIR BUTTS." The increase in volume and intensity as she said the last four words set off an impromptu celebration among the three players who were then standing on the sideline. Creager did jumping high-fives with Healy and Butler, bodies and arms getting incredible extension. Healy and Butler then gave each other some quick, hefty chest bumps. Our spirit was back. We took it with us to Drury, showing them, and ourselves, that we were major contenders again.

Rockhurst is another three hours north and west of Drury's campus, in Kansas City. Their team was at the other end of the GLVC West standings, at 2–10 in the league, 8–12 overall. Even so, they had played well at home, where their record was 7–3. This was a game we should win, even on the road. We did win, by 52 points, 93–41. Of the 12 games Rockhurst had lost, their largest margin of loss had been 20 points. We were ahead by 28 at the end of the first half, 45–17.

The first five minutes of the game created visions of that perfect game again, as NKU led 11–0. By the end of the first half, Brannen, Winner, and Creager had 10, 9, and 9 points, even though Winstel had already substituted freely. Rockhurst came into the game with three players averaging in double figures, but they scored 2, 2, and 0 in the first half, along with 0 and 0 for the other two starters. Our suffocating defense held them to 25 percent from the field for the game, compared with our 49 percent. NKU also led in rebounds, 52 to 35; in assists, 23 to 6; and in turnovers, 10 to 17.

Our offensive star was Brittany Winner, who scored 17 points on 7 of 11 from the field. Cassie Brannen had another fine shooting game, scoring 12 points on 4 of 6 from the field and 4 of 5 from the line while also getting 7 rebounds and 3 assists. Angela Healy had a double-double with 10 points and 10 rebounds. Nicole Chiodi had 8 points, 7 rebounds, 4 assists, and 2 blocks while committing only 1 turnover as our point guard.

This was a game in which all our bench players got some decent playing time in return for their 12 hours of bus travel across three states. No one played for less than 8 minutes. Everyone got 3 points or more. Everyone got at least one rebound. Everyone got at least one assist. Among the subs who played 14 minutes or more, Butler had 8 points, Graham 6, and Clark 3. Among those who played 13 or fewer, Brackman had 6, Finnell and Lantry had 5, and Echoles had 4.

While we were beating Rockhurst, Lewis was beating St. Joseph's, as expected. But there were some surprising scores. Drury beat Bellarmine by 16, Indianapolis beat Parkside by 10, and Missouri–Rolla beat Southern Indiana by 17. We were now suddenly alone in second place in the GLVC East, three games behind Lewis. Bellarmine and Kentucky Wesleyan were now tied for third, a game behind us, and Parkside was a game behind them. Playing all four of these teams at home in the next two weeks is just the right challenge at just the right time. Something will give this coming Thursday, when Lewis brings a 13-game win streak to Regents Hall against our 8 in a row. They will be as worried about us as we are about them.

February 8 and 10: Lewis and Wisconsin–Parkside

Again, this is the perfect test for our team. Lewis is the team that knocked us out of the national rankings five weeks ago. They are now 19–2, again ranked 7th in the nation this week, with 1 first-place vote and 546 total votes in the current poll. We have finally crept back into the bottom of the listings, in 37th place, with 4 total votes. A solid victory over Lewis tonight will probably lift us back into the top 25. Our friends from St. Rose in New York are currently number 23; Grand Valley is number 12. In this week's Great Lakes Region poll, Lewis and Grand Valley remain numbers 1 and 2. Our victory over Drury has moved us up to 5, with Drury still at 3, followed by Edwardsville. Bellarmine follows us at 6, and Wisconsin–Parkside is 8. Our next three games will put us in the heart, or at the margins, of the postseason picture.

Right now Lewis is the current favorite to host, and probably win, the eight-team Great Lakes Regional. They have already beaten Grand Valley, Drury, Edwardsville, Northern Kentucky, Bellarmine, and Parkside. They are the subject of an excellent February 2 feature story by Stephen Zerdelian on CSTV.com entitled "Lewis Flying High: The Flyers Have Evolved into a National Powerhouse." This is coach Lynn Plett's fifth year at Lewis; this is his first team consisting entirely of his own recruits. They had a disappointing season last year when they had been predicted to win the GLVC East and NKU had come out of nowhere to win the division and the conference, beating Lewis in its own gymnasium as well as in Regents Hall. Lewis hopes to return the favor this year. Its two stand-out seniors, Mary Moskal and Darcee Schmidt, have never won here, and they want this one badly. (At least that is what Winstel told her team in the huddle at the end of practice the day before the game.) Schmidt is the player who killed us with 32 points in their 75–64 victory up in Romeoville. And Moskal's 23 points kept us from closing the gap in the second half. Those 55 points between them are more points than seven of our last eight opponents have scored, so this game will be a real test of how much our defense has improved.

Looking back at that earlier game, the most notable fact is that Lantry had started in place of Chiodi (who had struggled against Parkside and was scoreless in 11 minutes off the bench against Lewis). Since then, Nicole has been back in the starting lineup and playing well; a strong performance from her should make a big difference. Another difference, looking back, is the play of Cassie Brannen in the last eight games. In the game against Lewis she had played only 15 minutes off the bench. Since then she has started every game and been central to our success. On Monday of this week she was named GLVC Player of the Week for her outstanding play on both offense and defense against Drury and Rockhurst, the first time a player on our well-balanced team has won that honor this year.

In Monday's practice Winstel assigned Chiodi to Brittney Diener, Lewis's superlative play-making point guard, telling her to stick with her even when she runs through our matchup zone. Most of the practice was spent defending against Lewis's offensive sets, making all the little adjustments that will give us a better chance of forcing Schmidt out beyond her comfort zone—and of reducing Moskal's ability to drive and pick up fouls. On Wednesday we were still working on some of these adjustments, which involved some complicated and unconventional switching. Seeing that the new approach was still difficult for the players to execute, Winstel stopped the practice and asked them if they would rather go back to the basic "11" defense they had used against Lewis before. When they said yes, she dropped all the new experimentation and went with their recommendation, saying, "I didn't realize you liked the 11 that well."

On the next play in the scrimmage the starting team defended exceptionally well against the Lewis play the scout team was running. "That was just beautiful," Winstel yelled excitedly, voicing the praise that is always eager to fly from her lips when the play inspires it. Brittany Winner had given her personal journal a rest during the eight-game win steak. She caught up with it as we were practicing for Lewis. "There's no secret strategy to this game—we just need to come ready to play and execute and compete the way we know we're capable of."

This was a terrific basketball game. The first half ended 35–35 with both teams playing exceptionally well. The score was tied six times as each team matched great plays by the other. NKU started off well: Brannen got the opening tip to Chiodi, who passed to Winner for a three. At the other end Moskal got blocked by Healy but recovered the ball and passed to Mooberry for a three. Our motion offense then got in gear when Healy passed to Brannen for two and Brannen returned the favor a minute later. After Diener tied the game at seven, Winner stole the ball and passed to Chiodi, who immediately passed to Creager for a three. Winner scored on our next possession, but then Schmidt made two shots in a row. When a three-pointer by Diener gave Lewis a 16–14 lead with 13:00 remaining, Winner immediately answered with a three of her own. Additional baskets by Winner and Brannen gave NKU a 5-point lead with 10:00 left. Lewis then fought back for a 3-point lead with 5:40 remaining on 10 straight points by Darcee Schmidt. Her last two were free throws after Healy's second foul.

With Angela having to sit out for the rest of the half, Lewis was in a position to really take over. Instead, our defense kicked in. Creager blocked a Moskal shot, got the rebound, and passed to Brannen for two. With 2:52 remaining Brannen blocked Moskal, and Winner got the rebound. Brittany then raced to the other end of the court to receive a pass from Cassie and make her third three-pointer of the half, giving us a one-point lead. Then came the most beautiful play of the game. Lewis missed a three-pointer, and Butler got the rebound. She passed to Chiodi, who immediately rifled a pass half the length of the court into the hands of Winner, who was sprinting full tilt on the way to the layup, just as in the 4:04 drill in practice. It was not any kind of set play, Brittany told me after the game. "I know that Nicole pushes it fast upcourt and she knows that I like to run, so I took off and she saw me. Her pass was perfect, and we scored." Another team might have been deflated by a play like that, but Lewis answered with a three-pointer by Mooberry with 13 seconds remaining, to tie the game at 35.

This was the best half of basketball, by two teams, we had seen in Regents Hall for a long time. (I hate to say this, but the only game to rival it so far this year was the first half of Emporia State versus Grand Valley in our December tournament.) Winner had taken over as she had in the championship game against Drury last year, this time scoring 15 points in the first half, one more than Schmidt scored for Lewis. Almost all the statistical categories were even: each team had 16 rebounds; one shot 46 percent from the floor, the other 45; one had 9 assists, the other 11; one had 4 turnovers, the other 5 (exceptionally low numbers, given the intensity of the play). The one noticeable advantage was in blocked shots, where NKU had 4 and Lewis none. It certainly seemed like the second half could go either way. Until the second half started. We took the game in hand and outscored Lewis 38–26 for the 73–61 victory.

Again, Winner set the tone, scoring our first basket on an assist from Chiodi. At the other end of the court, Healy blocked a shot by Schmidt and Chiodi got the rebound; she pushed it up to Winner for another three. NKU took a 10-point lead with 8:30 remaining on an offensive rebound and muscular stick-back by Chiodi. Schmidt and Moskal cut the lead to 6 with 6:22 remaining, but then our defense kicked in again. Creager stole the ball from Moskal, resulting in two free throws by Chiodi. Winner stole the ball from Schmidt, resulting in two free throws by Graham. From there on we did everything needed to preserve a double-digit lead.

Winner's leadership was self-evident and exceptional. She scored 22 points on 8 of 11 from the field and 4 of 5 three-pointers. In addition, she had 4 rebounds, 4 assists, 3 steals, and only 1 turnover. John in the faculty section had been calling her "our Larry Bird" for quite a while, and this was yet another game in which

Brittany lived up to the name. All the starters, however, played an exceptional game, individually and as a team. Cassie had 14 points in addition to 5 rebounds, 4 assists, and 3 blocks. Angela had 11 points, 5 rebounds, 3 assists, and 2 blocks. Karyn had 9 points and 7 rebounds. Nicole had 8 points and only 1 turnover. She also had 5 assists and 9 rebounds. For a point guard to lead the team in rebounds as well as assists was impressive. Nicole's 9 rebounds in this important game tied Darcee Schmidt, one of the best rebounders in the league. The combined 16 rebounds by guards Chiodi and Creager enabled us to outrebound Lewis 38–33 for the game; Nicole and Karyn had combined for only 6 rebounds in the game we lost in January. All the drills in the early season, when Winstel was insisting that her guards, like everyone else, crash the boards if they wanted to play, were paying off.

Winstel mentioned in her postgame comments that she was running relatively few drills in practice at this point in the season. She could devote most of her time preparing for the upcoming games because of how well her players had internalized the drills they had done during those intense preseason and early-season workouts. She had not yet studied the stat sheet for this game closely, but the one thing she noticed right away was the assist-to-turnover ratio of 18 to 9. We did an exceptional job of distributing the ball as well as protecting and rebounding it, and each of our starters was in on the act. This was not that perfect game Winstel dreams of. But it was as close as a team could come against a team as strong as Lewis.

Today we got the 200 minutes of intensity from five players at a time for 40 minutes at both ends of the court. Clark, Butler, and Graham all had effective and important moments off the bench, but this was a game for the starters. Winner, Creager, Chiodi, and Brannen played 39, 38, 34, and 33 minutes each; Healy was limited to 20 minutes by foul trouble. These starting five were now finding their strength, rhythm, timing, and cohesion, not to mention stamina. This was the first game in which our team showed they were capable of achieving their long-desired goal of becoming even better than last year.

It would be nice to rest on our laurels for a few days after this one, but Parkside is here on Saturday, so we have only one day to prepare for avenging that other intolerable loss in early January.

Parkside came in wanting to sweep us for the season, something they had never done. We wanted, of course, to avenge our loss on their court, where we had led 29–27 at halftime and then collapsed in the second half. This week Parkside was ranked eighth in the Great Lakes Region, but they had lost at Bellarmine on Thursday, so they were now, more than ever, playing for their postseason chances.

We started strong in the first half, with Winner making our first five points. We led by five with 13:31 remaining after two baskets by Brannen. We led by seven with 8:46 remaining when Chiodi made a three-pointer. Three minutes later Winner hit a three to open the lead to nine. After a three-pointer by Creager we still led by seven with three minutes remaining. We then allowed five unanswered points in the last minute and a half, reducing the halftime margin to three, 29–26, nearly identical to our halftime lead at Parkside in January.

This was an unusual first half in that we made 4 of 5 three-pointers. It was also unusual in that our motion offense was severely out of sync. The passes in to the post that had been so flawless on Thursday were all over the place on Saturday. We were throwing the ball away, it seemed, as much as we caught it. The eight points we got from both Brittany and Cassie were all that enabled us to hold on to that halftime lead.

The second half began as a disaster for us. Kari Score, the D-I transfer who had scored 20 in the January game but only 6 in the first half tonight, made the first 6 points of the half to give Parkside a 3-point lead. Her supple defense in the first half had again and again disrupted our interior passing, and now she was taking the lead offensively as well. We managed to tie the score at 41 on a shot by Creager with 9:48 remaining, but Score answered with 4 consecutive points, the last two on free throws after Chiodi's fourth foul. This brought Betsey Clark into the game to replace Nicole.

Betsey immediately hit a three-pointer to reduce the lead to 1. One minute later Betsey hit another three-pointer, again on a pass from Angela Healy, to give us a 4-point lead.

Now it was Parkside's turn to rally. A three-pointer by Ashley Ferguson gave them a four-point lead with four minutes remaining. Winner made two free throws that were answered by Mackenzie Heise. Brittany immediately reduced the lead to two on a pass from Katie Butler with 1:24 remaining. Each team missed opportunities to score, leaving Parkside with the ball with 20 seconds left and a two-point lead. When Heise missed a layup, Betsey Clark got the rebound and threw it downcourt over the Parkside defenders to a streaking Creager, who tied the game with 15 seconds left.

Parkside had the ball with plenty of time to score, and they got it to Kari Score, who had already scored 15 points in this half. Her attempted shot was smothered by Cassie Brannen with four seconds left, resulting in a jump ball that went to us on the possession arrow. This was Cassie's fifth block of the game and the third time she had blocked Score in the last eight minutes.

We had staved off what had seemed sure defeat. We would now have a chance to win in overtime. But before that we had four seconds to try to score from the far end of the court. Winner threw the ball in to Brannen. Cassie was hoping to pass the ball up beyond the center line, but everyone was covered, so she passed it back to Brittany, now driving past her. Three-quarters of the court away, Brittany sped around anyone between her and the basket, floating up a shot as she flew past the backboard and the buzzer sounded. Spinning off the glass, the ball spun longer on the edge of the rim before diving down and in. A miraculous play by our living gyroscope, leaving the entire gymnasium in momentary shock before the crowd went wild and Brittany was mobbed by her teammates.

The miracle shot at the buzzer released a roar of joy from the crowd such as we had not heard all year. Brittany had scored 6 of our 8 points in an 8–2 run that had stolen the game from Parkside in the last two minutes. Parkside had played its heart out and had outplayed us for nearly all the second half. But Brittany and Cassie and Karyn and Betsey made the big plays when we needed them. Brittany finished with 17 points, including 3 of 3 three-pointers.

Cassie had 12 points, 7 rebounds, and 5 blocks. Karyn had 11 points, including the 2 that had tied the game. Karyn, Brittany, and Cassie played 37, 36, and 36 minutes for us. Betsey played 24.

These may have been the best 24 minutes of Betsey's career. In addition to two critical three-pointers for her six points, she had six rebounds and two assists, all of them extremely timely. Brittany's, Cassie's, and Karyn's last-second heroics would not have been possible without the plays Betsey made. As Winstel pointed out to Betsey's teammates at the start of the next day's practice, Betsey had gotten that rebound for the long pass to Karyn after being knocked to the floor. During the practice before this game she had told Betsey that she expected Parkside to pack their defenders in on our post, challenging our guards—and especially Betsey, who was not known for her offense—to shoot the three. She told her to be ready and to take the shot if they gave it to her, and Betsey did. So did our other guards, Brittany making 3 of 3, Nicole 2 of 3, and Karyn 1 of 1 as we made 8 of 12 three-pointers as a team.

After watching the team preparing for this game the day before, I had noted, "Betsey really sharp in practice today." I had also seen Nicole and Karyn come back out, after the rest of the team had left the gym, to practice their three-point shots. Nicole had made only 2 of 11 three-pointers earlier in this season before making 2 of 3 in this game. Betsey had made 5 of 12 earlier before making 2 of 4 today. The way they, Brittany, and Karyn shot three-pointers in this game reminded me of our first practice after the loss to Lewis in early January, when Winstel had pointed to the floor beyond the three-point line and challenged her players by saying, "That spot is open for whoever wants it. DOESN'T ANYBODY WANT IT? I don't understand."

The way Brittany ran the entire length of the floor in the last four seconds reminded me of the way she ran every lap of the 4:04 drill during the weeks before and after the Kentucky Wesleyan game. Her all-out speed and concentration, enabling her team to convert 68 full-court layups in just four minutes and four seconds, had helped prepare for the challenge she faced at the end of the Parkside game. When Winstel was asked to comment about her strategy for that last full-court, in-bounds play, she said simply this:

"We felt that 4.2 seconds was a pretty long time, and we just ran our special press break. We just wanted to attack the basket if we didn't get anything long. The ball got in Brittany's hands, and Brittany did what she does best: take the ball to the rack. What an incredible play by her!"

Another memorable moment, for a different reason, came in the first half. During a time-out after Karyn Creager had scored on a power layup against Parkside's strongest defenders, Coach Winstel had given her probably the longest frontal hug I had seen all season. When I later asked Karyn what had prompted that hug, she explained, "We had a time-out right before that play, and Coach told me that my defense has been great, and to keep it up, but I need to be a little more aggressive on offense. I had taken two jump shots earlier in the game that just didn't fall. So I was determined to drive hard to the basket and draw a foul or make a shorter jump shot. That is when I made that play. It actually ended up being a more difficult shot than the other two I had taken previously, because it was against their big post players, but this one went in. Afterwards coach gave me that hug and told me, 'Good drive.' She said that was what she was talking about. She told me to 'Keep it up' because that is what the team needs me to do. I just think everyone was really excited because after that we started to make more plays and started to get the momentum."

Against Parkside we were a little flat compared to the Lewis game. But we pulled it out against an inspired team playing their very best. The way that spinning ball dropped down into the net at the end made one wonder whether this team, after all the disappointments earlier in the season, was becoming a team of destiny. Of course, Winstel would not confess to such thoughts before the season was over. Her emphasis is always on the here and now. In the postgame interview Mike Tussey pointed out that two very special former players just happened to show up at Regents Hall for this weekend's games—Michelle Cottrell and Michele Tuchfarber, stars of the 2000 national championship team. Winstel said she was honored to have these great players here to support this year's team, but right now she wanted to talk about Betsey Clark. "She's a senior and a veteran. She understands what's going on. She's not a starter but she's always mentally prepared. She works her butt off every day in practice and when you do that good things are going to happen to you. Today, Betsey Clark showed the reason why you're always prepared and ready to go. I'm happy for the team but I'm really happy for her."

These two victories gave us 10 in a row. We will now have to endure at least one more week of the various superstitions by which coaches, players, and fans have been trying to keep the win streak alive. Assistant coach Matt Schmidt wore the same gold-striped tie for these two games that he had worn for the previous eight. He had also arranged for his octogenarian grandfather to travel from near Pittsburgh to attend these important games because he had never seen our women lose a game. Karmen Graham's mother, Kay, came to both games with the trays of freshly baked brownies that she has brought for the players and their parents since the first game of the win streak. Her husband, John, brought four of his brothers to Saturday's game with Parkside, they and their families providing vocal support for Karmen whenever she stepped out on the court. She continued to contribute in spite of the knee injury that has severely hampered her senior year, playing 18 minutes against Lewis, 9 against Parkside.

I did not have any direct evidence of the superstitious habits by which the players themselves were trying to keep their win streak alive. But manager Erica Ziegler did mention that she had not seen a single change among the diverse colors of the sports bras and other undergarments in the laundry since the streak had begun. As for me, my personal contribution to the longevity of the streak had been to religiously observe Coach Winstel's request to "take a step back." After the Lewis game I had moved my folding chair four feet back from the scorer's table and kept my pen and legal pad zipped up in my Toni Morrison tote bag. We hadn't lost since.

February 15 and 19: Kentucky Wesleyan and Bellarmine

Brittany Winner began her journal entry the day after her heroics at the end of the Parkside game by writing, "Sadly, it was our last team breakfast at Bob Evans. We always eat our pregame meal there on Saturday mornings, and Feb. 10th was our last Saturday home game." After celebrating the big plays by her teammates near the end of the game—the threes by Betsey, the block by Cassie, the pass from Betsey to Karyn—she wrote this about the last four seconds and their aftermath: "In the end, we were able to squeak out another victory with a layup at the buzzer to win 60–58. The aftergame celebration was the best—everyone jumping around and screaming! I've never been a part of anything quite like that before." One more sentence finished the entry: "We can't let up yet though; we've got two more big games this week—Bellarmine on Tuesday and then KWC on Thursday for Senior Night!"

The big rematch with Bellarmine on Tuesday had to wait. Snow, sleet, and ice drove over Highland Heights for two days, canceling class on Tuesday and Wednesday and ending just in time for Kentucky Wesleyan to make it here from Owensboro for the Thursday evening game. The Bellarmine game was rescheduled for the following Monday, which would now be Senior Night for Brittany, Karyn, Karmen, Betsey, and Katie. After being frozen out of Regents Hall when the Tuesday storm shut down the entire campus, the team was able to schedule a Wednesday practice for the Thursday game against Kentucky Wesleyan.

The storm had evidently disrupted the NCAA Division II national offices in Indianapolis too. For the first time during the current season, the new week's national ratings were not posted on the D-II Web site on Tuesday. When the rankings were released on Wednesday, NKU was finally back in the top 25. Our victories over Lewis and Parkside elevated us from deep among "Others Receiving Votes" to number 24. Lewis is now 11 and Grand Valley 15. We moved up in the Great Lakes Regional standings too. We are now number 3, behind Lewis and Grand Valley. If we keep playing as well as we are now, there is nothing we cannot dream of or hope for. On Monday, Brittany Winner had been named GLVC Player of the Week. In addition to averaging 19.5 points against Lewis and Parkside she had made 7 of 9 three-pointers. This from a player who, until about midway into this season, had not been considered much of a three-point threat.

Kentucky Wesleyan was now in the position NKU had been in when we visited Owensboro a month ago—hoping for a big game that would lift them into strong contention for the conference and regional tournaments. They had scored four impressive victories after the loss to us. They buried both Bellarmine and Indianapolis under furious second-half rallies after trailing each team by eight at the half. If they beat us in this game, we would have identical 11–5 records in the conference, and their overall record would be one win better than ours. They played a good first half—and were obliterated in the second.

Cassie slapped the opening tip to Nicole, who got it to Brittany, who made a three. When McClintic answered with a three, Winner answered with a two. When Henry answered with a two, the score was tied for the last time. With 13:22 remaining in the half, Winner made a three-pointer to give us a 14–7 lead. After Wesleyan scored five unanswered points to reduce the lead to two, Chiodi got a defensive rebound that she followed with two offensive rebounds, keeping our possession alive until she passed to Winner for another three. Wesleyan trailed by six with 1:44 remaining in the half and was threatening to close the gap, but Winner blocked a shot by Latoshia Lawrence, and Brannen blocked one by LaTasha Henry, to preserve our 29–23 halftime lead. These were 2 of our 12 blocks in the game, tying a school record; five of them were by Brannen.

NKU opened up the second half with 9 unanswered points for a 15-point lead. We were leading by 21 with 8:14 remaining. Brackman, Finnell, Echoles, and Lantry played much of the rest of the game. They more than held their own with the Wesleyan starters, most of whom stayed on the floor. Brackman ended the game with a three-pointer that gave us our biggest lead, 31 points, in a 76–45 victory.

This was a big night for Minster, Ohio. Brackman's 11 points late in the second half matched Winner's 11 in the first half. Brittany finished with 18 overall. She made 4 of 6 three-point shots, giving her 11 of 15 three-pointers in the last three games. Chiodi was our other double-figure scorer with 11. She and Winner led in rebounds with 8 each. Brannen had 5 rebounds, 5 blocks, and 9 points. Katie Butler had 7 points, 3 blocks, and 6 rebounds. I asked her after the game about the inspired play she has been bringing us with her blocks and rebounds down low. "My offense has struggled a little bit lately," she said, "so I try to pick it up on the defensive end because that is something I can control."

Defense was certainly the key. In Owensboro Wesleyan had scored 38 points in the second half after we held them to 16 in the first. This time they scored 23 in the first half, only 22 in the second. Overall we held them to 17 of 70 from the field, for 24 percent. From three-point range they made only 3 of 22, for 14 percent. Karyn Creager played 28 minutes of inspired defense against Laura Mc-Clintic, holding her to 1 of 9 on three-pointers and 11 points overall (compared with 6 of 9 three-pointers and 22 points when she heated up in the second half at Owensboro). Wesleyan's first shot of the game was the only three-pointer McClintic made. For me, the signature defensive moment of this game came when Karyn not only fought through the narrow opening of a high screen being set for McClintic but also managed to keep her arms waving like a windmill as she did so. Here were months of concentration and execution in a variety of defensive drills paying off in applied athleticism of the most impressive kind.

This was another great team effort, breaking the game wide open against a quality opponent. We appear to be ready for Bellarmine on Monday. They will be ready for us. It is a perfect matchup for Senior Night and the last home game. As Winstel reminded the players when going over the scouting report, "We have a special relationship with Bellarmine. We have played them every year we have had a program here. The rivalry is so old we even played them back when I was on the team." Our current players were thinking more keenly about how Bellarmine had outplayed them 85–78 back in December. That was the first decisive whipping we had received from a team we had hoped to beat.

When Bellarmine arrived to play on Monday, February 19, they were third in the GLVC East with a 10–6 record and 17–7 overall. They were currently ranked eighth in the Great Lakes Region, a position they would have to hold to make the eight-team tournament. We had begun to prepare for them the previous Monday, before the snow and ice arrived. We were much preoccupied with stopping the perimeter play of their slasher Taylor Kopple (who had driven past our defenders for 24 points in December) and their three-point killers Angela Smith and Dana Beaven (who had scored 38 points between them, each making 3 of 4 three-pointers, each of those threes answering an important score of ours). Our white team spent much of that practice defending against Bellarmine's complex series of interlocking screens, deftly run by our black team of reserves, including one in which a Bellarmine post player is known for stripping off the defender with her muscular buttocks. Katie Vieth was playing that position for our black team, and suddenly Karyn Creager was picking herself up off the floor, sore and sheepish. Everyone got a good laugh from this one, as Winstel said, "I told you that's what they do."

When discussing the rescheduled game, Winstel reminded her players that traditionally, all the seniors are in the starting lineup on Senior Night. On game day, however, Karmen Graham, Betsey Clark, and Katie Butler came to Winstel and said they would rather not start. "Coach, we've won 11 in a row, and we don't want to screw it up." So these three seniors came off the bench, as they had for most of the season, Graham having joined Butler and Clark as a consummate role player. This gesture, as much as anything all year, showed the heart and the cohesiveness of this team.

Immediately before the Bellarmine game the five seniors *were* out on the floor together. One by one, each walked out with her parents to be hugged by her coach and honored by her fans. Having come to know the parents almost as well as the players, I loved seeing each successive threesome walk out together, forming a line of 15 imported Ohioans to whom our northern Kentucky fans will be ever grateful. As the sound of applause filled the building, fans in the stands waved paper fans on little wooden grips, each imprinted with our five seniors' names and faces.

The game itself was no anticlimax. It was a replay of the recent Lewis game—an absolutely tight and well-played first half after which NKU pulled away in the second. The first half of this game was fast and furious, with one great play topping another until we went to the locker room with a 39–35 lead. Winstel had put Creager on Kopple, who had hurt us so badly in December, and this worked. Their prodigious D-I transfer was scoreless in the first half. Yet for all our preparations, we could not stop Beaven or Smith, who were both deadly with three-point shots. Beaven made her third three-pointer with 11:21 remaining in the half to give Bellarmine a 21–17 lead. We stormed back with a 13–2 run to take a 30–23 lead with five minutes remaining, but Smith made three straight threes at the end of the half to reduce our lead to four. She finished the half with 17 points, along with 9 from Beaven, the two of them making 7 of 10 three-point shots. These two were as red-hot as they had been in December.

How did we counter this incredible display and manage to lead by four at the half? By making 72.7 percent of our shots from the field, 50 percent of our three-point shots, and 100 percent of our free throws. At the Monday practice one week earlier, Winstel had placed great emphasis on trying to stop Bellarmine's deadly transition offense. One way, she said, was to "GET OFFENSIVE RE-BOUNDS." Another was to "MAKE OUR SHOTS." We made 16 of 22 field goals in the first half. Bellarmine coach Dave Smith told me after the game, "I had been tickled to death at halftime when I looked and saw that NKU didn't have an offensive rebound. Then I got discouraged when I saw they hadn't missed a shot!"

Our leading scorers in the first half were Chiodi and Healy with nine and eight. Nicole was driving more aggressively than she had all year, and she made assists to five different teammates in the first half alone. Angela was playing her best game at both ends of the court since her monster game against St. Rose back in December. Cassie Brannen was again a terror on defense. She blocked four shots in a two-minute period beginning at 15:40 in the first half, enabling us to turn a two-point deficit into a four-point lead. First she blocked an attempted layup by Beaven. Then she swatted a layup from Kopple, who was visibly stunned, apparently thinking she could drive in unmolested. Nine seconds later Cassie blocked Beaven again. Half a minute later she blocked an attempted layup by Smith. Our three younger starters, Angela, Cassie, and Nicole, fully justified the faith our seniors had in wanting them to start this game.

The game took a bad turn for NKU at the beginning of the second half. Beaven made a jumper, Smith made a three, and suddenly we were down by one. Winstel called a time-out with 18:22 remaining. We faculty fans could not hear the words she said from our perch 10 rows up on the other side of the court, but the pantomime was clear. So were the results. NKU went on a 10–2 run to lead by 7 with 15:34 remaining. We then withstood two Bellarmine runs to win by 12. With 1:32 remaining Winstel substituted Graham and Butler for Healy and Brannen so that all five seniors could be on the floor of Regents Hall one last time. A Bellarmine turnover with 17 seconds remaining allowed Winstel to bring them off the floor as a group too, replaced by the reserve bench players who had helped us prepare so well for this game.

Apart from Cassie's deadly blocks and Angela's emphatic rebounding, the defensive key in the second half was Winstel's half-time decision to move Creager from Kopple to Smith. After the three-pointer Smith made on the second play of the half, Karyn shut her down. After scoring 17 points in the first half, Smith had only 5 in the second. Creager herself, after scoring 4 points in the first half, scored 7 in the second, all of them coming during a five-minute period in which she answered one Bellarmine shot after another, the last being a three-pointer that restored our 7-point lead with 11:02 remaining. We responded to Bellarmine's next run, which reduced our lead to 1 with 7:48 remaining, with a brilliant offensive show by Healy and Brannen. Three times in a row, in a two-minute period, Angela passed to Cassie for layups. Graham, who had answered Smith with a three-pointer near the end of the first half, now made the move that put the game out of reach. Taking a great pass from Chiodi, she went up for one of her patented I-was-there-but-now-I'm-here power layups, fouling Beaven out of the game and converting the three-point play.

The final statistics showed the balance and intensity with which the whole team played. Junior Angela Healy had a double-double, with 15 points and 10 rebounds. Nearly as impressive, for a post player, were her 4 assists and 4 steals. Junior Nicole Chiodi had 13 points and 7 assists while making every shot (4 on the floor and 5 from the line). Sophomore Cassie Brannen had 11 points, 5 rebounds, and 6 blocks. Senior Brittany Winner had 11 points, 5 rebounds, and 6 assists. Senior Karyn Creager had 11 points during 38 minutes of intense defense, first on Kopple, then on Smith. Senior Karmen Graham's 6 points and 3 rebounds off the bench were extremely timely contributions. So were senior Katie Butler's 7 points after coming in midway through the first half. As a team, NKU made all 16 free throws. When an interviewer asked Karyn Creager if her free-throw prowess was rubbing off on her teammates, she simply described what happens at practice. "Everyone has to shoot free throws in a game situation, and we have to make so many in a row before we are done." Winstel usually requires 15 in a row to end a practice. The 16 in this game were only one shot more.

After the game Winstel kept her entire team on the court so she could give her final tribute to each of the seniors before the home crowd. Speaking through a microphone to the full house, she began by announcing, in her left-handed way, "Not one of them is a bad girl." Each player received a helium-filled star-shaped balloon as the coach warmly praised and lightly roasted her (telling Brittany, for example, she would love to bring her back for an alumni game 10 years from now and see if she can do the same thing in four seconds that she did at the end of the Parkside game). This was, indeed, the last time for these five seniors to be honored by their adoring fans on their home court—unless, by some currently unforeseen sequence of events, we would get a chance to host the NCAA Regional.

Winstel and Dave Smith, the Bellarmine coach, are tough competitors. As Winstel had told her players at practice a week earlier, "He and I will chit-chat before a game, but we are RIVALS. Once the game begins we are no longer friends. We both want to win and we would not have it any other way." Smith had been gracious after Bellarmine's victory in December, saying that NKU might have won if the game had gone five minutes more. He was doubly gracious this night in defeat. First he told me, in a wonderfully facetious way, "I think Nancy was outcoached tonight, but her kids overcame the coaching to pull the game out." After going over a few specifics of the game he declared, "There isn't anybody in the Region who wants to play Northern right now on any court, let alone on Senior Night, in a televised game, having beaten them before."

Quite a bit later, as I was leaving Regents Hall to go home and write up this game while the men's game was still being played, I saw coaches Winstel and Smith talking quite comfortably with each other in a back hallway. Once bitter rivals when he coached for St. Joseph's, they were now chatting about the league, the upcoming conference tournament, common opponents, everything they share in the honor of the game. They could have been two whaling captains in a heavily hunted part of the ocean, not having seen each other during two strenuous months in which each had been chasing the same elusive White Whale.

February 22 and 24: St. Joseph's and Indianapolis

In an interview after the victory over Kentucky Wesleyan last week, Winstel confessed how happy she would be for her players if they would win 20 regular-season games. The emotional Senior Night victory over Bellarmine on Monday gave them number 19. Hopefully, number 20 would come against St. Joseph's in Rensselaer, Indiana, on Thursday night. NKU was entering that game with a 12-game win streak. St. Joseph's had *lost* 11 games in a row. Our GLVC record was 13–4. Theirs was 1–16. Our homecoming win over them on January 27 had been one of the most lopsided games of the season—a 79–54 victory in which we had absolutely crushed them in the first half, taking a 41–12 lead into the locker room. Yes, St. Joseph's had upset us 50–47 in their weird airplane-hangar gym early in the 2005–06 season. But that would only keep our team from taking St. Joseph's too lightly. Or so it seemed.

This game started off as so many had in recent weeks. Cassie got the opening tip to Nicole, who got the ball to Brittany, who made a layup. Our offense continued to excel for the next three minutes. Brannen and Healy each made baskets on passes from Chiodi; Winner made a three on a feed from Creager. NKU led 9–0 with 16:50 remaining in the first half. We were outplayed by St. Joseph's for the rest of the game. Allison Hughes tied the game at 12 on a layup with 12:31 remaining in the half. Her free throw with 3:53 remaining gave her team a 6-point lead, 24–18. NKU, after scoring 9 points in the first 3 minutes, scored only 9 more in the next 13. Two layups by Healy and another by Butler kept us within 2 at the end of the half, 27–25. Quite a difference from our 42–12 lead four weeks earlier.

St. Joseph's never trailed for the rest of the game. Michelle Bova made the first two shots of the second half, and Allison Hughes kept the game out of reach, scoring 13 more points for a total of 23. We had no answer for Hughes the whole night. Her ability to drive resulted in 10 of 12 free throws on two fouls by Creager, one by Chiodi, and three by Winner. In the first half we were hurt by 10 unexpected points from Whitney Cole, a 5-foot-8 freshman guard who was averaging about 3 points a game. She was 4 of 6 from the field as St. Joseph's made 41 percent of its field goals and 44 percent of its three-pointers, compared with 31 percent and 12 percent for NKU.

Angela Healy was the only NKU player who played a consistently strong game at both ends of the court. She scored 20 points and had 12 rebounds. Chiodi was 0 of 8 from the field, and Creager was 3 of 13. Karyn was 1 of 7 on three-point shots, and Katie Butler was 0 of 5. Even our free throws were bad in this game, apart from Healy. Angela made 10 of 11 from the line, but her teammates missed 8 of 16. NKU led St. Joseph's in assists, blocks, and steals, but we lost to them in points, rebounds, and intensity. The final score was 65–58. More shocking than the loss itself was how we were outplayed by a supposedly inferior team. Yet one also had to give credit to St. Joseph's for playing so well during the last week of a season that had been such an extreme disappointment.

Last year we had been rudely upset by cellar-dwelling Parkside on the front end of the road trip that ended our regular season, breaking our 16-game win streak. After that game we had come back to beat Lewis in Romeoville, setting the stage for our brilliant play during the following week at the GLVC Tournament in Evansville. One can only hope we will be able to bounce back the same way with a victory over Indianapolis on Saturday.

FINDING WHAT WE NEED

This will be a Saturday evening rather than a Saturday afternoon game. This will be Senior Night and "Pack the Arena" night at Nicoson Hall, where we have played so many dramatic games over the years. I could not go to Rensselaer because of my teaching schedule, but on Saturday I will be riding to Indianapolis with my faculty colleague John, discussing all the nuances of the surprising loss to St. Joseph's while driving west on I-74—and hopefully savoring victory number 20 on the way back home.

Indianapolis had scored an impressive victory over Bellarmine on Thursday night, 66–52, giving them a record of 9–9 in the conference and 16–10 overall. They needed a victory over us to have a chance to make the GLVC Tournament. For the first half it looked as if they would get it. NKU opened with a 6–0 lead, as Cassie controlled the tip and Winner made a three-pointer on the first play of the game. But Indianapolis tied the score at six with 15:00 remaining—on a play in which Healy committed her second foul. This put Angela on the bench for the rest of the half. Butler replaced her for much of the half, during which she was herself called for three fouls. The only player who kept us in the game underneath was Cassie Brannen, who blocked six shots in the first half, five of them by senior Amanda Norris, the All-Conference player who had burned us with 19 points in our game at Regents Hall—and who had recently scored her 1,200th career point for the Greyhounds. On two of these blocks Cassie smothered the ball before Norris could even begin to release it.

Apart from Cassie's play, the game looked much like the St. Joseph's game had sounded on the radio. Indianapolis's tenacious defense, ranked with ours as the strongest in the conference, pushed our offense way out high and entirely took our motion offense out of its rhythm. We trailed for 10 full minutes after Healy's departure until a three-pointer by Betsey Clark tied the game at 16 with 5:03 remaining. Karla Mast then answered with 10 points in two minutes, giving Indianapolis a 28–21 halftime lead. NKU was shooting as badly as at St. Joseph's; we had made only 28 percent of our field goals.

Winner made a three-pointer at the beginning of the second half, sparking a 9-point run that gave NKU a 30–28 lead. Indianapolis then surged to a 36–30 lead on back-to-back layups by Norris and Mast. Creager answered with a three-pointer, and Brannen blocked Norris twice in 23 seconds. After two layups by Brannen and a jumper by Creager, Karyn made another three-pointer to give us a 4-point lead with 9:49 remaining. Creager's third three-pointer with 5:35 remaining gave us a 10-point lead at 55–45. We were pulling away like we had in the second half against Indianapolis in Regents Hall, but the Greyhounds had not given up yet.

Five unanswered points by Mast and Norris cut the lead to five with 2:30 remaining. Indy played furious defense on the next possession and drove Chiodi extremely high on the right wing with only 1 second left on the 30-second clock. Her only option appeared to be a desperation three-pointer. But Nicole saw Healy cutting toward the basket and drilled it to her for a perfect pass-catch-and-score just as the buzzer sounded. This was Nicole's seventh assist of the game, four of them in the second half.

After this our defense kept up its pressure with one great play after another. Cassie blocked Mandy Geryak for her 12th block of the game (breaking our school record of 7; in this game she blocked Norris alone 8 times). On Indianapolis's next possession Creager reached high to nab an upcourt pass with one hand, bringing it directly down for a steal. Winner closed the game by blocking Mast's attempted three-pointer. Winstel had assigned Winner to Mast after Karla's 10-point explosion in the first half, and Brittany held her to 5 in the second. After trailing by 7 at the end of the first half, NKU outscored Indianapolis 37–25 in the second. We held them to 28 percent of their field goals in the second half, while we made 55 percent.

The balance of our team, especially in the second half, was again admirable. Winner had 14 points with 5 rebounds and 2 blocks while also defending Mast. Brannen had a rare kind of double-double, 12 points and 12 blocks (validating Winstel's last-minute gamble to see whether Cassie could defend Norris better than her more senior post players had done in the earlier game).

Creager scored all of her 11 points in the second half, putting her over the 1,000-point career mark with 1,009. She also finished with 5 assists and 6 rebounds. Angela Healy played nearly all of the second half after sitting out most of the first half; her 9 points included the split-second two she converted on the feed from Chiodi.

Nicole scored only two points but led us in assists with seven and in rebounds with nine, her floor game making all the difference in the second half. She and Winstel both agreed that we had let Indy shove our offense too far out in the first half. In the second half we moved and we drove and we cut and we dished, and when Indy tried to stop all this by shifting into a zone, Karyn killed them with her threes.

This was an extremely important game for our chances in the NCAA Regional Tournament. If we had lost to Indy after losing to St. Joseph's, and then happened to drop the first game in the conference tournament, we might not have made the regional. This game gave us that coveted 20th regular-season victory. Its second half restored our confidence and our rhythm going into next week's conference tournament. Most of the other Saturday games in the conference went as expected. The pairings for the tournament in Evansville were announced as John and I were driving back home through the snow, sleet, and slush that had coated the parking lot of Nicoson Hall during the first half of the women's game. As the number-two seed in the East, we are playing Missouri–Rolla, the number-three seed in the West. If we win, we will meet the winner of Drury and Kentucky Wesleyan. Lewis and Edwardsville are the top seeds in the other bracket.

In a way, tonight's Indy game symbolized our whole GLVC season. We were underachievers during the first half of the game, as we had been in the first half of the season. But then we came out with extremely strong play when we needed it. Since the loss to Lewis we have completed a 13–1 run, lifting our record from 7–5 to 20–6. Our conference record has improved from 1–4 to 14–5. After dropping out of the regional and national rankings during the first week in January, we are now ranked 3rd in the region and 24th in the nation. We have regained the dream of defending our GLVC championship and even of winning the Great Lakes Regional and playing for the national championship. These young women had indeed dug deep and found the passion. They had completed the regular season in "badass fashion." They had found what they needed inside themselves and one another. They were now again a team to be feared.

By what magic had this transformation occurred? Some things were self-evident. The team had found the defensive tenacity that both Winner and Winstel had been seeking after the loss to Bellarmine in December. Brittany had taken over in game after game, showing the same power to carry the team she had shown in the upset over Drury a year before. Cassie had blossomed as our starting center, breaking out of that cocoon of kindness to become our "baby-faced killer" (as John in the faculty section began to call her as she calmly stuffed shot after shot). Karyn had continued the precision shooting she had always shown, but she also became our defensive stopper on the perimeter to a degree we had not seen before. Angela on the inside remained a force all season at both ends of the court. Nicole showed more and more leadership as her shoulder continued to heal, protecting and dishing the ball as well as any point guard who had played for Winstel, and rebounding it better than any. The five starters had carried the team during its 13–1 streak, but they had unforgettable support off the bench: Katie Butler scoring 20 against Rolla at home. Karmen Graham turning around our games at both Kentucky Wesleyan and Drury. Betsey Clark playing the game of her life as we beat Parkside at home.

To go 13–1 against opponents as strong as Lewis, Drury, Bellarmine, Parkside, Kentucky Wesleyan, Southern Indiana, Missouri–Rolla, Indianapolis, and UMSL was an exceptional achievement, especially after all the disappointments in the early part of the season. Some of the team's on-court success could be traced to their off-court initiatives: Negotiating the later arrival on game day and the time to themselves in the locker room. Getting the heartfelt poem from Angela just when they needed it most. Going in to see the coach when things needed to be clarified. All these things had helped the team get to where they were now. Challenged and supported by their coaches, they had stayed together and played themselves back into contention for both the conference championship and the NCAA Tournament.

As an assistant coach, Matt Schmidt has to attend closely to what is happening both on and off the court. One of his informal roles is to work with the cocaptains to keep the necessary information flowing between the players and the head coach. He is often the one who hears what the players have in mind and who offers suggestions as to what might or might not be acceptable to the coach. With regard to the pregame changes the players requested after the loss to Edwardsville, Schmidt feels that "young women these days need to feel they are making some decisions about how the team is run." It is also important for them to go in and see the head coach if something needs to be talked out. "They need to learn to have that type of conversation" for situations they will encounter later in life. But it is also the kind of conversation where "you'd better have some thought behind what you're going to say." The thinking a player does before such a conversation is another way in which the team grows. Karmen Graham observed, "Whoever goes into the office, Coach listens and responds."

Coach Winstel does value such conversations with her players. She tries to listen and to respond honestly, even when she might have "a hard time relating to their plight. The dynamic of the 20-year-old mind today," she says, "is an interesting phenomenon." In these conversations, "sometimes there are tears, and sometimes we both cry." Sometimes, she finds, players are surprised by what she will agree to. But she has her limits as well. "You do want them to take ownership of the team. But at the end of the day, it might be their team, but it's my program." That, too, is important to learn.

These shifting exchanges by which players, either individually or as a group, sift out their needs, frustrations, or desires and then express them to the coaches, and hear the latter's needs, frustrations, or desires in return, contribute to the evolving dynamic by which the team as an organism is able to grow and flourish. This delicate, yearlong process of conversational give-and-take involves a different "complex consciousness" from the kind the players employ in the heat of the game. But it is another essential ingredient if they are going to actualize the "aptitude to fly" (in the words of Dickinson's poem).

After that furious second-half performance against Indianapolis, in which Cassie's killer blocks had stuffed some of that team's biggest wings back into their cocoon, I wandered back toward the visitor's locker room under the stands in Nicoson Hall, hoping to get a quick interview or two as the players emerged. Coaches Winstel and Schmidt both came out quite soon and shared with me a bit of what they had said in the locker room before the second half. I waited and waited, but the players did not come out. From deep inside the locker room I faintly heard a sustained medley of strange whooping sounds I had never heard before. These were not the squawking seagull sounds with which these beautifully conditioned athletes had been performing their daily and weekly drills for years on end. No, these were entirely different sounds, probably originating in some of the pain they had felt after that intolerable, last-second, one-point, home-court loss to Edwardsville. They were now blending the pain of all those early-season losses with the passion for the game they had loved as children, and the passion they had harnessed as a group during the last two months, into a powerful improvisational chant that was now finding its impromptu, communal release. They had produced another pearl of a season, one that probably brought them even closer together than last year's magic had.

These young women had won a game that was terribly important to themselves—even more than to their coaches, program, or fans. They were going to savor this private moment among themselves as much as they had savored the public celebration on the floor of Roberts Stadium after winning the conference championship a year ago. Having seen the ice and sleet that were already covering the parking lot as darkness had descended at halftime, I decided it was time to find John and begin our drive home. We were two happy fans who would never know the full inside story but who could fully savor what we had seen out on the court—and, in Cassie's case, about nine feet above it. The nighttime precipitation was still a mix of snow, sleet, and rain. The roads were alternately treacherous and sloppy for about 10 miles out of Indianapolis. We were then home free in the blessed rain.

It is hard to believe it was only four short years ago that John and I were driving back from Nicoson Hall after freshman Sharell Snardon led NKU to the upset over Indianapolis in March 2003, the game in which she lost two teeth but helped inspire the subsequent run that took her team all the way to the national championship game. At that time, Amanda Norris, one year younger than Sharell, was a high school basketball star in Springport, Indiana. She would begin a college career at the University of Indianapolis in the fall. At the same time, Karmen Graham, Karyn Creager, and Betsey Clark were high school stars in Kettering, Leipsic, and Cincinnati, Ohio. They would begin their college careers at Northern Kentucky University in the fall. Also at the same time, Katie Butler in Findlay, Brittany Winner in Minster, and Keri Finnell in Cincinnati were preparing to take their basketball talents to the University of Dayton, Elon University, and the preparatory school for West Point. On this one night four years later, the angled road of experience had brought all these players and their teammates together one last time on the floor of Nicoson Hall, the postseason dreams of both teams, as usual, hanging in the balance.

9

GIVING ALL WE'VE GOT

Best gains must have the losses' test
To constitute them gains.
—*Emily Dickinson*

Just like last year, Rudy, John, Bill, and I drove straight to Evansville for the GLVC Tournament after our Thursday afternoon classes. This time Jon and Cheryl followed in their van. We saw every variety of wind and rain during the first three hours, feeling on the windshield the brutal bursts that had appeared only as the colored edges of storm fronts on the TV weather forecast. With half an hour to go, our first blue pocket of light opened high in the sky. As the higher sky slowly broke, an orange band of light became brighter and brighter under the dark wall of clouds over the western horizon. Ten minutes before we turned south toward Evansville the sun dropped beneath that high horizontal wall, blinding in its clear-skied beauty. Our first-round opponents for tomorrow's game, Missouri–Rolla, were probably riding beneath those distant, clear skies as they traveled toward us from the opposite direction.

The GLVC All-Star Team had been announced on Wednesday. Brittany Winner made the first team, along with Molly Carter from Drury, Amber Shelton from Edwardsville, and Mary Moskal and Darcee Schmidt from Lewis. Schmidt was GLVC Player of the Year and her coach, Lynn Plett, was Coach of the Year. Angela Healy made second-team All-Conference, along with Amanda Norris from Indianapolis, Angela Smith from Bellarmine, LaTasha Henry from

Kentucky Wesleyan, and Whitney Sykes from Edwardsville. Cassie Brannen was one of 10 players named to the honorable mention team. Karyn Creager did not make honorable mention this year, as she had last year, in spite of the fact that her offensive productivity and defensive tenacity were both stronger this year.

If we beat Rolla in the first round on Friday, we will play either Drury or Kentucky Wesleyan on Saturday. We will have to wait for the championship game on Sunday to play either Edwardsville or Lewis, who play Bellarmine and Southern Indiana, respectively, in the first round. We are still ranked third in the Great Lakes Region, behind Lewis and Grand Valley, but our loss to St. Joseph's has dropped us out of the top 25 in the national rankings. We have fallen back into the "Others Receiving Votes" category, in 29th place overall. We fought back impressively, but we still have something to prove to ourselves and to others.

March 2, 3, and 4: GLVC Tournament

Rolla is entering the tournament on a roll. Last Thursday they upset Edwardsville at Edwardsville by a surprisingly large margin, 71–51. On Saturday they beat Quincy at Quincy by 14 points. In both games Rolla outrebounded their opponents by 10 or more. Nicole Dierking, Katie Bunge, and Tamara McCaskill scored in double figures in both these games, as they had for much of the year (Dierking and McCaskill were both named, with Cassie Brannen, to the GLVC honorable mention team). They will give us plenty to handle today. In practice on Wednesday Winstel had stressed Rolla's large rebounding advantage in last weekend's games and also their ability to draw fouls and make free throws (Rolla had made 24 of 28 free throws on Saturday). If we can defend against them as well as we did in Regents Hall in January after our loss at Lewis, our chances should be good.

Dierking made Rolla's first shot of the game, a three-pointer. Winner had left her too open a look, so Betsey Clark entered the game with 18:48 remaining in the first half. Dierking did not get another field goal. Clark, Creager, and Butler combined to hold her to 0 of 11 attempts for the rest of the game. Our defensive pressure on the entire team was strong for the whole game, holding Rolla to 34 percent of field goals, while we made 53 percent. We also won the rebounding battle 34–31 and outblocked the Miners 8–1. Three of our blocks were by Katie Butler, who scored 8 points in 11 excellent minutes off the bench. Her three-pointer with 5:32 remaining in the first half gave us a 24–17 lead and closed off a 5-minute rally that had brought Rolla within 1 point before Healy and Butler gave us the momentum again. Rolla never got closer than 5 points the rest of the way.

This was another game that Healy and Brannen absolutely dominated in the post. Healy had 23 points on 8 of 12 from the field and 7 of 8 from the line while also blocking 3 shots and getting 7 rebounds. Brannen had 14 points while blocking 2 shots and grabbing 10 rebounds. Our passing in to the post was some of the best we had seen all year. Winner, Creager, and Chiodi all threw pinpoint, split-second passes to Healy or Brannen, who would catch the ball and finish the basket with acrobatic motion or surgical precision. Bunge, McCaskill, and Dierking are all rangy players who were defending hard, but there was no stopping us inside in this game. Butler's big shot was our only three-pointer in the first half, but Butler, Chiodi, and Creager each made a three in the second half to keep the defense honest. Two of those threes provoked sideline gestures I had not previously seen from Winstel this year. When Butler made her killer three in the first half, prompting Rolla to call a 30-second time-out, Winstel actually jumped for joy as Katie ran to the bench. After Karyn made a timely three to give us an 11-point lead five minutes into the second half, Winstel sent a full-court smile to Karyn that was received and quickly returned from the other end.

Winner missed most of the first half with two fouls, but Clark on defense and Butler on offense ably filled in for her. Healy and Brannen were our only double-figure scorers, but Creager, Chiodi, and Butler had 9, 9, and 8. This was a very satisfying first-round victory in which we played very well at both ends of the court. Winstel praised Healy in her postgame comments. "Angela carried us in November and December when we were struggling and she is starting to play that way again. She understands how to get open, how to finish, and she is also a great free-throw shooter if you foul her. Angela and Cassie both played well in this game, and we did a good job of getting the ball in position to score." This was a game in which all our practice at passing, catching, and finishing paid off. The passes that were just missing early in the season are finding the right hands now, and those hands are taking the ball in and up with exceptional quickness, power, and beauty.

After a pizza party to which parents and fans were invited to join in celebrating the victory, Winstel's team got back on the bus and returned to Roberts Stadium to scout out tomorrow's opponent—the winner of the Drury–Kentucky Wesleyan game. Winstel invited our faculty group to ride on the bus with the team. We saw Drury, the number-one seed in the West, beat Kentucky Wesleyan, number four in the East, 74–63. Drury led by eight at halftime and played a very impressive game. Guards Becky Flippin and Molly Carter and forwards Greta Wiersch and Lauren Gregory kept up the pressure at both ends of the court. Tomorrow, Drury will want revenge for our victories this past February and last March. This is what you want in a conference semifinal: two excellent teams playing a game that each badly wants to win.

Drury and NKU have been jostling back and forth in the regional rankings all season. Entering this week we were third and they were fourth. Lewis and Grand Valley were still ranked first and second. But Grand Valley was upset by Michigan Tech in the first round of the GLIAC Tournament. Already, certain postseason expectations and projections are beginning to shift.

Well, a little ground shifted out from under us tonight. Drury not only beat us but beat us badly, 68–57. We kept it close in the first half, trailing 34–31, in spite of having Healy on the bench with her second foul with 12:55 remaining. For the first 10 minutes this was the kind of game NKU fans were hoping to see. Each team matched the other with strong plays. When Flippin or Gregory would score for Drury, Creager, Healy, or Graham would answer for NKU. When Gregory answered a basket by Graham, NKU executed its most powerful press break of the day, as beautiful as in practice, each step of which I suddenly found myself calling out from the stands.

The ball was thrown "in," "to the center," "to the side," "downcourt," "across," and "three" (the three in this case coming from Creager in the corner). This lightning-quick break of Drury's fabled press gave us a three-point lead with 13:59 remaining in the first half.

We still led by three when Winner hit a three with 9:40 remaining. Carter answered that with her first three of the game. Winner answered with another three-pointer, putting us up by 22–19 with 7:44 remaining. We were still holding our own even though Healy was on the bench with that second foul. But then Molly Carter took over. She led Drury on a 13–2 run by scoring 11 points in the next three and a half minutes. Creager had been doing a fine job guarding her until this point, but Carter's quick bursts of speed, and her ability to scoot forward and then jump backward for a quick release, were too much even for Karyn at her best. Five clutch points by Chiodi, including a three-pointer in the final minute on a pass from Graham, reduced Drury's lead to three at the half.

With Healy back to start the second half, we were still in a good position to win the game. Instead, Drury outplayed us in every way, sparked by Molly Carter. She finished with 27 points in an absolutely all-star performance. Last year we beat Drury in the conference tournament in spite of her 28 points—in part because we had 30 from Winner, in part because no one else was scoring much for Drury. This time, forward Lauren Gregory scored 17 points, 12 of them coming in the second half, giving Drury a one-two punch for which we had no answer.

We had balanced scoring by the end of the game, with 13 points by Creager and Healy, 11 from Winner, and 9 from Chiodi. But Drury played us tough inside, holding Brannen, Butler, and Graham to 5, 4, and 2. Once Healy departed in the first half we never found the rhythm on those passes to the post that have become such an effective part of our game. In the first half Drury outshot us 60 to 39 percent. We had both layups and three-pointers spinning in and then out of the basket. It was much the same in the second half. They outshot us 42 to 27 percent. The frustration grew in our section of the stands as call after call went against us and shot after shot rimmed out.

In the second half Angela's mother, Marcia, usually quite con-

strained during games, kept shouting at the ref, "THEY'RE BREAK-
ING HER BACK!" Karyn's father, Dale, also quite a restrained
spectator, could not help shouting "MOVING PICK" each time one
was set to help Carter get free. Nicole's mother, Susan, sometimes
sits in the far reaches of the arena so she can walk off the tension
during the course of a game, but this time she sat it out with the rest
of us as Nicole led our defense with a steal and a block in the closing minutes as we gave all we had to try to close the gap.

The result of this game was a big disappointment. But we had
played hard against a team that today was simply better than we
were. Drury had a special incentive, in that we had defeated them
on their own court in February. Because of that, Winstel recalled
months later, "they were very fired up when they played us and I
don't think we matched that. They played us like we played them in
the conference tournament the year before." This game evened the
score for two great programs. A rematch at next week's regional
tournament would be great to see.

We will still qualify for the NCAA Tournament after the loss to
Drury, probably as the fourth or fifth seed. We are still capable of
beating anyone we play for the rest of the postseason, whether that
lasts for one more game, six more, or something in between. Drury
will play Lewis tomorrow to see who succeeds us as GLVC champion. Later in the day the seeds for the Great Lakes Regional will be
announced.

March 9, 10, and 12: NCAA Division II Great Lakes Regional Tournament

I was wrong about the seeds. We are seeded second to Lewis, which
beat Drury 69–52 to win the GLVC Tournament. Lewis will be hosting the Great Lakes Regional at its Neil Carey Arena. Drury is
seeded fourth, Edwardsville fifth, and Bellarmine eighth. From the
GLIAC, Grand Valley is seeded third, Gannon sixth, and Ferris
State seventh. We are in the bracket with the GLIAC teams, playing
Ferris State in the first round. If we win that game, we will play the
winner of Grand Valley versus Gannon. Only if we make it to the
final will we play another GLVC team—whichever one emerges

from the bracket that begins with Lewis versus Bellarmine and Drury versus Edwardsville.

The loss to Drury in Evansville cost us another of our goals for the season: to defend our GLVC Tournament championship. But we still have every reason to think we can win the Great Lakes Regional from which Grand Valley eliminated us last year. Practice on Tuesday, March 6, is spirited. When Winstel calls for the free-throw drill—the one that does not end until we make 15 in a row—we make the first 15 free throws that we shoot. When she calls for the 4:04 drill at the end of the practice, 33 sprinting layups at each end of the floor, we make the 66 with a couple to spare. While the team is stretching at the beginning of practice, Winstel presents Angela Healy with her award for making the GLVC All-Tournament team.

The next day we learn that Brittany Winner has made second-team All-Great Lakes Region. With her on the second team are Molly Carter from Drury and Amber Shelton from Edwardsville, in addition to Crystal Zick from Grand Valley and Mandi Johnson from Lake Superior State. Darcee Schmidt and Mary Moskal from Lewis made the first-team All-Region. So did Rachel Folcik, a 6-foot-1 post player we will get to know in our NCAA opener against Ferris State. She is averaging 19.1 points and 8.2 rebounds a game and is shooting 56.6 percent from the field.

Ferris State enters the tournament with a 21–8 record, compared with our 21–7. They finished second to Grand Valley in the GLIAC North, just as we finished second to Lewis in the GLVC East. They won their first game in the conference tournament and lost their second, as did we. They come into the NCAA Tournament having won six of their last seven games, including a 64–62 victory over Grand Valley on February 24. They are familiar with the Neil Carey Arena, having lost to Lewis here on November 21 by only three points, 72–69. One week later they beat Drury at Drury by four points, 91–87. These games with common opponents show that they are evenly matched with us, even though they are the seventh seed and we are the second. We are going to have to play at or near our very best to win in the first round.

On Thursday, March 8, the day before the first round, each of the eight teams is allotted a 55-minute practice session on the

Lewis floor. Our session is at noon, immediately after Gannon and before Ferris State. After the normal warm-up activities, Winstel devotes most of the practice to a scrimmage in which her white team continues to work against Ferris State as impersonated by our scout team in the red jerseys they wore in Regents Hall on Tuesday and Wednesday. Winstel's most direct intervention in the scrimmage comes when she says to the white team, "Any time our post player gets the ball in the block, I want you to make a power move to the basket. Not a turnaround jump shot. But a power move." Later she stops the scrimmage to say to Cassie, "We need you to be aggressive on offense. You are too good not to be." She clearly thinks her post players can score against Folcik and her fellow post player Audrey Thwing—and maybe get them in foul trouble too.

On the short bus ride to this practice Winstel was regaling her assistant coaches with stories of how much fun the game used to be when she was a kid on the West End of Newport. She and her brothers would get up in the morning and play whoever was out on the streets as long as they wished. There were no uniforms, no rules, and no coaches, just kids making their own decisions minute by minute as long as there were people to play. She remembered how upset her father would be when she came home with a big black eye and how much she enjoyed even that. Against Ferris State tomorrow we have only 40 minutes to play. If we lose, that is the end of the season.

We play the second game of the afternoon session. In the first game, Gannon upsets Grand Valley, 66–59. The defending national champs, who had looked so unbeatable when we played them in December, have now been beaten in the first round of both the GLIAC and the NCAA tournaments. This is another measure of the increasing parity in the entire Great Lakes Region. The familiar faces and numbers were on the court for Grand Valley, and they showed moments of greatness. Erika Ryskamp powered an impressive first-half comeback after Gannon sprinted out to an early 12-point lead. In the second half, however, Gannon took the game over and proved to be the superior team.

The NKU–Ferris State game was a different story. For the last

17 minutes the score was tied eight different times as the lead changed hands following one great play after another. The score went from 44–44 with 16:23 remaining to 69–68 with 0:09 remaining. The one-point lead belonged to NKU. Angela Healy got it for us on a power move to the basket on a pass from Katie Butler. On the previous play of the game Angela had blocked a shot by Rachel Folcik with 0:25 remaining.

Ferris State used its last nine seconds without calling a timeout. Sam Johns drove the length of the court and missed a contested layup. The rebound disappeared into a falling wall of players from both teams who scrambled for it on the floor until suddenly it squirted out into the hands of Teghan Thelen on the other side of the basket. As she said in her postgame interview, "Pretty much, it was like a hot potato because I had no idea how much time was on the clock." She tossed it up and it hit the rim as the buzzer sounded. It hit the rim again before it fell through, ending our season.

You could not have asked for a more cleanly played, strongly contested game. It was a clash between their high-powered offense, averaging 80 points a game, and our stingy defense, giving up 58 a game. The 70–69 result split that difference exactly. Coming into the game, junior Rachel Folcik was their offensive leader at 19 points a game. But senior guard Kristin Reinhart was scoring 15 a game, senior guard Erin Miller 11 a game, and senior forward Audrey Thwing 10 a game. When Ferris State came out on the floor, 5-foot-11 Thwing was nearly the mirror image of 6-foot-1 Folcik, two powerful swans who looked like dark-haired versions of Xavier's All-American Tara Boothe. Erin Miller was not on the floor. She had suffered a severe knee injury in the GLIAC Tournament and was replaced by sophomore Teghan Thelen, averaging only 6 points per game. The hot potato that Thelen tossed up at the buzzer gave her 14 points for this game, 6 of them on timely three-pointers.

The player who most determined the outcome of this game was Kristin Reinhart. A 5-foot-5 guard in the mode of Molly Carter and Erika Ryskamp (all three are blonde, exceptionally quick, and able to take over a game), Reinhart scored 22 points, 18 of them in the second half, swinging the momentum to Ferris State after NKU had dominated much of the first half. She scored 10 of her points during a 13–2 run early in the second half in which she led Ferris State from a 42–34 deficit to a 47–44 lead in only two and a half minutes. The teams essentially traded baskets for the rest of the game.

NKU's run had come in the first half, when Katie Butler entered the game. The score had been tied at 6–6 and 12–12. Ferris State led 17–16 with 10:40 remaining, but then Karmen Graham made two consecutive layups on passes from Angela Healy. And then Butler went to work. She made a jump shot, a three-pointer, a second three-pointer, and a third three-pointer, giving us a 10-point lead, 33–23, with 3:27 remaining. Ferris State then closed out the half with an 11–4 run of its own, 6 of its points coming from Folcik, two of ours from Butler again. Katie had scored 13 in the first half, including 3 of 3 from three-point range.

Butler was our high scorer for the game, with 15 points. Losing her last game as a senior on a last-second shot in the NCAA Tournament made her think, in the postgame interview, of how hard it must have been last year for the Michigan Tech seniors who had lost to us by 1 point in the first round of the NCAA: "Last year, we won at the buzzer, and now I kind of know how the Michigan Tech girls felt." She again said how happy she was, after having begun her career at the University of Dayton, to have finished it at NKU.

In addition to Butler's exceptional play off the bench, we had many other performances to be proud of. Cassie Brannen scored 14 points on 6 of 8 shooting from the floor, several of those on the kind of power drives Winstel had challenged her to take. She also had 2 blocks against Ferris State's powerful post players, as did Angela Healy. Healy scored 11 points, 7 of them in the second half, and she led our team with 6 assists while also getting 5 rebounds (in addition to what had appeared to be the game-winning block and basket). Nicole Chiodi scored 11 points, 7 of them in the second half; she also pulled down 10 rebounds, 8 of them in the first half. She had 4 assists and only 1 turnover in another nearly flawless floor game in which she played all 40 minutes.

The biggest disappointment in the game—and certainly to themselves, because they are self-critical to a fault—was the play of our senior starters Brittany Winner and Karyn Creager. Brittany was scoreless in the first half, although she scored 8 in the second, 6 of them coming on three-pointers that gave us important leads. She also had 7 rebounds, 3 assists, and a steal. Karyn scored only 4 points, 2 in each half, but she was occupied the whole game trying to keep Reinhart in check, which she did in the first half, holding her to only 4 points, before she exploded to finish the game with 22.

This loss was all the more painful since we fans were so close to the floor. The Neil Carey Arena seats only 855 fans. The NKU contingent was perched right over our team's bench. Our cheering section was led by the parents of our five seniors. The parents of many of our younger players were here as well. Our cheerleaders and our mascot were here. So were NKU president Jim Votruba, athletic director Jane Meier, and vice president for student affairs Mark Shanley. Also noteworthy among our fans were Chuck Hilgeman, who has attended every NCAA Tournament game Winstel's teams have played back to 1986, and Ray Rack, who has attended nearly *every* game, home or away, regular or postseason, for the last 15 years. Even for fans with this much postseason experience, the abruptness with which this game ended was a shock.

We would have liked to meet and greet the players as we often do after a game, but this game completed the afternoon session of the first round, and we were forced to clear the building without a chance to mingle. It was all so sudden that the players' parents did not know where to meet their daughters. Fans who had planned to stay through the championship game on Monday night now suddenly had to decide when, and in some cases how, to head back home. It did not help that we all got stuck in a 50-minute traffic jam on the 12-minute ride back to the hotel owing to an accident on the suddenly rain-soaked highway.

It was a low-key night for those players whose parents were not here to take them out to dinner (and who, for the most part, had not played in the game). They had seen a China City Buffet where they wanted to eat, but they were not sure exactly where it was, so the bus headed out one way in the rain, turned back, went another way, turned back, and finally figured out the first way was right, only we had turned around a few blocks too early. By then everyone was starving enough to momentarily subordinate the shock of the loss

to the need to eat, choosing item after item from five entirely different double-sided buffet lines.

The team bus would be leaving for the five-hour ride home at
7 A.M.

Sitting in the lobby after bringing my suitcase down to load, I
somehow knew it was the coach when I heard a rolling suitcase
thumping down the stairway from the second floor, loud enough to
wake whoever was behind the door with a "Congratulations Drury"
sheet stuck under it at the head of the stairs. (Drury had defeated
Edwardsville in the game that followed ours.) As soon as Nancy got
to the bottom of the stairs she saw that Herb, Matt Schmidt's grandfather, was about to roll his own suitcase out to the bus even though
last night's rain had turned to fog and ice. She absolutely would not
allow him to do it. She insisted that he sit at her table until Zach,
the manager, could take his suitcase for him.

When I returned to the lobby a little closer to the departure
time, the players had all gathered, some of the seniors with their
parents. Karmen's father, John, was sitting with Karmen and Karyn
Creager at a table close to Winstel's.

Coach was still being protective of Matt's grandfather. Gestur-
ing to Herb, she asked Karmen's dad, "Aren't you glad that when you
are his age you will have someone like Matt to take care of you?"

Caught off guard so early in the morning, John's expression
meshed with the immediate rise of Karmen's eyebrows. "I'm not so
sure of that," he said.

"I guess it will be straight to Shady Pines, then," the coach said.
"With that Christmas card once a year."

We all felt a little better knowing that the coach, in her caring
for Herb, had it all in perspective.

As for her caring for the players themselves, with the season
suddenly over, that had been shown in the locker room, among
themselves, after the game.

The rain was gone, the fog burned off, and the bus moved smoothly
through the sunny farmland as we rode diagonally down and across
Indiana, with a food stop near Indy.

As we turned the corner onto the campus drive, Winstel carried a little box back to the middle of the bus and said to her players, "You each get this award for being in the NCAA Tournament."

After passing them out, she reminded her players that spring break was ending, that classes began again on Monday. She reminded those who were not seniors that registration for their fall classes would be coming up at the end of March. She said she did not expect any recruits to be coming in for open gym next week, or probably the week after that.

Winstel told her players that she would be in touch with them. There would be some kind of gathering before the end of the semester when they could all get together with family and friends. And she told any of the seniors "who would like to" that she would enjoy "having your help" when next year's team got together for some workouts before the semester ended.

On the day that our team rode back from Romeoville two days earlier than they had hoped, Ferris State overwhelmed Gannon, 80–61. In the other semifinal game, Drury upset Lewis 67–62, surprising the Flyers on their own floor. Drury won the championship game against Ferris State, 79–69. Drury traveled to the University of Nebraska at Kearney to represent our region and conference in the Elite Eight. They lost in the first round to Southern Connecticut State, the eventual national champion. Southern Connecticut, after beating California–San Diego in the semifinal game, upset previously undefeated Florida Gulf Coast for the championship. Southern Connecticut finished the season 34–2. They had been undefeated in their first 20 games. Their first loss had been to the College of St. Rose, one month after NKU had defeated that team in Florida.

The three Division I teams that NKU had played in advance of the 2006–07 season finished the season, like us, with many accomplishments, but fewer than they had dreamed of. The University of Kentucky, in spite of being nationally ranked in the preseason, did not make the NCAA Tournament. Neither did Indiana University. Both teams played in the Women's National Invitational Tournament (WNIT). Each advanced to the third round. Kentucky ended its season with a record of 20–14. Indiana finished at 19–14. South Dakota State, which eliminated Indiana from the WNIT, is the team that four years earlier, as a Division II program, had defeated NKU for the national championship.

Xavier University, our summertime scrimmage partner, did make it to the NCAA Tournament. They lost to West Virginia in the first round. Xavier finished the season with a record of 26–9, tying for second best in the history of the program. Amber Harris set new school records for freshman-year scoring and rebounds in a season; she also set a record for career blocked shots. If Xavier comes to NKU for open gym again next summer, it will be fun to watch her and Cassie underneath.

During and after the NCAA and WNIT tournaments, the annual round of coaching resignations and terminations began. Much national attention was given to Pokey Chatman's resignation at Louisiana State University because of an alleged relationship with a former player. Local basketball fans were shocked by the abrupt resignations of Mickie DeMoss at the University of Kentucky and Laurie Pirtle at the University of Cincinnati, one after 4 years on the job, the other after 20. GLVC coaches who resigned after the 2006–07 season included Nyla Milleson at Drury, Lynn Plett at Lewis, Larry Just at Quincy, Teri Moren at Indianapolis, Amy Siegel at St. Joseph's, and Lee Buchanan at Missouri–St. Louis.

Here at NKU, however, Nancy Winstel will be back as head coach for her 25th consecutive year. She remains a bastion of stability in a college basketball world in which commercialism, celebrity, and the pressure to win sometimes overshadow the continuity of a program or the education of its student-athletes. When I asked Matt Schmidt to choose the single word that best sums up Nancy Winstel, his answer was immediate: "educator." This makes her "a dying breed in this business. She is a great educator and she teaches her players, yes, about basketball, but she also teaches them about life."

Winstel is losing five seniors for the upcoming season. She will have three returning starters: Healy, Chiodi, and Brannen. Coach Schmidt is shocked by those fans who feel that the team record of 48–13 in the last two seasons is not something to be proud of. He is bemused by one fan who wanted to commiserate with him because only three starters are returning for the next season. To him, a team with Healy and Brannen in the paint and Chiodi on the point has an exciting foundation to work with. As for the departing seniors, they made this "the finest group of young people I've ever got to coach."

For the five seniors, the ride back from Romeoville was quite different from the one two months ago. Then their struggling team had been beaten badly two games in a row, making them question themselves as never before. Now, after two brilliant months in which they had played themselves back into national contention and regained their self-respect, they had seen their regional dreams evaporate with one crazy bounce of the ball. This was a bitter blow. It was also a fluke, almost an accident. It did not take away from what they had achieved or who they had become in this last year together. Now, not only basketball but also their days at NKU were about to end. No doubt, during the long, quiet bus ride, each senior minutely replayed everything that could have gone differently in that last game. Probably each was also beginning to look ahead— maybe more expansively than ever before—to her life beyond the game, beyond the school.

Brittany Winner had not duplicated her postseason heroics of the year before. She had, however, carried her team during much of their 13–1 run. She had also provided the season's defining moment of miraculous joy for players and fans alike—when her fly-by last-second shot against Parkside had spun down into the net. Back in October she had vowed to "make the days count." She had done so—and the hours, minutes, and seconds, too.

For Karyn Creager, this season, like every season she had played, "ended too soon." She never got that state or national championship for which she had worked so hard through both high school and college. Nor did she have the pleasure of making another last-second, game-winning shot in an NCAA Tournament game. She *had* set career records for free throws at NKU. More impressive than that was the way she had improved every aspect of her game day by day in all four years. Equally impressive was the increasing leadership she had given her team as her best friend, Karmen, was struggling with one bitter misfortune after another.

Karmen Graham had had everything to look forward to this year, for her team and for her own superlative career. Instead, the young woman who had led her team to such an exceptional year as a junior had to watch much of the action from the sidelines as a senior. It had been hard enough as an incoming freshman to "go from this person who was everything on the team in high school to one who, if you didn't play, it doesn't matter." It must have been infinitely harder to make a similar transition from a junior All-American to a senior substitute. Then it was due to inexperience, now to injury, but Karmen averaged fewer minutes and started many fewer games as a senior than as a freshman. Yet she retained her zest for the game and her love for her teammates.

Betsey Clark, the third senior to spend all four years in the program, had her disappointments, too, during her last three years. Yet she continued to bring the perimeter defense we needed even when the shoulder socket, the subsequent bursitis, or the serious knee injury kept her from playing all-out. That all her virtues could be showcased in the stirring victory over Parkside in one of her last games in Regents Hall was something for which her fans will always be grateful.

Katie Butler, the senior who was here for only two years, is the one who ended up sitting next to Coach Winstel at the mandatory NCAA press conference after the devastating loss to Ferris State. She is the senior who did the most to give us a chance to win that game, again showing her uncanny ability to turn a game around with poise and firepower off the bench. In the NCAA press room, no less than in the Florida hotel lobby, Katie found the right words to say, sympathizing with the Michigan Tech seniors who had lost to us at the buzzer the year before, and saying how grateful she was to have transferred to NKU.

More of the team's preseason goals had now fallen by the wayside. These seniors and their teammates had not made it to the Final Four or won the national championship. The gains they made the year before were now much greater for this year's losses. Both post-season tournaments were deeply disappointing, but the team had certainly finished the regular season "in badass fashion." They had done so in a way that would have made it most difficult to choose a Most Valuable Player. On one level, it could be Karmen Graham for remaining such an inspiration to her teammates in spite of all she was going through. On another it could be Brittany Winner for carrying the team through so much of its resurgence. Or Karyn Creager for her day-by-day leadership in practice as well as in games. Or Angela Healy for anchoring the team at both ends of the court during the entire year. Or Cassie Brannen for playing like a superstar after our star went down. Or Nicole Chiodi for providing the pulse that kept it all in balance at its best. From the start of the game on Senior Night through to the end of the Ferris State game, Healy, Brannen, and Chiodi had certainly shown they were ready to be team leaders during the next season.

All these players, as well as those who played more supporting roles, some of them brilliantly at times, could be proud of what they and their team had accomplished. Individually and together, they had overcome doubts and disappointments, injuries and medical conditions, bruised emotions and dashed hopes, the deaths of friends and loved ones, and all sorts of other unexpected eventualities. Each had endured the seemingly endless day-after-day and week-after-week challenge of maintaining the concentrated effort by which each shaped herself on the court. Each had continued to make impressive progress in her studies. The team's cumulative grade point average for this season was 3.385, 15th in the nation. This year's gains, too, will give all our players much to savor and treasure when the soreness leaves the heart, the bounty floods the soul, and the legacy lives on.

10

FAREWELL TO FIVE

This world is not conclusion.
—*Emily Dickinson*

Two of our seniors had found their parents in the lobby of the Neil Carey Arena before the building was cleared for the evening session. Betsey and Katie were both sobbing convulsively. The tears at the farewell banquet a month later were of a different kind. Like those of Isabel Archer after the loss of her cousin Ralph at the end of Henry James's *The Portrait of a Lady,* "they were not the tears that blind." Ralph had given Isabel two kinds of legacies—the fortune that had made her the victim of a fortune-hunting husband, and the generous love that had prompted that ill-fated gift. Even though Ralph was gone, the love remained.

This team leaves its fans many legacies besides the sounds of "Fergalicious" filling Regents Hall during the pregame warm-ups: Their record of 48 wins against 13 losses in the last two seasons. Their two trips to the NCAA Tournament. Their GLVC championship. The 1,088 career points by Karmen Graham. The 1,035 career points by Karyn Creager. Karyn's school-record 34 free throws in a row. Cassie Brannen's school-record 12 blocks in a game. Brittany Winner's miraculous moments against Drury and Parkside and Bellarmine and so many more. Katie Butler's being the best sharpshooter Winstel ever had off the bench. Betsey Clark epitomizing the role of the unheralded defensive specialist essential to the success of the team. Angela Healy anchoring us underneath for two full seasons. Nicole Chiodi throwing the breathtaking passes that only she and her receivers can imagine and make real.

Each of the above players has made a distinctive contribution to D-II women's basketball. But it is the way they have done so as a team, not individually, that will be their lasting legacy, for themselves as well as their fans. The joy they have in the game, and in one another, remains their defining quality—whether in the heat of a game, the purgatory of practice, or the pleasure of being together away from the court. The five departing seniors had done much to sustain this joy, keeping it alive during some of the toughest trials that a team this talented could have. But essential leadership had come from some of the younger players as well, both on and off the court. The team stayed together as its dreams fell apart, remaking themselves to be stronger than ever in spite of circumstances that could have diminished their love for the game or one another. Twelve young women, pushed and inspired by their coaches, turned a season of adversity into one of empowerment.

The awards ceremony was scheduled for 1 P.M. on Sunday, April 22. This turned out to be one of those sweet, beautiful springtime days in northern Kentucky when everyone indoors would love to be outdoors, the kind of day on which I had arrived for my campus interview as a faculty recruit in April 1972. When Coach Winstel opened the ceremony in the University Center Ballroom, she immediately alluded to the beauty of the day, saying she would do her best to keep the program short so everyone could get outdoors. The program was certainly more streamlined than it might have been (she rightly said she could have talked about these five seniors all day). Yet there were many memorable moments during the event itself—and much extended mingling before anyone felt ready to leave the room.

Before giving her gifts and tributes to each of her 12 players, Winstel announced the team's choices for this year's special awards. Cassie Brannen is Most Improved. Brittany Winner wins the Hustle Award. Angela Healy receives the Outstanding Offensive Award. Karyn Creager shares the Outstanding Defensive Award with Cassie Brannen. Coach Winstel calls on Cassie to step up for a very special award, one she warns her not to drop, because it is heavy. It is a large trophy whose sculpted athlete is anchored by 12 heavy, solid metallic blocks, one for each of Cassie's blocks in the Indianapolis game. Winstel says she does not ever expect that record to be broken, unless by Cassie herself.

As the coach went on to recognize each player, she began with Rachel, the lone freshman, and worked her way up to the seniors. When she came to the juniors she gave a special tribute to Keri Finnell, who "has decided she's not going to play ball next year"; she will use her remaining time to prepare more directly for the business world or graduate school. Winstel recalled "the privilege of meeting Keri at summer camp probably when she was in the third or fourth grade." After going away to the army prep school, Keri joined our team "with a knee injury that made it kind of tough for her to compete, but every day she came in and worked hard and did everything in her power." This season she "played the point on our scout team," and she has been "a 100 percent pleasure to coach. This young lady has so many opportunities academically and she will be a success at whatever she does."

After each individual tribute, Winstel presented each player with three gifts: a DVD set of the five games that were televised during this season, a compilation by Coach Schmidt of newspaper stories written about the team, and a copy of this year's highlight video, again put together by Coach Schmidt. The screening of the video was one of the highlights of the entire ceremony. Advances in technology allowed the inclusion of more video clips from the games we had played this year. Schmidt certainly had plenty of outstanding footage from which to select our most outstanding shots, blocks, steals, and fast breaks, but I noticed that most of those at the beginning featured players in a reserve role this year who will presumably have more playing time next year. The section on the Florida trip showed, predictably, a long row of 6-foot sunbathers standing with the Gulf behind them. Interspersed through the video were photos of the entire team enjoying such random activities as bobbing for apples and carving pumpkins.

In keeping with this team's great love of music, this year's video was filled with a sequence of songs whose lyrics spoke to the experience of this particular season:

"We are family. I've got all my sisters and me."

"Won't back down. Stand my ground."

"A, B, C. Do, re, me. Easy as 1, 2, 3."

"The Midwest farmers' daughters . . . I wish they all could be California girls."

"We're not going to take it. . . . There ain't no way."

"What you want . . . What you need . . . All I'm askin' . . . a little respect."

"I'm moving on. . . . I've lived in this place, and I know all the faces / Life has been patiently waiting for me."

The most touching element of the video for me, and I expect for most in the room, was "A Tribute to the Seniors through the Years." After the name of each player and the number of her jersey was a sequence of photos of her as a little girl: Brittany, number 10, standing in front of a wheat field taller than she is. Betsey, number 15, riding a bicycle up a sidewalk. Karyn, number 24, dwarfed by her beloved grandfather. Katie, number 30, asleep on that bench in the gym. Karmen, number 34, a baby in her daddy's hands. These photos became even more meaningful after I had completed my exit interviews and read the poem that Angela had attached to everyone's locker. These photos, like Angela's poem, evoked the precious childhood years behind the number on each senior's jersey. They conveyed to the whole room the "childish love of the sport" that had enabled the entire team to connect with one another in a way that helped them save their season. How did such photos, dug out from who knows how many old albums, get in Coach Schmidt's hands in time for him to put them in the video? He had asked the parents of each senior to supply such photos. This part of the video was as much of a surprise to the seniors as to anyone else.

But now it was, indeed, their time to leave. Before introducing them individually, Winstel said she hated to say good-bye to "these fine outstanding ladies who have meant so much to our program." But the whole point of the program is to "prepare your players to go out in life. It's hard to see them go but it would be worse if you weren't prepared. So the good news," she says, looking at them, "is that *you are prepared*. You're even more prepared than you *even know* you are. Because you've been involved in a team sport that requires discipline, requires you to be on time, requires you to be dedicated, requires you to communicate with people, requires you to look people in the eye when you really do not feel like it, requires you to use your time well. It requires you to do lots and lots of things. So when you go out into the world I truly believe you are going to be okay. And I think you probably feel that way too. You come to a university to get an education and move on."

That was exactly what Winstel had done at NKU exactly 30 years ago, when she had completed her college education in 1977 and moved on to Bloomington to follow her dream of becoming a basketball coach.

Along with her spoken tribute to each senior, Coach Winstel gave her an engraved plaque in the shape of the state of Kentucky so each of these Ohioans would remember where they had come to play ball. She began with Katie Butler and Brittany Winner, the most recently arrived of the five seniors.

With Katie, she gave credit to Matt for recruiting her when he heard she was going to leave Dayton. She praised Katie for having the rare versatility to shoot like she did from the outside while being able to post up inside. She shared her favorite moment of Katie during her two years on the team: that three-point shot in St. Louis that bounced high enough in the air for Karmen to be fouled for the five-point play before the ball fell through.

With Brittany, she recalled how strongly we had recruited her at Minster, how disappointed we were she had gone elsewhere, and how happy we were when she did join our program. She emphasized how in this past season in particular Brittany had again and again shown that rare combination of "speed, quickness, and power" that can "take over a game." Her favorite moment: Brittany streaking the full length of the court in only four seconds to make the game-winning shot against Wisconsin–Parkside.

With Betsey Clark, Winstel stressed the versatility that she brought to us from McNicholas High School. Not only did she have the ability to play all five positions on the floor; she also understood each of those positions better than anyone else on the floor. Her favorite image of Betsey: coming off the bench against Wisconsin–Parkside to make those two three-point shots, without which Brittany's game-winning shot could not have occurred.

With Karyn Creager, Winstel began by saying how lost she had felt when Brian Neal drove her up to that little town in northern Ohio where Karyn lived. She explained how Karyn had arrived here as a shooter but had made herself into an "all-round player" by "coming to practice every day and working hard to get better—every single game, every single day in practice." The result: a "phenomenal year and a phenomenal career."

Grammy came last. Winstel stressed that Brian Neal had "recruited her hard" because we really wanted her in our program. After paying tribute to Karmen's junior year as an honorable mention All-American, followed by everything she had suffered and worked through as a senior, she told Karmen how deeply she was admired by everyone who has "witnessed your journey this year and what you went through to try to play." She then said she wanted her to have "one special award." This turned out to be a custom-made plaque onto which a shoe was mounted, the sight of which brought immediate laughter from all of Karmen's teammates.

"As some of you know," Winstel said, "we had a little shoe incident. This is *the shoe*. It really is. There are two different stories about this, and mine is the true one" (more laughter from members of the team). Looking directly at Karmen again she said, very deliberately, "Grammy, number 34, I *knew* I wouldn't hit you." The bursts of laughter that followed that assertion were the therapeutic climax of the entire ceremony. Angela and Nicole presented a tribute to the seniors from their teammates, and the seniors said their parting words. The official part of the ceremony, and of their roles on the team, had ended.

Soon after the exciting Senior Night victory over Bellarmine in February, I had asked Coach Winstel how special she considered this team to be, after all they had been through this year. "They are probably one of the most loving teams to one another that I have coached ever," she said. "They don't like to let each other down.

There really isn't anyone on the team that nobody likes." When I asked about the difficulty of replacing the five seniors, she used a memorable phrase to summarize why, even though she will miss them greatly, she would not want them to stay: "they came here to leave." The whole point of their education, and of their playing on the team, is to prepare them to leave when the time comes.

The five seniors had now done that for which they came. In the words of Brittany's journal entry on the first day of practice six months ago, they had completed "their last year of basketball. Ever." We had watched them grow before our very eyes, and now they were going. None of them had achieved everything she had hoped for during her senior year, but each had discovered new strengths she did not know she had. After being challenged and nurtured in the intense cocoon of NKU women's basketball, each could now feel that cocoon "tighten" as she expanded from the inside. From that "dim capacity for wings" with which each had arrived in Regents Hall, each had now developed the "aptitude to fly" somewhere else altogether.

I conducted my exit interviews with most of the players during the two weeks before the April awards ceremony. Again I was impressed with how articulate and forthcoming these young women were. I was happy to see that they had great pride in their season—and themselves—in spite of their disappointments at both the beginning and end of the season. I was especially happy that the seniors felt that way. In spite of unfulfilled dreams during their "last season ever," they expressed undiminished devotion to the game and one another; they spoke of the "great experience" and "tremendous opportunity" of playing on this team, and each was grateful for the way basketball had "shaped" her as a person.

I asked some of my questions to all the players to get a spectrum of responses across the team. When I asked each player to choose the single word that she felt best characterized Coach Winstel, half of them chose "intense." The other words were "passionate," "determined," "demanding," "respected," and "outspoken" (in the sense of "telling you what she thinks"). More than one player said she hopes one day to be as passionate about her work as Coach Winstel is. Many emphasized that "she will do absolutely anything for you."

I wondered how they felt about the intensity with which Coach Winstel gets on them in practice. When I asked whether that kind of intensity is necessary for the results she gets on the court, Angela Healy gave a classic answer: "I like that style, even if I don't like it at the time." A coach has to push because "that's what a leader does."

What if you feel the coach is riding a teammate, or even a close friend, too hard?

"I try to make it seem that I'm not on either person's side. I might try to explain to a teammate that Coach is not telling you this because she doesn't like you. She wants you to be better. It's for you." It can be "tough," but "you see both sides and you do whatever you've got to do."

When I spoke with Nicole I wondered whether she remembered an encounter in Australia after her freshman year in which the coach had got on her so much about her defense that she had cried. She did remember it. She did not particularly like the way the coach had done it, but "it was important for her to tell me, to let me know what I need to do better in order for me to play for her. And I guess the way she did it is beside the point. You just have to take it and go out there and get it done. It happens to everybody and we're just all there for each other."

I got two kinds of answers when I asked each player for the single word that best characterized her teammates as a group. Half of them stressed their idiosyncratic differences with words like "unique," "crazy," "eclectic," "charismatic," "random." The others chose words about qualities they have in common: "exciting," "enthusiasm," "close-knit," "never-give-up" and "family" (the "functional" kind). Many had trouble choosing a single word to characterize the team as a whole, but each enjoyed elaborating on whatever word she had chosen. They all enjoyed talking about their teammates and what they had accomplished.

Coach Winstel once told me that "the most important thing about a season is how the players feel"—that how she feels as the coach is "immaterial." Lynn Plett, the Lewis coach, had said something similar when we spoke before the February game in Regents

Hall: "As a coach you remember the losses, but you hope your players will remember the victories." Winstel's players were remembering all the victories at the end of this season. They were deeply disappointed not to get farther in the NCAA Tournament, but they felt evident pride and success in what they had accomplished. Winstel was proud of her team, too. But she, like Plett, remembers the losses. When I asked her for the single word that best summarized the 2006–07 season, the first word she chose was "frustrating." After thinking a bit about the challenges that had been overcome, she modified it to "challenging."

When I asked each player what she thought would be the best measure of what the team had accomplished during its last two seasons, two looked back to 2005–06, when the team had achieved so much when nobody expected it, especially upsetting Drury for the conference championship. Others chose examples from the current season—when they beat Drury at Drury or when they came back to beat Lewis, Parkside, and Bellarmine after being beaten by each of them earlier. Another chose the two win streaks—16 in one year, 12 in the next.

Other players defined the team's achievement not in terms of specific games or seasons but in more abstract, intimate terms: "playing like we're capable of," "growing as a team," "how we played as a team," "playing well together," "sticking together through ups and downs," and "dealing with all the stuff that we have and working through it every time." These players were defining themselves not so much by their wins and losses as by what Dickinson calls that "internal difference, / Where the meanings are." The internal and external components are both essential in evaluating the success of a team.

Years and decades from now, the friendships and relationships are probably what the players will remember most. When I asked each player to describe what was most fun about being on this team, I expected to hear about certain hilarious moments or episodes. Instead they emphasized "just being with the girls," "the closeness of everybody," "making it fun even in practice when the coach is having a bad day and getting on you," "meeting people who will be friends forever." When I interviewed Keri's father at halftime of the

Northern Michigan game and told him how happy I was that her knee was strong enough that she could play now, he said, "Whether she plays or not, it's the relationships that matter." Angela had condensed those relationships into one line of her poem: "by team I mean best friends from near and far."

But these players and their fans will also remember those special moments in which they transcended themselves and lifted us with them into temporary ecstasy: The astonishing upset over Drury at the conference tournament in 2006. The suspended moment in which Brittany's miraculous shot spun into the basket against Parkside in 2007. The moments when Karmen started hitting game winners at NKU after never having done so in high school. The game in which Cassie blocked the ball like no one we've ever seen. Athletes and fans live for such moments, such spots of time in the flow of life. Once we taste them, we hunger for more. Coach Schmidt compares this craving to a kind of addiction. "When you win a big game, you want another one. When you score a big bucket, you want to make another one. Whenever you catch any of the big highs, you want another one." You want another "taste," in Dickinson's words, of "a liquor never brewed."

On the other side of the ecstasy of transcendence is the agony of preparation. When I asked Nicole what had been the most difficult thing as a member of this team, she said, "Just the wear and tear of practices every day. It's not like a job where you can walk in and get things done without too much energy or emotion. The emotions you go through, and just the stress of constantly being ready to go, takes a lot out of you." The physical part is "a lot on your body, but the good thing about our team is that everyone wants to win, whether it's in a drill or a huge game. That's just part of our passion as athletes. But when you are feeling 'emotional' about things, and you have to bring that every day, it's more draining than you can ever imagine.

"And it doesn't end. You have to work on it all year long. You have high and low emotions all through basketball—winning and losing, having good days of practice and bad—and it takes a toll on you sometimes. It's a lot, but in the end it's worth it when you accomplish things. You have to have a good balance for it, and having

274

close family and close friends that are on the team really helps you to be able to deal with it all."

At the time of the awards ceremony on April 22, only 5-foot-5 guard Diondra Holliday, from Clark Montessori in Cincinnati, had signed for the 2007–08 season. By the middle of June Schmidt and Winstel had also successfully recruited two more freshmen, Kendra Caldwell, a 6-foot post player from Xenia High School in Ohio, and Rita Stéfan, a 5-foot-9 Hungarian-born guard from Mount de Chantal Visitation Academy in Wheeling, West Virginia. They also signed Jessie Slack, a 5-foot-11 junior transfer from East Carolina University, a native of Mount Perry, Ohio, who appears to be very well suited to our wing position.

Each of these recruits will find out next fall what it means to "listen to what Nancy says." Each will learn, as Cassie Brannen did as a freshman, that this woman who "comes off as a real sweetie" will "yell at you." Each will discover, as Rachel Lantry did, that Winstel will not "ask you to do anything that you are not able to do." And that she would not have recruited them if she did not know what they *could* do. And that all she really wants from her players is intense, concentrated effort for 40 minutes of every game and 150 minutes of every practice.

I saw Coach Winstel at a campus event in mid-June, during a short break from the first of her many 2007 summer camps for girls. I congratulated her on the new players who were signed for the upcoming season. Her eyes were again bright with expectation as she told me of the challenge of bringing these new players in together with her returning ones. "Sometimes that can be even more fun than when you have everyone coming back." She, her team, and her fans should be in for another exciting year. Next year's team will have only two seniors rather than five. Having just said good-bye to this year's seniors, I do not want to even think about saying good-bye to Healy and Chiodi next year. But that day, too, will come. And they, too, will be prepared.

When I began writing this book I did not expect to be quoting Emily Dickinson all the time. But once her words began to associate themselves with what I was seeing and writing about, there was no end to it. Poetry and basketball are certainly different worlds. The popular image of Emily Dickinson as a pale recluse in a white dress writing thousands of poems in isolation in the middle of the 19th century certainly contrasts sharply with the public, physical lives led by the young women of this book early in the 21st century. Yet they do have common ground. Dickinson was giving explicit expression to exactly those themes of female identity and empowerment that Winstel's players are expressing implicitly in the most public arena of their own private lives.

Dickinson shaped her identity and empowered herself while writing and revising the 1,770 poems she left unpublished at her death in 1886. Winstel's players shape and empower themselves in the practice sessions the public never sees. In each case, the process is as important as the final result. That is why Winstel believes that the successful coach must love not only the game and her players but also the "process" of "becoming a team." As she writes in the afterword to this book, "some coaches hate to practice; me, I love practice. It's the time when I get to do what I love the best, 'teach the game.' If you truly want to prepare your team to compete, the place you do it is at practice. That's where teams are made! That's where they learn to win!

"There is no greater reward to me as a coach than to have a group of young ladies go through the process of preseason conditioning, practice, and game preparation and then, on game day, go out and play the game as 'one' and, yes, be successful doing it. It is great for me to be a small part of that performance. It's like putting the pieces of an orchestra together to make a great symphony, or watching a dance recital where everyone moves in perfect harmony. To me, it's poetry in motion."

Dickinson presented her most concise account of her own artistic process in these lines written during the Civil War:

> I made slow riches but my gain
> Was steady as the sun
> And every night it numbered more
> Than the preceding one.

This is exactly how it works with Winstel and her players. The day-after-day practice eventually adds up to a body of work, a sequence of accomplishments whose "slow riches" mean more than one had originally envisioned. I am grateful to have witnessed, for one entire season, its day-by-day accretion as much as its week-by-week display.

Two years before describing her poetic process in the lines above, Dickinson wrote about her inspiration:

> It was given me by the gods
> When I was a little girl.
> They give us presents most, you know,
> When we are new and small.
> I kept it in my hand
> I never put it down.

Born three decades apart, Nancy Winstel and the members of her 2006–07 team had received comparable girlhood gifts. Each had cherished and developed her individual gift until the angled road of experience brought them together on one rectangular floor where they could learn to share, strengthen, perfect, and display the gift the gods had given. Working together on the same court that had been Winstel's home court in 1974, each had learned to take her power against the world, yes, but with one another.

Thirteen strong women. Playing for more than they know. Including all those who had come before. And those who would return to Regents Hall for one last season.

CONCLUSION
March 2008

A bird came down the walk:
He bit an angle-worm in halves
And ate the fellow, raw.
—*Emily Dickinson*

In 2008 March Madness lasted the whole month. The shock of last year's last-second loss to Ferris State receded deeper and deeper into the past as this year's team won one game after another all the way to the national championship game in Kearney, Nebraska, on March 29. In that game unranked NKU upset the highly favored University of South Dakota, duplicating the feat of Winstel's team in upsetting North Dakota State for the national title eight years earlier. Led by senior cocaptains Angela Healy and Nicole Chiodi, the 2007–08 team achieved all that had been hoped for the year before, without being expected to do it.

The season had started well. The team had a 13–3 record and was ranked 14th in the nation when they left for a road trip into Missouri in late January. NKU was expected to beat Missouri–St. Louis. The Riverwomen were having a difficult season, with a 4–10 record, but they upset us 56–51. We knew it would be hard to beat Missouri S&T, the new name for the university in Rolla. They were having a terrific season with a 12–2 record and were leading Drury in the GLVC West. They beat us 66–42 in one of our worst performances in memory, knocking us out of the national rankings for the rest of the season.

CONCLUSION

The team bounced back to win five straight games at home. These were the last regular-season games ever to be played at Regents Hall (next year's team would be playing in the brand-new Bank of Kentucky Center). In the very last game, against Indianapolis on February 16, NKU wore retro uniforms to match those worn by Nancy Winstel and her teammates in the very first game at Regents Hall in 1974. This was our most important game thus far in the season because we were tied with Indy for first place in the GLVC East. NKU won a very hard-fought game 68–60. The turning point came when junior Danyelle Echoles made a three-pointer with 4:10 remaining to break a 57–57 tie. She had earned a starting guard position through her exceptional defensive play; now her offense helped us win a critical game on Senior Night for Healy and Chiodi. These were the best 40 minutes the team had played all season. I e-mailed the publisher of this book, already in production, to ask whether there would be time to add a postscript should something remarkable happen in this year's postseason.

After the stirring victory over Indianapolis, the team faced four games on the road to end the regular season. We lost the first of them to Bellarmine, always difficult to beat in Knights Hall. Then we lost at Kentucky Wesleyan in one of the worst games we had played all season. Those losses dropped us out of first place in the GLVC—and from number five to number nine in the regional poll. We would now have to win both remaining road games to have a chance for the NCAA Tournament. Those games were at Wisconsin–Parkside and Lewis, two places where we have difficulty winning even in the best of years. Both teams were battling Bellarmine, Indianapolis, and NKU for the top of the GLVC East.

Winstel was so disgusted with the way the team played at Kentucky Wesleyan that she gave the players two days off and challenged her cocaptains to fix whatever was wrong with the chemistry of the team. The team responded with a powerful 15-point win over Wisconsin–Parkside and a good 6-point win over Lewis. We finished the regular season with 20 wins and 7 losses. Our conference record of 13–6 tied us with Indianapolis for first place in the GLVC East, but we won the title because we had beat them both at home and away. Our players finally had a happy ride home from Romeoville.

One reason we beat Parkside so handily is that Echoles held Kayla Ming, averaging 18.5 points a game, to 4 points. Another reason is that their senior guard Mackenzie Heise was able to play only a few minutes because of a knee injury that had essentially ended her season. Winstel had mentioned before the game that Heise was entering the game with 997 career points. She hinted to her players that it would be okay to give her an open three if we should have a big enough lead at the very end of the game. Heise missed a three-pointer with 12 seconds left. Rachel Lantry got the rebound and passed to teammate Jessica Wendeln, who passed to a surprised Heise. She had just enough time to gather herself, launch a three, and make her 1,000th career point. The statistician has no category for a gesture such as Jessica's. The official play-by-play charges a turnover to Wendeln on a steal by Heise.

March 4, 8, and 9: GLVC Tournament

This year the conference tournament was played at local sites rather than at Roberts Stadium in Evansville. As the first seed in the East, NKU played one more game at Regents Hall, hosting SIU–Edwardsville in the first round. Drury, with a record of 24–3, was the first seed in the West and the top seed overall. If they won in the first round they would host the semifinals and the championship game. They were currently ranked first in the Great Lakes Region and eighth in the nation.

NKU won its first-round game against Edwardsville in very impressive fashion. We broke open a very close game by holding Amber Shelton and her entire team scoreless for the last 10 minutes. This victory avenged that last-second loss in Regents Hall the year before when Shelton had scored after we threw the ball away. We had balanced scoring from Slack (17), Echoles (16), Brannen (14), and Healy (12).

One more victory in the conference tournament would give us a good chance to make the NCAA. It would have to come against Missouri S&T on Drury's court. This time we beat them resoundingly, 79–67, avenging the disastrous drubbing they had given us on their own court in January. All five starters were in double figures. Healy had 21, Brannen 17, Slack 16, Chiodi 12, and Echoles 11. Chiodi also had 11 rebounds for a double-double.

Playing this well made us believe we could beat Drury in the championship game. They had beat us by three points in Regents Hall in January. This time they beat us by four, 71–67, primarily because their pressing defense forced us into 26 turnovers. Slack, Echoles, and Chiodi scored in double figures, but we had such difficulty getting the ball up the court and in to either Brannen or Healy that they scored only 10 points between them.

This was a very disappointing loss because we had played so poorly. But this team still had much to be proud of. They had already outperformed last year's team by winning the GLVC East and making the finals of the conference tournament. Angela Healy made first-team All-Conference. She was averaging 14.6 points and 9.8 rebounds a game, with 14 double-doubles. She led the league in rebounds, was second only to Brannen in blocked shots, and was shooting 52.1 percent from the floor and 83.6 from the line. None of these statistics, impressive as they are, could measure the personal leadership Angela brought to the team.

Cassie Brannen and Jessie Slack were both averaging 12.8 points a game. Cassie was leading the league in blocked shots and was second in field goal percentage (56.4). Jessie was our leading three-point shooter, but she could also spin and drive, sometimes filling up the net as fast as Katie Butler had. She and Chiodi both made the All-Tournament team. Nicole was averaging 9 points and 6.2 rebounds a game. She was fourth in the league in defensive rebounds, a remarkable achievement for a point guard. She was second in the league in minutes played per game, having had several games in which she played all 40 minutes without a single turnover.

All these individuals could be proud of their play during most of the season, but the motto of this year's team was "One Body, One Team." Like their coach, they knew they had not yet reached the consistency and toughness they would need to succeed in the NCAA Tournament. Too often they had played brilliantly only to fall into six minutes of lethargy. Too often they had played really well only in the second half. Too often they had thrown the ball away under pressure—or not under pressure. They were still a work in progress, but they were progressing. Their two victories in the conference tournament earned them the fourth seed in the Great Lakes Regional. Now they would see how far they could go.

March 14, 15, and 17: NCAA Regional

As expected, Drury hosted the NCAA Regional Tournament. Only two GLIAC teams qualified, the other six coming from the GLVC. Our first-round game was against Indianapolis, and we played a terrible first half. The defense was as bad as the offense, and they outscored us 33–20. In the second half Healy scored 7 points in the first five minutes to key an 11–2 run. But we were still behind 44–36 with 9:10 remaining. Echoles kept the season alive by making three three-pointers in the next four minutes. Her teammates then took over, and NKU held on to win 55–54. Healy led the team with 18 points and 10 rebounds. For the third year in a row NKU had won or lost by 1 point in the first round of the NCAA. Now we would have to face Drury again on their own court.

During this season I had enjoyed being a regular fan again. I did not have to worry about bringing tape recorders, arranging interviews, or scheduling my life around practices. But I still wrote a little summary of each game on my score sheet. My summary for this one began: "Another strange game from this team, playing terribly in the first half, then coming back to win by one." Looking ahead, "the advantage would seem to be with Drury, but this crazy team might pull it out the way the 2003 team did in the NCAAs."

The next day we totally outplayed Drury, 84–65. Cassie Brannen had the game of her life when we needed it most, scoring 29 points on 9 of 13 from the floor and 10 of 10 from the line. She dominated the way Brittany Winner had when we upset Drury for the conference title in 2006. This victory, however, was in the second round of the NCAA. That was the same round in which Grand Valley had beat us so badly on this same Drury court back in the year of the tornadoes. This year's team had suddenly surpassed the achievements of that magical 2005–06 season as well.

This loss was devastating for Drury and its fans. Their team had every expectation of defending its regional title and returning to Kearney, Nebraska, for the Elite Eight, this time hoping to advance beyond the first round. It was a tough way for Molly Carter, such a splendid athlete and courageous competitor, to end her career. I could not get NKU's Webcast on my computer at home, so I found the one by Drury's announcers. They greatly admired Cassie's amazing game, but they called her "Casey." At one point they announced, "Hannah's on the floor and we don't know what happened." Any NKU fan would have known that Molly Carter's younger sister Hannah had run into one of Healy's immovable backcourt picks. This year Angela has gotten into the habit of helping up those who run into her.

Our opponent for the Great Lakes Regional championship was Missouri S&T, who had beaten Quincy in the semifinals. We beat them decisively, 60–52, to advance to the Elite Eight. Again, Cassie Brannen was the star of the game, scoring 25 points on 8 of 9 from the field and 8 of 8 from the line. She was named the tournament's Most Outstanding Player. Jessie Slack also made the All-Tournament team. Angela Healy was chosen first-team Great Lakes Region.

Winstel admitted that if you had asked her in November whether this team would be going to the Elite Eight, "I probably would have laughed." As recently as the loss to Kentucky Wesleyan, our chances had seemed poor for even making the Great Lakes Regional that we now had won. Since then the team had elevated its game to a higher level. All year these young women had enjoyed playing and just being with one another. Now they were challenging one another to surpass all expectations.

March 26, 27, and 29: Elite Eight

No teams returned from last year's tournament in the Health and Sports Center of the University of Nebraska at Kearney. Six of this year's teams were ranked in the most recent national poll. Undefeated Delta State University (32–0) was ranked first in the country. The University of South Dakota (31–1) was ranked third. They were followed by the University of Alaska–Anchorage (number 9, 29–4), Franklin Pierce University (number 17, 27–5), California University of Pennsylvania (number 23, 27–6), and Washburn University in

Kansas (number 24, 26–6). Wingate University (North Carolina; 27–6) headed the list of "Others Receiving Votes," with 33. NKU (25–8) was last on that list with a single vote, compared with 647 for Delta State and 597 for South Dakota.

The Elite Eight bracket had been preset according to region, so NKU from the Great Lakes Region opened against Wingate from the South Atlantic. Wingate came in with an 11-game win streak that ended 78–65. They had been averaging 78 points a game and were led by junior guard Anna Atkinson, who was averaging 14.9 points and 8.3 assists per game. We had a height advantage up front and would have to slow the tempo to be successful. We were leading 21–18 when Healy got her second foul with nine minutes remaining in the first half. We were in danger of losing the lead with her on the bench, but sophomore Rachel Lantry and freshman Kendra Caldwell came off the bench to help us expand the lead to 33–27. Lantry immediately made two assists and hit two straight threes. Caldwell had four points, two rebounds, and two blocked shots filling in for Healy.

With Angela back for the second half NKU found its rhythm. Slack hit three three-pointers to spark a 16–6 run that put the game effectively out of reach. She finished with 20 points, 5 assists, and 4 steals. Healy had 16 points, 8 rebounds, and 4 assists. Brannen had 15 points, 6 rebounds, and 3 blocks. Chiodi played 38 minutes at the point with no turnovers and 3 steals; she led all rebounders with 9. This was an excellent performance by the team's upperclass leaders, but the result might have been different if Lantry and Caldwell had not played so well off the bench. Each finished with 8 points.

Our Final Four opponent, Alaska–Anchorage, had outlasted Franklin Pierce 71–65 the night before in overtime. This powerful team presented an entirely different kind of challenge. They had upset previously unbeaten Seattle Pacific to reach the Elite Eight. Six-foot-two center Rebecca Kielpinski was their anchor underneath, averaging 12.2 points and 8.8 rebounds per game. She had keyed the overtime victory over Franklin Pierce with 28 points and 14 rebounds. Five-foot-seven guard Kalhie Quinones was averaging 10.5 points and 3.8 assists per game. She had 16 points, 10 rebounds, and 4 steals in the win over Franklin Pierce. Guard Maria Nilsson and forward Ruby Williams were averaging 10.1 and 9.5 points a game. This extremely well-balanced team had been scoring 71 points a game while holding its opponents to an average of 51. Our differential was half as wide, 69 points to 59.

In one very important way, this game was like the one with Wingate: Healy drew her second foul with 10 minutes remaining in the first half. We had built up a very impressive 17–10 lead. Without Healy to battle Kielpinski underneath, we seemed in danger of losing it quickly. But Kendra Caldwell again provided exceptional play off the bench to help preserve a 26–21 halftime lead. This was our toughest game inside all year. Kielpinski and Williams held Healy and Brannen to 1 of 7 field goals in the first half. But Caldwell helped hold Kielpinski to 1 of 8. Two consecutive three-pointers by Echoles and another by Slack gave us the halftime lead. We shot only 37.5 percent from the field in the first half, but we held Alaska–Anchorage to 25 percent.

The second half was a game of fierce runs. Alaska–Anchorage opened with five straight points to tie the game at 26. NKU took the lead for the next six minutes, but Dasha Basova tied the game at 36 with 10:21 remaining. NKU went on a 7–0 run to lead by nine with 6:49 remaining. We seemed to be in control. We still had a nine-point lead, 50–41, with 3:53 remaining. But Alaska–Anchorage made a six-point run on four free throws by Kielpinski and a jumper by Quinones. After Healy and Brannen responded with four consecutive free throws, Basova drove for a powerful three-point play and fouled Brannen out of the game, reducing our lead to 54–52 with 1:13 remaining. Slack answered with two consecutive free throws, but Quinones drove for a layup and fouled Healy out of the game with 0:48 remaining. With Caldwell and Brackman playing for Brannen and Healy, we held the Seawolves scoreless the rest of the way for a 57–54 victory.

It took an extraordinary defensive effort by NKU to hold Kielpinski to 2 of 13 from the field. But she made all 12 of her free throws and helped foul both Healy and Brannen out of the game. NKU got balanced scoring from all its starters in the second half. Echoles was our leading scorer with 13. Slack finished with 12, Healy and Brannen each had 10, Chiodi had 9. Chiodi's 12 rebounds led both teams; Healy and Brannen followed with 8 and 7. We hit 57 percent of our field goals in the second half, compared with 33 percent for Alaska–Anchorage. It was an imposing exhibition of team defense. Our entire team embodied Melville's declaration that "in everything imposingly beautiful, strength has much to do with the magic."

Immediately after the NKU-Anchorage battle came what was billed as the marquee matchup of the tournament: undefeated Delta State, ranked first in the nation, versus South Dakota, ranked third. Many assumed that whoever won this game would win the national championship, especially now that unranked NKU was to be the opponent. South Dakota won with a strong finish, 68–58. In doing so they extended their record to 33–1 and their win streak to 31. Our win streak was currently 5, with one more needed to become the best in the nation. No team with 8 losses had ever won the national championship. Cal Poly Pomona had won the very first tournament in 1982 with a 29–7 record. Since 1987, when Winstel's team got to the Final Four on her first trip to the Elite Eight, no team had won the national championship with more than 5 losses.

Winstel loves the underdog status. She used it to her team's advantage in the 2000 victory over North Dakota State. The fact that her unranked 2007–08 team, with only 1 vote in the final national poll, was playing the third-ranked team, with 597 votes, almost guaranteed that South Dakota would underrate us. Adding to the David and Goliath dynamic was the fact that Vermillion, South Dakota, is only four hours from Kearney by bus, guaranteeing that the bleachers and end zones of the Health and Sports Center would be filled to overflowing with red-sweatered South Dakota Coyote fans. They would be certain to drown out the 40 or 50 parents, fans, and cheerleaders who had traveled more than 17 hours from Highland Heights by car or bus to make the opening game on Wednesday. These included Chuck Hilgeman, who had seen every Elite Eight game Winstel had coached back to 1987, and Ray Rack, who had seen almost every home or away game she had coached for more than a decade.

On Saturday these die-hard fans would be supplemented by the pep band and additional fans on a second bus, and by President

Votruba and other dignitaries arriving by air. After all the excitement of the last two days, it would be hard to wait all day Friday and most of Saturday for the championship game. In Kearney, one of the best ways to spend a day and a half of waiting is to watch the birds.

To wait on an abandoned bridge over the Platte River on a frigid, overcast morning for nearly an hour before sunrise to see all the cranes you can hear but not see finally decide to rise from the sandbars into the sky in weaving necklaces—in strings of dozens and hundreds that turn into thousands upon thousands, first from the east of the bridge and then from the west—is an experience never to forget. I had not known before arriving in Kearney on Tuesday night that 500,000 sandhill cranes populate the shallows of the Platte River for three weeks every March on their way to Canada, Alaska, or Siberia. Theirs is one of the most majestic migrations in the hemisphere, drawing viewers from across the nation and around the world. And here I was on that free Friday morning, seeing and feeling and hearing what it was all about. The entire multitude ascends every morning at sunrise, preceded by a raucous squawking that grows to an absolute roar as their bodies rise to the sky.

After gorging themselves all day on waste grain in widely scattered crop fields, the cranes return like clockwork as the sun is setting to roost for another night along the shallows of the river. The sun this evening is warm and brilliant as the birds glide down through a blue, breezy sky. The squawking intensifies as the darkness descends. The river has been shrinking in recent decades as its waters are diverted to irrigation upstream—causing more birds to compete for less space as they alight from the sky and fight for a place on the sand.

I could not watch the powerful, coordinated flight of these sleek, streamlined creatures without thinking of the imposing beauty, strength, and grace of the female athletes we had come to watch in Kearney—each creature combining freedom and discipline in a deeply instinctual way. Nor could I listen to the squawking of the congregated cranes as they salute the morning together, or fight for roosting spots at night, without thinking of raucous fans roosting on bleacher seats game after game as we claim our space and defend our kind. March Madness is a national ritual in which we root and roost for the teams we love.

Doing so connects us with something more primal than we are aware of. I first began to sense this a year and a half ago when Winstel's players were squawking like starving seagulls and waddling like sedated penguins at the beginning of that conditioning session in which Danyelle had lost her breath and Cassie had gone lightheaded. For three magical weeks every March the players we love to watch link us vicariously to deep, primordial rhythms until that last championship game is finally played, leaving this manifestation of our biological imperative barren and at rest until the return of the birds and the brackets brings the madness again.

How could the players stand to wait until 5 P.M. Saturday? It was hard enough for the fans to wait. Finally the doors opened an hour before the game. On Wednesday and Thursday we had shown our tournament tickets and walked right in. So we arrived about 15 minutes early only to find hundreds if not thousands of red-sweatered South Dakota fans jamming both hallways waiting for the doors to open. Fortunately, one section of the bleachers behind our players' bench had been reserved for us. Otherwise we would have been scattered to the winds in a sea of red. All but a few hundred of the 3,000 who filled the stands were South Dakota fans.

Like Alaska–Anchorage, South Dakota is a powerful team on both offense and defense. They were averaging 76 points a game and giving up 59. They have a unique offensive alignment in which all five players spread out beyond the arc. All their starters are adept at shooting the three, driving one-on-one, or swinging into a wonderful weave that seems to unbraid whenever they want it to. Jeana Hoffman leads them in scoring with 17.4 points a game, hitting 41.5 percent of her three-point shots. Five of her teammates average between 11.5 and 7.7 points a game. We have a height advantage with four 6-foot starters, but it is hard to imagine in advance how that will play out against their offensive spread.

This game would certainly test our perimeter defense because their offense is *all* perimeter. Our nose-on-ball defense has improved all year with the emergence of Echoles as a defensive specialist. Slack, too, after coming in primarily as a shooter, has been learning to play Winstel defense. When I asked her dad at the reception after the game whether it had been difficult for her, as a junior transfer, to adjust to Winstel's methods, he said, "No, it wasn't a problem for Jessie. She does fine with people like that."

The game started well for NKU. When Jeana Hoffman hit a three-pointer for a 3–2 lead, Slack matched it for a 5–3 lead. Soon after Jeana's twin sister, Jenna, made a three for an 8–5 lead, Lantry, in for Echoles, made one for a 9–8 lead. When Jeana Hoffman tied the game at 13 with another three, Chiodi immediately answered with a rare three-pointer of her own. After two power layups by Angela Healy, NKU led by 21–14 with 6:27 remaining in the half. But now we turned cold and South Dakota heated up. They outscored us 12–2 to take a 26–23 lead into the locker room. In addition to missing field goals at the end of the half, we were missing free throws. Healy, Slack, and Brannen missed 4 of 6 in those closing minutes.

One reason they missed may be that they were shooting into an end zone filled with red-sweatered fans who were doing everything they could to distract them, waving long tubes or balloons that I had not noticed when they were jamming the hallways before the game. We would be shooting into a more neutral crowd in the second half. Many of the Kearney locals behind the other basket were cheering for the upstarts from NKU. These included the class of fifth-grade students that our players had visited the day before the tournament began. They were in the first row, wearing black shirts with NKU taped on the front and ESPN2 on the back. The meltdown at the end of the half was worrisome, but Healy had played the whole half with only one foul. The refs were letting them play, position, bump, and battle.

South Dakota showed what a strong team they were during the first five minutes of the second half. They outscored NKU 12–3 to take a 12-point lead, 38–26. Their defense was forcing us out of our rhythm. During this stretch we missed three layups as well as three

three-pointers. This was going to be a very difficult game to win. Maybe the polls, the national television audience must have been thinking, were right.

Suddenly the game turned back our way. After Brannen made two straight free throws at the "good" end of the floor, Echoles made eight straight points on a three-pointer, a pair of free throws, and another three-pointer. She had reduced the deficit to only three points, 39–36, with 10:50 remaining. It now seemed to be anybody's game. But South Dakota answered with a 10–4 run to lead by nine, 49–40, with 5:52 remaining.

Now NKU surged back with a 10–1 run to tie the score at 50 with 3:11 left to play. The first five of those points came on a jumper and a three-pointer by Slack, each sparked by a steal by Lantry. Then Brannen broke open for two strong layups, being fouled on the second for another good free throw. When South Dakota took the lead for the last time with a pair of free throws, Brannen answered with four more points on a layup and two free throws. Cassie fouled out blocking a layup with 1:12 remaining, but her teammates closed out the scoring with a basket by Healy and free throws by Lantry, Slack, Echoles, Healy, and Echoles. Our poise and power during those last six minutes were unbeatable as we made play after play and shot after shot to close the game out, 63–58. In those closing moments the red-sweatered end zone was as quiet as the riverbank when the birds have flown.

A remarkable end to a remarkable season. Angela Healy finished the game with 14 points and 13 rebounds and was named Most Valuable Player of the national tournament, the honor Michelle Cottrell had won eight years earlier. Cassie Brannen finished with 18 points, 15 in the second half, a performance that put her on the All-Tournament team with Healy. Danyelle Echoles had 12 points, all in the second half, when she kept us in the game while no one else was scoring. Jessie Slack had 11 points, 7 in the second half, and also finished with 5 assists. Nicole Chiodi scored only 4 points, but she had 5 assists and 8 rebounds while playing all 40 minutes without a turnover. NKU as a team had only 10 turnovers, one of its lowest totals of the year against the toughest team it had faced. Our inner strength was shown on the most bizarre of those turnovers. Slack was wrestled out of bounds by two Coyotes after grabbing a defensive rebound with 1:19 remaining. Instead of calling the foul, the referee called Jessie out of bounds and returned the ball to South Dakota. They immediately made the play that fouled Cassie out of the game. Any team might well be flustered by such a turn of events, but our team continued to play with authority and total concentration.

Our long, lean players, who had shown impressive strength against Alaska–Anchorage under the basket, showed impressive length against South Dakota beyond the arc, playing them close and high to deny both the shot and the drive. They were making 42.6 percent of their field goals during the season, but we held them to 32.2. They were making 37.7 percent of their threes, but we held them to 23.3. After missing 6 of 10 free throws in the first half, we made 19 of 23 in the second half. Cassie made 8 of 9 for the game. The one free throw she missed in the first half was the only one she missed in the NCAA Tournament, in which she made 37 of 38!

At the press conference after the game a reporter asked Winstel about a moment in the second half when she had some words for Echoles, who was benched after being called for a charge. Not wanting to answer directly, she said, with the barest hint of a smile, "I probably said something like, 'Keep up the good work.'" Unsatisfied, the reporter asked Echoles if she remembered it the same way the coach did. She shrugged and said, "Yeah, it was probably something like that." But then she went on to say, "Coach and I have an understanding about how I need to be an emotional player and sometimes my teammates feed off that. So I have to feel I can be myself out there to play as well as I can."

Winstel, after mumbling something like, "Channel that emotion," spoke a little louder as she went into a mini-dissertation on how "it used to be you could be tough on your players. You could really get onto them when you needed to do it. I still do that but I'm more careful about the way I go about it. With young women today you've got to make it so they want to listen to you. Sometimes you've still got to kick them, but if you do, you'd better hug them too. You'd better hug them more than you kick them."

Winstel, Healy, and Chiodi had gone through a lot since those two incoming freshmen from opposing high schools had arrived at the first open gym an hour early and found a way to get along. Now the two seniors had been best friends for four years and had put themselves, their teammates, and their coach in the record book right alongside Cottrell and Tuchfarber and the team of 2000. During the last three years Angela had become the team's spiritual leader as well as its physical enforcer. She finished her career with 1,262 points and was named honorable mention All-American. Nicole played 1,286 minutes during her senior year, the most ever by an NKU player in a single season. This was her ultimate gift to all those fans who would have loved to see her play more minutes during that difficult freshman year.

I did not want to say good-bye to Healy and Chiodi last year, and I did not have to. Now I am ready to, because they are ready, ready to leave in the way their coach wants each of her players to be ready. In Dickinson's poem, after the bird came down the walk, bit the angle-worm in halves, and ate the fellow raw, "he unrolled his feathers" and "divided" the sky "too silver for a seam." She is "one of the smoothest athletes I have ever seen at NKU," athletic director Jane Meier said of Chiodi as we watched the cranes glide through the evening sky high above the bridge near Kearney.

Photographer Tim Downer was on the bridge too, sharpening his eye for the victory photos he would be shooting the next day. Angela and Nicole together had epitomized our combination of length and strength and our ability to rise to the occasion, making us the best in the nation (see his championship photo). I had assumed they were the ones who had challenged the team to elevate its play after that disastrous loss to Kentucky Wesleyan back in February. The senior cocaptains *had* said some words to the team. But Cassie had also stepped forward, calling a team meeting to which Angela and Nicole were not invited, exhorting her teammates to dig deeper and play harder so their two seniors could have great memories to the very end.

At a festive reception back in Highland Heights, Coach Winstel still had to let people know she hates to lose, beginning her remarks by saying, "This makes me 2 for 25." In the fall she will begin a new season with Cassie and Jessie and Danyelle and Rachel and Karen and Kendra and Diondra and Jessica and some new recruits. The tradition will continue, but a new one will also begin. On November 8 NKU will inaugurate its Bank of Kentucky Center with a double-header against the female and male Cardinals of the University of Louisville. Healy, Chiodi, and their teammates closed out the Regents Hall era maybe even better than their coach had expected. Look for their successors to be playing some very exciting basketball by the time the cranes fly back to Kearney next March. Whatever the result of March Madness 2009, Winstel's returning players already will have scored a unique kind of double-double in November by inaugurating a new era of women's basketball at NKU after having completed the first one in such emphatic fashion in March of the same year.

Winstel's players "come here to leave," but they do not stay away forever. Cottrell and Tuchfarber and Shannon Smith came to a lot of games at Regents Hall this year. At a reception following the last regular-season game at Regents Hall on February 16, Winstel was surrounded by players from every team she had coached as well as by teammates from the school's original team. At halftime of that hotly contested game with Indianapolis, I got photos of Winner, Clark, Graham, and Butler perched on a single bench—and of Mobley, Jensen, Smith, and Flanagan all standing tall.

Kearney, Nebraska, is far, far away and not easy to get to, but three former teammates got there in time to see Healy and Chiodi play their last game. Karmen Graham had a big "NKU" painted on one side of her face as she watched Angela, the incoming freshman she had taught to play the post in the absence of Snardon, complete her career. Also present were Liz Burrows and Nikki Perkins, guards who had helped Nicole learn to work within Winstel's system during her difficult freshman season and some trying times in Australia too. You may have seen the sign Burrows was holding on national TV. The letters in gold on black said, "Chiodi kills Coyotes."

This year's awards ceremony on April 27 was longer than usual. There were two highlight videos—one for the season, another for the postseason. Winstel thanked the supporters of the team, the athletic department, and her coaches and staff. She commented on each player as she presented their awards, with special tributes to Nicole and Angela, her two graduating seniors. Angela and Nicole asked to make their farewell presentations to the coach and their teammates "now, before we start crying." This day the most visible tears were from the coach herself, during the closing seconds of the two-hour ceremony as she gave one last tribute to her two seniors and their teammates for a season in which the team was truly "one."

AFTERWORD

Nancy Winstel

I have been asked to contribute my coaching philosophy to this book. I can't say that I have ever sat down and written out my philosophy on coaching. I have, however, given much thought to the coaching process over the years and have formulated some strong feelings and opinions on the subject. In these next few pages, I will attempt to give the reader some insight into the areas I feel are important.

I believe that a very important role for the coach is to assist student-athletes in making their dreams come true. My job is to help them achieve. I try to do this by preparing them for competition, by giving them the tools to be successful at a high level. This may mean teaching them fundamentals, getting them in shape, or instilling mental toughness.

I believe that coaching at any level is a tremendous challenge. This challenge seems to me to become more and more difficult every year. I'm not sure why that is; it might be because "kids" are different than they were years ago or because I am different. Nonetheless, coaching to me is a great challenge, and I must say, I love challenges. It can consume the heart and the soul. For me, it's all about the team. Yes, there are times when you must put an individual above the team; however, for the most part, team is everything! As a coach, I often must ask myself, is this best for the overall good of the team? Our players know that if they have a problem, I have a problem. If anyone messes with them, they mess with me. We are one! Even though from time to time we have our ups and downs, we can always count on each other. That is a bond that cannot and will not ever be broken!

I believe that in order to be an effective coach, you must have some "loves." First of all, you must love your players; second, you must love the sport you coach; and last, it helps to love the process that it takes to become a team. If you possess these three loves, then you have a chance to be effective in the "challenge." If you do not possess these loves or if you lose these loves, then in my opinion, you are going to have a difficult time being an effective coach.

Love number one—love your players. To me, this is an absolute *must*. I think it's sort of like being a parent. You don't have to like your players all the time; however, I think you must love them. And, this love must be unconditional. You can't turn it on and off like a faucet. This may sound a bit corny, but this is the way I feel. I also think that your players have to know that you love them. You sometimes need to say it, but you really have to show it. Personally, I happen to think that you can show you love your players in many ways. Sometimes with a hug and, yes, sometimes with a kick.

The second love I think you need to have is the love of your sport. No matter which sport you coach, you must have a passion for it. Love watching it, love teaching it, love it! This is the way I feel about the game of basketball. I just love it! The skill it takes to play the game, the conditioning you must have to be successful in the game, and the overall teamwork involved in mastering the game are what make basketball special to me. All coaches should be passionate about the sport they coach.

Third, love the process. Some coaches hate to practice; me, I love practice. It's the time when I get to do what I love the best: teach the game. If you truly want to prepare your team to compete, the place you do it is at practice. That's where teams are made! That's where they learn to win! One of my greatest struggles is in dealing with talented players who don't want to practice, or want to practice only when they feel like it. The great players love practice, and they want to improve; the *really* great players carry those great practices into great play.

I have been very fortunate throughout my career to coach some great practice players who, when game time came, played the game at a very high level. I am very thankful to those young ladies for their hard work during games. However, I am especially thankful to those players who brought it every day in practice and gave their all; in my opinion, they are the real champions. There is no greater reward to me as a coach than to have a group of young ladies go through the process of preseason conditioning, practice, and game preparation and then, on game day, go out and play the game as "one" and, yes, be successful doing it. It is great for me to be a small part of that performance. It's like putting the pieces of an orchestra together to make a great symphony, or watching a dance recital where everyone moves in perfect harmony. To me, it's poetry in motion.

I suppose that when a coach talks about her coaching philosophy, she should include her views on winning and losing. People who know me will tell you that I am not fond of losing. Winning doesn't make me feel superior; it makes me feel worthy. It gives me a sense of accomplishment. This day and age we are all about winning. I really don't think that I am. I think I am somewhat misunderstood when it comes to this subject. I believe in excellence. My goal in coaching every year is not to win every game but to be the best team we are capable of becoming. Now, that standard is very high, so it does involve a score, but at the end of the day, if you do your best, then you have nothing to be ashamed of and no one to explain anything to.

Some people don't want to compete because they are afraid of losing. For me, I don't think that I have ever been afraid of losing or that my team has been (I sure hope that I didn't teach them that). We really don't think about winning or losing. We merely think about competing at the highest level we can and being our best in doing so. Even though in my profession there is so-called pressure to win, I don't really feel that anyone has ever put more pressure on me to win than I have put on myself. I have a competitive drive that is sometimes a very good thing, and other times not so good. It is said that some of your greatest strengths can also be your greatest weaknesses, and I kind of think my competitiveness may be just that.

I guess that's my philosophy. Respect is earned. You cannot demand it. The only way you can lose your integrity is if you give it away. No one can take it from you!

ACKNOWLEDGMENTS

I am grateful, first of all, to Coach Nancy Winstel and her 2006–07 team for all the ways they made this book possible. Although the process of writing about the team turned out to be somewhat more complicated than either the coach or I had originally imagined, the access I was granted for much of the season to practices, open gyms, bus trips, and team meetings gave me insights about the making of the team that I could have gained in no other way. The interviews I had with each of the players in May 2006 introduced me to 12 young women it has been a pleasure to know; my exit interviews with most of the same players in April 2007 deepened my appreciation of what they had achieved on and off the court. Similarly, the interviews granted to me by Coach Winstel and her assistants Matt Schmidt, Katie Vieth, and Travece Turner through the entire time of my project (13 taped interviews with Coach Winstel over an 18-month period) were extremely helpful in understanding the team in ways I could not have perceived from the stands. I trust that my text makes abundantly clear my admiration of the talent and dedication of the players and coaches alike.

I am particularly grateful to Coach Winstel for the afterword she wrote for this book, to Brittany Winner and Angela Healy for allowing me to quote from the journal and poem they wrote during the season, to Keri Finnell and Betsey Clark for providing photographs for possible use in the book, and to Matt Schmidt for sharing his photo archive and other information. I am grateful to Tim Downer for his excellent photos of the players in action, to Joe Ruh and the NKU Sports Information Office for the photos they provided, and to the commissioner's office of the Great Lakes Valley Conference for images provided for use in the book. I am grateful to the parents of the players who took the time to meet with me for taped interviews before, during, or after games at Regents Hall so that I could learn more about who their daughters were before and during their years at NKU. The players themselves provided me with the most important ingredient for this book—the pleasure of watching them play and of watching the team grow.

Many others in the athletic department helped me in the course of this project. I am particularly grateful to athletic director Jane Meier, senior associate athletic director Scott Eaton, strength and conditioning coach Livey Birkenhauer, sports medicine specialist Noriko Masamoto, and team managers Zach Cook and Erica Ziegler. Others at the university who assisted me include sports information director Don Owen, broadcaster Mike Tussey, former men's basketball coach Ken Shields, former sports information director Rick Meyers, photography professor Matt Albritton, and director of the Learning Assistance Center Paul Ellis. Jennifer Gregory, Cynthia Valetta, and Lois Hammill in the Schlachter Family Archives all helped me find photographs for use in the book. Historian Jim Ramage and NKU president Jim Votruba both provided essential encouragement and support.

I am grateful to Danny Miller, chairperson of Literature and Language, who encouraged me to make this brief detour from my long-term research interests. I am equally grateful to the "faculty section" in Regents Hall, with whom I have had the pleasure of watching Winstel coach for more than two decades now, especially John, Rudy, Bill, Karen, Prince, Frank, Jim, Nina, Jon, and Cheryl.

Getting access to the team, the practices, and the support personnel is one thing; to make a book from what one has seen and enjoyed is quite another. First I want to thank Stefanie Harrison for her excellent transcriptions of all the player interviews in May 2006 and many of my subsequent interviews with players and coaches. Rose Curtin and Jenn Conner also transcribed several interviews for me. Many friends and colleagues read early drafts of the book as it evolved. I am particularly grateful to Ron Ellis, Jock Edwards,

ACKNOWLEDGMENTS

Tom Kearns, Scott Eaton, John Alberti, Jim Votruba, and Nancy Winstel for reading large sections of the book and making suggestions for improvement. Other readers who were helpful at various stages of the writing process include Jon Cullick, Jim Ramage, Pat Moynahan, Holly Doyle, John Braden, Blaise Weller, Vicki Prichard, Wyn Kelley, Beth Schultz, and Bob Levine.

Among those who have written about women's college basketball, I am particularly grateful to Pamela Grundy and Susan Shackelford for their pioneering book *Shattering the Glass: The Remarkable History of Women's Basketball* (2005). Among Nancy Winstel's rival coaches in the Great Lakes Valley Conference and its sister conference the Great Lakes Intercollegiate Athletic Conference, I am grateful to Dave Smith of Bellarmine University, Lynn Plett of Lewis University, and Dawn Plitzuweit of Grand Valley State University for granting me interviews during the heat of the season. I am also grateful to Lois Webb, athletic director of Florida Southern University, for granting me an interview during the holiday tournament on her campus in December 2006, and to Timothy M. Southers, head basketball coach at Midway College, for providing information about Nancy Winstel's years as a coach there. I am also grateful to Annalee Ferrante for information she provided in the course of my research.

I am grateful to Steve Wrinn, director of the University Press of Kentucky, for the guidance he provided during the evolution of this book. The readers who read the manuscript for the press made helpful suggestions for improvement. I am grateful to the design staff for their work on the cover design and to Ila McEntire for her guidance during the editorial and production process.

During all my work on this book my greatest support came from my wife, Joan Ferrante. She was gracious about all the time I spent at practices and sometimes traveling with the team; she provided her own keen insight into my subject as a former collegiate tennis player; she also provided helpful insight and advice as a writer, sociologist, and fellow fan. She is the best companion and colleague a husband and writer could have.

NANCY WINSTEL'S RECORD AS A PLAYER AND COACH

Nancy Winstel joined NKU's first women's basketball team in 1974–75, never having played on a basketball team before. More than 30 years later, her career average of 8.3 rebounds per game remains third in school history. Shooting free throws was more of a challenge, but she improved greatly during her senior year. Her win-loss percentage as a player at NKU (75.9 percent) is only slightly ahead of her current career record as a coach at NKU (75.7 percent). In both rebounds and points per game, she put up impressive targets for her current players to shoot at.

Career Statistics as a Player at NKU

Season	1974–75	1975–76	1976–77	Total
Games	27	26	30	83
FG Made	116	104	121	341
FG Att.	250	243	310	803
FG %	46.4	42.8	39.1	42.0
FT Made	47	18	40	105
FT Att.	118	50	71	239
FT %	39.6	36.0	56.3	43.0
Rebounds (per game average)	253 (9.4)	160 (6.1)	275 (9.2)	688 (8.3)
Assists	41	47	57	145
Points (per game average)	279 (10.3)	220 (8.5)	282 (9.4)	781 (9.4)

Career Win-Loss Record as a Player at NKU

Season	Record	Postseason
1974–75	19–8	AIAW National Tournament
1975–76	28–2	AIAW Regional Tournament
1976–77	19–11	AIAW Regional
Total	66–21 (75.9%)	

Career Win-Loss Record as a Head Coach

Season	Record	Postseason
Midway		
1978–79	8–14	
1979–80	14–13	KWIC Championship
1980–81	17–14	KWIC Championship
Midway total	39–41 (48%)	
NKU	Overall; GLVC	
1983–84	17–10	
1984–85	19–9	NCAA Regional Tournament
1985–86	22–6; 13–3	GLVC Co-Championship; NCAA Regional
1986–87	25–5; 14–2	GLVC Co-Championship; NCAA Final Four
1987–88	25–3; 14–2	GLVC Co-Championship; NCAA Regional
1988–89	21–7; 12–4	NCAA Regional
1989–90	20–7; 13–5	
1990–91	22–6; 16–2	GLVC Championship; NCAA Regional
1991–92	19–9; 13–5	NCAA Regional
1992–93	19–8; 12–6	
1993–94	20–7; 13–5	NCAA Regional
1994–95	18–9; 14–6	
1995–96	18–9; 14–6	

Career Win-Loss Record as a Head Coach (cont'd)

Season	Record	Postseason
1996–97	17–10; 14–6	
1997–98	18–10; 13–5	
1998–99	30–3; 20–2	GLVC Championship; NCAA Final Four
1999–2000	32–2; 19–1	GLVC Championship; NCAA National Championship
2000–01	25–5; 17–3	NCAA Regional
2001–02	26–7; 17–3	NCAA Elite Eight
2002–03	26–8; 15–5	NCAA Championship Game
2003–04	17–11; 12–8	NCAA Regional
2004–05	16–12; 13–7	
2005–06	27–5; 16–3	GLVC Championship; NCAA Regional
2006–07	21–8; 14–5	NCAA Regional
2007–08	28–8; 13–6	NCAA National Championship
NKU total	548–184 (75.7%); 329–100 (76.7%)	
Career total	587–225 (72.3%)	

Appendix 2

TEAM AND INDIVIDUAL RECORDS, NOVEMBER 2005–MARCH 2008

The figures below are traces left in the record book by young women whose pleasure in the game, devotion to the program, and achievement as student-athletes exemplify the nature of top-tier Division II collegiate basketball.

2005–06 Season

Women's Basketball Schedule
(27–5 overall; 16–3 GLVC)

Date	Opponent	Result
Nov. 16	Wilberforce	W 71–40
Nov. 22	Northwood (Mich.)	W 81–55
Nov. 26	at Wayne State (Mich.)	W 76–48
Dec. 1	Rockhurst	W 70–57
Dec. 3	Drury	L 45–56
Dec. 8	at St. Joseph's	L 47–50
Dec. 10	at Indianapolis	W 58–56
Dec. 19	W. V. Wesleyan	W 68–48
Dec. 20	Hillsdale	L 52–58
Dec. 22	Loyola (Ill.)	W 74–55
Dec. 29	Brescia	W 63–42
Jan. 5	Kentucky Wesleyan	W 62–47
Jan. 7	Southern Indiana	W 62–43
Jan. 12	at Missouri–St. Louis	W 66–57
Jan. 14	at Missouri–Rolla	W 62–50
Jan. 19	Lewis	W 62–51
Jan. 21	Wisconsin–Parkside	W 68–62

Women's Basketball Schedule (cont'd)

Date	Opponent	Result
Jan. 24	Georgetown (Ky.)	W 57–51
Jan. 28	Bellarmine	W 66–64
Feb. 2	at SIU–Edwardsville	W 72–55
Feb. 4	at Quincy	W 73–70
Feb. 9	Indianapolis	W 81–62
Feb. 11	St. Joseph's	W 76–51
Feb. 14	at Bellarmine	W 82–70
Feb. 18	at Kentucky Wesleyan	W 62–60
Feb. 23	at Wisconsin–Parkside	L 62–70
Feb. 25	at Lewis	W 75–65
Mar. 2	vs. Missouri–St. Louis*	W 72–62
Mar. 4	vs. Quincy*	W 67–49
Mar. 5	vs. Drury*	W 86–73
Mar. 10	vs. Michigan Tech**	W 67–66
Mar. 11	vs. Grand Valley State**	L 70–91

* GLVC Tournament, Evansville, Indiana
**NCAA Great Lakes Regional Tournament, Springfield, Missouri

Team Achievements
Champion, GLVC East Division, 16–3
Champion, GLVC Conference Tournament
First-round winner, NCAA Great Lakes Regional Tournament
Ranking in final NCAA Division II national poll: 19
Team grade point average: 3.524 (fifth in the nation)

Individual Achievements
Leading scorers (per game): Karmen Graham, 14.3; Brittany Winner, 9.7; Karyn Creager, 9.1; Angela Healy, 8.8; Nicole Chiodi, 7.2
Leading rebounders (per game): Karmen Graham, 5.5; Angela Healy, 5.2; Brittany Winner, 5.1; Nicole Chiodi, 4.3
Karmen Graham: first-team GLVC All-Conference; first-team Great

Lakes All-Region; honorable mention All-American; national leader
in free throws made (177)
Brittany Winner: GLVC Tournament Most Valuable Player; second-
team GLVC All-Conference
Karyn Creager: honorable mention GLVC All-Conference
GLVC All-Academic team members: Cassie Brannen, Nicole Chiodi,
Karyn Creager, Danyelle Echoles, Angela Estes, Keri Finnell, Kar-
men Graham, Angela Healy, Brittany Winner
Nancy Winstel: GLVC Coach of the Year

2006–07 Season

Women's Basketball Schedule
(21–8 overall; 14–5 GLVC)

Date	Opponent	Result
Nov. 21	Midway (Ky.)	W 98–42
Nov. 25	Wayne State (Mich.)	W 97–56
Nov. 30	Quincy	W 65–63
Dec. 2	SIU–Edwardsville	L 64–65
Dec. 6	Georgetown (Ky.)	W 92–69
Dec. 9	at Bellarmine	L 78–85
Dec. 18	Northern Michigan	W 68–46
Dec. 19	Grand Valley State	L 58–74
Dec. 28	vs. St. Rose	W 74–63
Dec. 29	vs. Mercyhurst	W 76–50
Jan. 4	at Wisconsin–Parkside	L 57–66
Jan. 6	at Lewis	L 64–75
Jan. 11	Missouri–Rolla	W 72–51
Jan. 13	Missouri–St. Louis	W 67–44
Jan. 18	at Kentucky Wesleyan	W 61–54
Jan. 20	at Southern Indiana	W 70–56
Jan. 25	Indianapolis	W 62–54
Jan. 27	St. Joseph's	W 79–54
Feb. 2	at Drury	W 52–49

Women's Basketball Schedule (cont'd)

Date	Opponent	Result
Feb. 3	at Rockhurst	W 93–41
Feb. 8	Lewis	W 73–61
Feb. 10	Wisconsin–Parkside	W 60–58
Feb. 15	Kentucky Wesleyan	W 76–45
Feb. 19	Bellarmine	W 76–64
Feb. 22	at St. Joseph's	L 58–65
Feb. 24	at Indianapolis	W 58–53
Mar. 2	vs. Missouri–Rolla*	W 67–52
Mar. 3	vs. Drury*	L 57–68
Mar. 9	vs. Ferris State**	L 69–70

* GLVC Tournament, Evansville, Indiana
**NCAA Great Lakes Regional Tournament, Romeoville, Illinois

Team Achievements

Second round, GLVC Tournament
First round, NCAA Great Lakes Regional Tournament
Team grade point average: 3.385 (15th in the nation)

Individual Achievements

Leading scorers (per game): Brittany Winner, 11.3; Angela Healy, 11.3; Karyn Creager, 10.0; Cassie Brannen, 9.0; Katie Butler, 8.3

Leading rebounders (per game): Angela Healy, 6.9; Cassie Brannen, 5.1; Brittany Winner, 4.7; Nicole Chiodi, 4.6

Brittany Winner: first-team GLVC All-Conference; second-team Great Lakes All-Region; GLVC runner-up in three-point field-goal percentage (.471)

Angela Healy: second-team GLVC All-Conference; GLVC All-Tournament team; GLVC leader in defensive rebounds per game (5.97)

Cassie Brannen: honorable mention GLVC All-Conference; GLVC leader in field-goal percentage (.589); NKU school records for shots blocked in a single game (12) and shots blocked in a season (71)

Karmen Graham: 1,088 career points

Karyn Creager: 1,035 career points; NKU school records for consecutive free throws (34), free-throw percentage in a season (.888), and career free-throw percentage (.879); second-team District IV Academic All-American

GLVC All-Academic team members: Karen Brackman, Cassie Brannen, Nicole Chiodi, Karyn Creager, Keri Finnell, Karmen Graham, Angela Healy, Brittany Winner

Nancy Winstel: 500th career victory as a coach at NKU

2007–08 Season

Women's Basketball Schedule
(28–8 overall; 13–6 GLVC)

Date	Opponent	Result
Nov. 15	Brescia	W 71–53
Nov. 20	at Mercyhurst	W 83–67
Nov. 29	at Quincy	L 66–83
Dec. 1	at SIU–Edwardsville	W 75–67
Dec. 5	Georgetown (Ky.)	W 72–58
Dec. 8	Ohio Dominican	W 75–63
Dec. 17	Fayetteville State	W 93–80
Dec. 18	St. Andrews	W 100–50
Dec. 20	at Wayne State (Mich.)	W 78–60
Dec. 29	at Grand Valley State	L 55–66
Jan. 3	Rockhurst	W 61–39
Jan. 5	Drury	L 52–55
Jan. 10	at Indianapolis	W 62–60
Jan. 12	at St. Joseph's	W 79–39
Jan. 17	Southern Indiana	W 59–54
Jan. 19	Kentucky Wesleyan	W 65–44
Jan. 24	at Missouri–St. Louis	L 51–56
Jan. 26	at Missouri S&T	L 42–66
Jan. 31	Lewis	W 73–42

Women's Basketball Schedule (cont'd)

Date	Opponent	Result
Feb. 2	Wisconsin–Parkside	W 73–55
Feb. 9	Bellarmine	W 72–59
Feb. 14	St. Joseph's	W 69–39
Feb. 16	Indianapolis	W 68–60
Feb. 19	at Bellarmine	L 60–73
Feb. 21	at Kentucky Wesleyan	L 66–74
Feb. 28	at Wisconsin–Parkside	W 69–54
Mar. 1	at Lewis	W 68–62
Mar. 4	SIU–Edwardsville*	W 68–56
Mar. 8	vs. Missouri S&T*	W 79–67
Mar. 9	at Drury*	L 67–71
Mar. 14	vs. Indianapolis**	W 55–54
Mar. 15	at Drury**	W 84–65
Mar. 17	vs. Missouri S&T**	W 60–52
Mar. 26	vs. Wingate‡	W 78–65
Mar. 27	vs. Alaska–Anchorage‡	W 57–54
Mar. 29	vs. South Dakota‡	W 63–58

* GLVC Tournament, NKU (March 4) and Springfield, Missouri
** NCAA Great Lakes Regional Tournament, Springfield, Missouri
‡ NCAA Elite Eight, Kearney, Nebraska

Team Achievements

Champion, GLVC East Division, 13–6
Championship round, GLVC Tournament
Champion, NCAA Great Lakes Regional Tournament
National champion, NCAA Division II
Ranking in final national poll (April 1): 1
Winner, first annual GLVC Sportsmanship Award
Team grade point average: 3.341

Individual Achievements

Leading scorers (per game): Angela Healy, 14.1; Cassie Brannen, 13.6; Jessie Slack, 13.3; Nicole Chiodi, 8.8; Danyelle Echoles, 6.9

Leading rebounders (per game): Angela Healy, 9.3; Nicole Chiodi, 6.9; Cassie Brannen, 5.4

Angela Healy: first-team GLVC All-Conference; first-team Great Lakes All-Region; honorable mention All-American; Most Valuable Player, National Championship Tournament; GLVC leader in rebounds (9.3 per game); 805 career rebounds (7th on NKU all-time list); 1,262 career points (15th on NKU all-time list); Jarchow International Student Teaching Scholarship (South Africa)

Cassie Brannen: third-team GLVC All-Conference; Most Valuable Player, Great Lakes Regional Tournament; Elite Eight All-Tournament team; GLVC leader in blocked shots (2.08 per game); second in field-goal percentage (55.6); 75 blocks (breaking her school record of the year before)

Jessie Slack: third-team GLVC All-Conference; GLVC All-Tournament team; Great Lakes Region All-Tournament team

Nicole Chiodi: GLVC All-Tournament team; 1,286 minutes played (NKU single-season record)

Nancy Winstel: second national championship as coach of NKU women's team

INDEX

INDEX